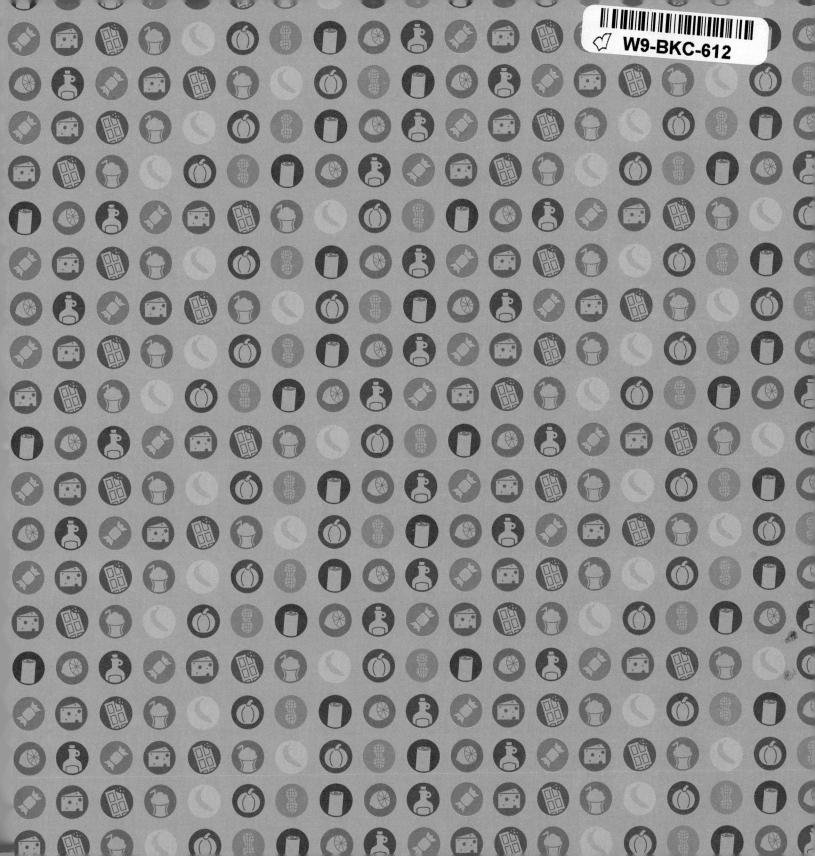

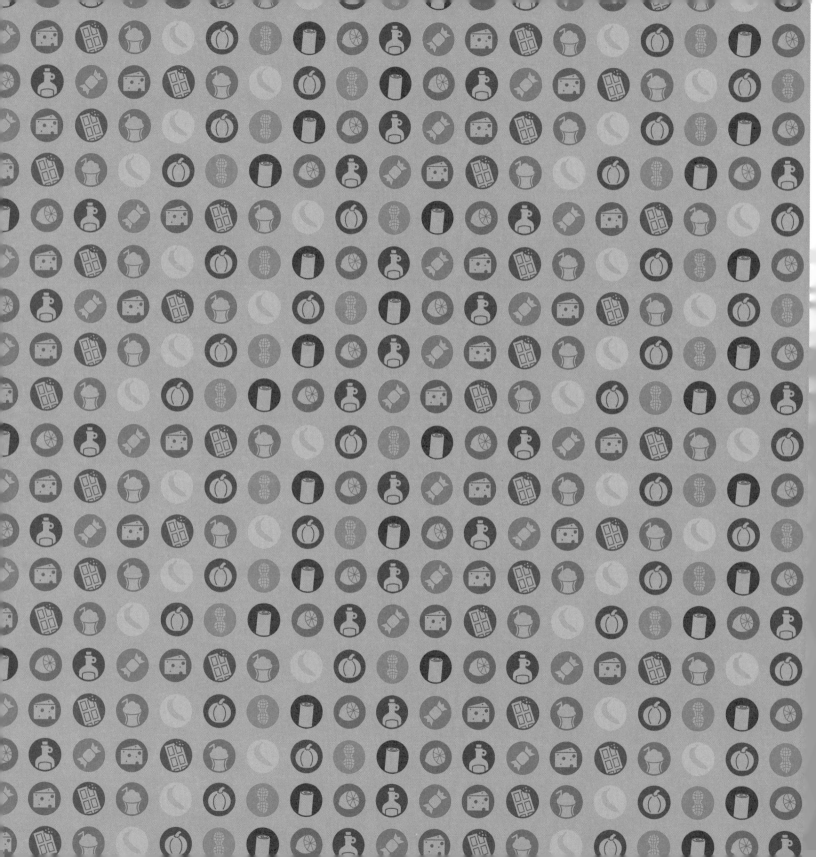

ESTABLISHED 2005

BAKED

ELEMENTS

ESTABLISHED 2005

BAKED
ELEMENTS

OUR 10 FAVORITE INGREDIENTS

MATT LEWIS & RENATO POLIAFITO
PHOTOGRAPHS BY TINA RUPP

STEWART, TABORI & CHANG   NEW YORK

CONTENTS

CARAMEL...56

PEANUT BUTTER...20

BOOZE...76

LEMON AND LIME...38

PUMPKIN...92

INTRODUCTION

Theoretically speaking, Renato and I should have killed each other by now. We work in extremely cramped quarters, see each other more than most married couples, and jointly run a decently sized (i.e., decently stressed) bakery operation. I like to imagine that we still respect, complement, and work well together because we've found some harmonious balance—a spiritual tipping point—but I suppose it is much less interesting than that. It's probably sheer willpower and our shared love of the same thing: sweets.

A TALE OF TWO KITCHENS

Thankfully, we run parallel with each other regarding all things pastry. Chocolate, peanut butter, caramel, and cinnamon play big roles in each of our daily lives, and they are never far from our reach. Also, both of us believe in eating dessert at least once (if not twice) per day, and we both feel that a bad chocolate chip cookie is one of the saddest things in the world.

That is where most of our similarities end—in the pastry corner. Our differences—the things that bring so-called balance into our hectic business lives—are just as apparent and just as necessary, and you only need to examine our respective home kitchens to understand our personalities.

My kitchen is orderly chaos. It is clean, but needs a trim. I have six-year-old candy bars in my refrigerator because I keep meaning to replicate them as desserts. I have whole-wheat flour, all-purpose flour, and bread flour stored in at least seven different bins and plastic containers throughout the kitchen without any rhyme or reason. Surplus cocoa powder is stored in the guest bedroom. Unusual or hard-to-find ingredients are put in unusual and hard-to-find places. Nothing is labeled, and yet I know where everything is. I rarely have more than three savory ingredients in my pantry at any one time, as I am comfortable making a dinner with just chocolate, cheese, and wine. I have too many cake pans, pie plates, and baking sheets, and yet I can't part with any of them. They are like old friends with whom I like to hang out in the kitchen.

Renato's kitchen is a study in obsessive-compulsive disorder. It is operating-room sanitary and hyperorganized. Things are washed as they are used and put back in their exact same place in the exact same way. Everything is labeled (courtesy of a handy label maker) and easily accessed. If you didn't know any better, you would assume by looking at his kitchen that Renato was a stereotypical New Yorker—that he didn't cook or bake at all, that he was the king of takeout—but looks can be deceiving. Though his kitchen looks barely used, he is an avid cook. In addition to making many pastries, he is also extremely comfortable with the savory—making Italian and German and American fare with great aplomb.

Our bakery kitchen, the Baked kitchen, for better or for worse (but mostly for better), has come to resemble a weird hybrid of both of our kitchens—though the bakery kitchen is more efficient, bigger, more gangly, as if on steroids. The detailed organization—the highly efficient systems and important folders and handbooks and time lines—that's a lot of Renato with a healthy dose of fantastic staff mixed in. The odd, semi-eccentric, big-picture ideas—the let's make something with wort (unfermented beer), the let's write a bunch of books under impossible deadlines, the let's create a shelf-stable, all-natural, hard-to-distribute product—that's a lot of me tempered by Renato and said staff. It's a big blended bakery. It's a beast, and we feed it. Then we go home and we think about it.

We are unaware of any other way to run a bakery. In fact, our entire baking venture is either earth-shatteringly easy or appallingly narrow: we only make and serve what we like and hope the customer is game. Perhaps we should broaden our menu horizons, experiment with ingredients we normally shun, take a walk on the nouveau side—but that would seem disingenuous, if not a little dangerous. Our bakery and our books are really just a version of us—the caffeinated, much sweeter version of us.

THE BAKED PYRAMID

(a plan for happiness through sweets)

DISCLAIMER: We are not proposing a radicalized revamp of years of nutritional advice.

peanut butter

lemon & lime

caramel

booze

pumpkin

malted milk powder

cinnamon

cheese

chocolate

banana

LUNCHBOX FREUD

Self-reflection through the lens of the contents of our fifth-grade lunch boxes is worthy of both analysis and concern. True, the historical data is fuzzy, but it is strictly a function of our individual memories. Had we cataloged and parsed our average grade-school lunches for deeper meaning, certain biometrics could have been distilled, a future of eating habits could have been foretold. In retrospect, our lunch boxes were much more than just vessels for carrying food—they were mini windows into our souls.

My lunch box (the contents, not the *Flintstones* decor) was the envy of many school chums: a very substantial peanut butter and jelly sandwich, a candy bar (cookies on Fridays), and either a banana or a bag of pretzels or both. No vegetables. No strange lunch meats like liverwurst. At one point, Mom might have halfheartedly pushed more nutritious meals—the kind that wouldn't attract the attention of Child Protective Services—but she eventually understood and gave in (she herself was quite happy with cake for lunch). I was already on my path, and my path was paved in peanut butter, bananas, and chocolate.

Renato's lunch box (*The Empire Strikes Back*) benefited from more rarefied sandwiches. Salami (not a circular slab of bologna, mind you) with mayonnaise on Wonder bread was a common theme. On rare occasions, he was able to eat a more nutritious (if you consider grilled cheese more nutritious than salami) lunch at home before returning to recess. However, the thermos was always filled with chocolate milk, and there was always a snack. That the snack was often the underrated Whatchamacallit candy bar seems somehow prophetic. It was my favorite as well.

Had we written a cookbook based on our ten favorite ingredients when we were eleven, we are certain the chapters would be identical to the ones in this book. For whatever reason—through sheer stubbornness or perseverance—we developed particular bonds with certain foods and ingredients, and we still pursue them with tenacity.

THE FOOD PYRAMID REORGANIZED

Despite our early childhood experiences, we respect and understand nutritional guidelines. We are completely—even hyper—aware of the physiological benefits of consuming many, many servings of vegetables, fruits, and proteins and the possible physiological dangers of consuming too many servings of sugar, fat, and caffeine. In short, basic nutritional science can be summed up as *asparagus is good, chocolate cake is very bad.* The trouble with this quick and easily dispensed nutritional advice is that it does not take into account the psychological effects: chocolate cake inevitably will make you happier than asparagus—probably a lot happier. Happier people live longer (or so we have heard), and at the very least, they are more enjoyable to be around. I imagine life would *feel* very long if it were lived solely according to nutritional guidelines—dark days of nibbling leafy greens and chalky yogurt in a dimly lit room.

The Food Pyramid of yore would have made more of a lasting impact (more of a connection to the target audience) if only it allowed for a few dietary sins. Instead of a stringent and rigorous schedule of dull, by-the-numbers eating, the pyramid should have been constructed to be more bearable. It should have been threaded throughout with nods to the foods that make life worth living: butter, flour, sugar, and chocolate.

I am not proposing a radicalized revamping of years of nutritional advice. I am just suggesting a mini update—a reorganization—of the dusty old Food Pyramid. We think you just might live a little bit longer and be a lot happier if you pick up that chocolate cheesecake muffin and put down that spinach smoothie (at least occasionally).

SELECTIVELY SPEAKING

Ever since I started organizing recipes—and long before we started writing cookbooks—I always sorted them according to main ingredient (banana, chocolate), as opposed to the more traditionally recognized recipe types (breakfast, lunch, dinner, pasta, poultry, meat). If I wanted to locate my favorite macaroni and cheese dish, I would flip to the cheese section of my otherwise haphazard recipe book. The idea being to answer an important question like "What can I make with chocolate (or cinnamon, or peanut butter, or cheese) today?" It seems beneficial, if not completely logical, to search for chocolate recipes in a chocolate section versus sifting through pages of dessert recipes or cake or cookie or brownie recipes. Simply start with a flavor, and form will follow.

Baked Elements, like my recipe book, is arranged by our favorite ingredients, ten distinct flavor elements from which to build a range of recipes. These are the ingredients that we would take to a desert island or rescue from a burning house. They are the basis of our bakery, our books, and to some degree, our lives. These ingredients, for better or worse, form the basis of our own food pyramid.

Finalizing our top ten list was both a simple and agonizing process. It was easy because we only had to look around our bakery and our home kitchens for the ingredients we used over and over again. Theoretically, we have consumed enough peanut butter to have a peanut farm named in our honor, and we cook with enough booze to nearly qualify our kitchens as bars. Bananas are scattered throughout our kitchens in various stages of ripeness, and our pantries are overrun with different varieties and forms of malt. These ingredients, including our other favorites (lemon and lime, cinnamon, caramel, cheese, pumpkin, and chocolate), were obvious. It took about seventeen seconds to list them. The difficult part was limiting our list to just ten ingredients. Though we adore almonds and oranges and blueberries, and we somewhat understand the appeal of coconut, we just don't use them as often as we do our top ten. Perhaps a book containing these ingredients—think classic B-sides or director's cut—will rear its head, but they won't be featured in this book.

As always, we strove to create recipes that are classic Baked: fun, delicious, interesting, and unpretentious. While we can't expect everyone's top ten ingredients to match ours, we do hope the recipes turn into new favorites. Enjoy.

EVERYTHING YOU NEED TO KNOW TO GET BAKED

KITCHEN TOOLS AND EQUIPMENT

OVER THE YEARS we have acquired many, many kitchen accessories, tools, and appliances. Our drawers are bursting with heirloom baking pans and antique (and some not so antique) rolling pins, and our countertops are altars to whisks, spatulas, and bench knives. This is not how normal people should live. In fact, this is not even how most home bakers should live. But we think it's fine. We just happen to accept our frailties and wrap them up in denial.

The home baker needs only a few must-have items to produce a multitude of cookies, cakes, pies, brownies, and bars. Simpler is always better, and less is always more. In other words, five whisks are nice (borderline hoarder) to have, but you really only need one good one. The following is a list of our favorite equipment and stuff you will need to bake almost anything from this book. (Also see Sources, page 215.)

Baking sheets: The simplest baking sheets are the best baking sheets. We use inexpensive, light-colored, rimmed half-sheet pans (18 by 13 inches)—the kind you find in a restaurant supply store. These basic pans are multipurpose and should last several lifetimes. Nonstick pans are not necessary; we always line our pans with parchment paper.

Bench knife: An ordinary bench knife, or dough scraper, is bliss in a kitchen, and we use it for everything (sweet and savory). Bench knives are usually made of a 3-by-5-inch sheet of metal attached to a wooden or plastic handle. We use them to cut, portion, and turn all sorts of dough. Additionally, they are great for scraping down and cleaning surfaces. In a pinch, I have even used mine for moving cookies from pan to cooling rack.

Blender: You don't necessarily need a blender for this book (except for our Bourbon, Vanilla, and Chocolate Milk Shakes on page 78 and the Malted Vanilla Milk Shakes on page 117), but we are fairly addicted to ours. Besides shakes, we use them frequently for soups, sauces, smoothies, and ice cream bases.

Brownie and bar pans: Over the years, for various reasons, we have baked in various pans (light-colored metal, glass, ceramic, dark-colored metal, and some of unknown material) and they all work reasonably well, though we tend to favor glass, ceramic, and light-colored metal, as neither of us is drawn to the crispy edges created by dark metal pans (though we realize that this is a personal preference).

Bundt pan: Somewhere along the line, our Bundt pan collection became an obsession and we started to acquire too many (be warned: this could happen to you). You really only need one Bundt (10- or 12-cup Nordic Ware) in any shape. Mini Bundts work well, but you will have to decrease your baking time (usually about half the recommended time). If you do opt for a more decorative pan, be sure to grease all the nooks and crannies extra carefully to prevent unsightly surface breakage or stickage (this is a made-up word).

Cake pans: As with almost all of our pan suggestions, simpler equals better. We use a variety of economical, professional aluminum cake pans available from almost any kitchen supply store.

Cake turntable: If you decorate enough cakes, you might want to invest in a cake turntable—basically a lazy Susan for decorating cakes. You don't *need* one, but it will make cake (or sugar cookie or cupcake or brownie) decorating that much easier. We recommend heavy-duty turntables for the more-than-occasional decorator. They are not inexpensive, but they will last a lot longer than the plastic versions.

Cooling racks: As we both live in New York (i.e., smallish apartments and even smaller kitchens), we both recommend using collapsible, stackable, cooling racks. As the name implies, the racks are necessary for letting air pass over and, more important, under baked goods. Additionally, we use cooling racks to temporarily store hot-from-the-oven baking sheets and to glaze cakes. Color and material do not matter, but you want to make sure at least one is large enough to hold a 12-inch cake or a tray full of cookies.

Cupcake and muffin pans: The explosion in popularity of cupcakes has given way to a plethora of cupcake pans. For testing purposes, we used the familiar 12-cup cupcake or muffin pan made of light-colored metal. If you decide to use a different cup size, you will have to adjust the baking time accordingly: mini muffins or cupcakes usually bake in half the suggested baking time (or less), while the jumbo pans usually require time and a half in the oven.

Food processor: The dreaded food processor is an absolute kitchen necessity. Yes, they are bulky, heavy, annoying to clean, and expensive, but they are also perfect for chopping nuts and malted milk balls, shredding pumpkin and cheese, and making some batters, icings, and pie dough. I use mine often (including for many savory tasks), and my only regret is that I didn't get one sooner.

Ice cream scoop: We use several different sizes of ice-cream scoops (the kind with the release mechanism) to make perfectly uniform cookie-dough balls. They are also perfect for portioning cupcake and cake batter.

Loaf pans: I am not even sure how I acquired my old, blackened, battered loaf pans (9 by 5 by 3 inches or thereabouts), but they appear very old, they will definitely outlive me, and they work

like a charm. If you can't pick up a set at a garage sale, search out inexpensive, heavy, and light-colored metal loaf pans from your local kitchen supply store.

Measuring cups and spoons: Liquid and dry cup measurements are completely different.

- **For liquid measurements**, I recommend Pyrex glass 2-cup and 4-cup sizes. I often use my larger liquid measuring cup to melt butter or chocolate (or butter and chocolate together) in the microwave, and often it is my default "small" mixing bowl.

- **For dry measurements**, I recommend a basic set of metal measuring cups, with sizes ranging from ¼ cup to 2 cups.

- **For measuring spoons**, use the most basic set of metal spoons you can find, starting with ¼ teaspoon and going up to 1 tablespoon. They usually come joined by a metal ring (which I remove because I find the clumping together of spoons to be annoying).

Microplane: *Microplane* actually refers to the brand of long, thin, graters commonly found in commercial and home kitchens alike. Use one for grating cheese and zesting citrus, and another separate one specifically for grating spices (you don't want the fragrant spices to affect the taste of your zest and cheese).

Microwave oven: Though the microwave is much maligned in foodie kitchens, we are proud to say we use ours constantly. It melts decent amounts of butter and chocolate (or butter and chocolate together) quickly, brings water to

a boil quickly (for recipes that require small amounts of hot water), and—most important—it reheats coffee. A microwave is not a necessity, but it is nice to have.

Mixing bowls: My idea of the perfect mixing bowl changes as I age. I used to only recommend nested, melamine, spouted mixing bowls. Then I was on a steel bowl kick (the wide kind you find in a restaurant supply store). But now I am falling in love all over again with vintage ceramic bowls. Regardless, we leave the bowl decision up to you—just make sure you have at least three sizes on hand to handle all sorts of recipes. Melamine bowls are lightweight and easy to maneuver, metal bowls are easy to clean, and vintage ceramic bowls are heavy but beautiful.

Panettone papers and molds: Panettone papers or molds are a specialty item. They come in a few different sizes, are created for the sole purpose of baking panettone, and are terribly hard to find, even at your average kitchen or restaurant supply store. Luckily, they are readily available online (even at Amazon.com), and we offer several substitutions on page 183.

Parchment paper: Parchment paper is essential for the home baker. We use it to line cookie sheets (you can reuse it at least once) and all manner of cake, brownie and bar, and loaf pans to aid in removing your baked goods in a clean manner. We don't use Silpat liners, so it is impossible for us to recommend them. We find it equally hard to hate them, however, since they can be used many times (one can argue the environmental benefit of this versus the less environmentally friendly material they are manufactured with) and they create a super-easy-to-clean, nonstick surface. Unfortunately, Silpat liners keep the bottom of the dough too far from the surface of the pan, thus not allowing the proper (at least in our world) browning, crisping effect we relish in our cookies.

Pie plates or tins: Use any pie plate or tin (though we are partial to glass and metal), but do not use the disposable tins, as they generally produce soggier crusts. Glass pie plates usually cost just a few dollars more than the cheap disposables, and you can reuse them endlessly.

Pie weights: Pie weights, or dried beans, help the pie dough hold its shape and prevent it from shrinking while baking. Most kitchen supply stores sell specially made (usually inexpensive) pie weights that you can use over and over again. If you make a lot of pies, buy some pie weights.

Soufflé dishes, molds, and ramekins: The ubiquitous white porcelain soufflé dish (or mold or ramekin) comes in various sizes, but we tend to use only a large 1½-quart dish and a set of 3- to 5-ounce ramekins for our soufflés. They also come in handy for puddings, individual casseroles, and even for serving ice cream on occasion. If you would rather use a vintage type of vessel to bake your soufflés, be sure it is high-sided, made of ceramic or porcelain, and can withstand high heat.

Spatulas: We have whole drawers dedicated to various spatulas. We are quite fond of the medium-size, heat-resistant rubberized spatulas (actually we recommend owning a few different sizes). They are essential for stirring, scraping

down bowls, mixing light batters, and folding in egg whites. We also are addicted to the long thin metal spatula for icing cakes and the offset metal spatula that works as a multipurpose, detail-oriented Swiss Army knife of sorts for smoothing batters in baking pans, loosening cakes from the sides of pans, removing the first brownie, and swirling and marbling batters.

Springform pans: We use a high-sided (2 to 3 inches high) 9-inch springform pan to create our Easy Candy Bar Tart on page 71. A springform pan is not quite a necessity for this tart (you could use a pie plate or a tart pan in its place), but it will not have the same visual appeal, and it won't unmold as easily. A springform pan will also come in handy for cheesecakes and flourless chocolate cakes.

Standing mixer: We could not live without our standing mixers. Even the casual baker should have one, as it simplifies almost every baking task. We both use KitchenAid models (they usually come with whisk, dough hook, and paddle attachments), and we use them often. Many recipes in this book require a standing mixer. Hand mixers are an adequate substitute in some recipes, though they often lack the power of standing mixers, and you will have to be extra thorough in making sure all of the ingredients are mixed properly (i.e., many, many rotations of the hand mixer around, up, and down in the bowl). If you are like my grandmother and insist on mixing everything by hand, we are mightily impressed with your strength and drive, though we still think you and your recipes would be better off with a standing mixer.

Tart pans: Tart pans with removable bottoms are an absolute must for the home baker. We constantly use a 9-inch version (both fluted and non-fluted—though it is entirely up to you) and a set of 4-inch mini tart pans for individual tarts. Store mini tart pans between layers of paper towels or parchment paper to make sure they do not stick together while nesting.

Thermometers: Even if you're only a casual baker or candy maker, we think you will be genuinely pleased to have a variety of inexpensive thermometers at the ready.

- **Oven thermometer:** Most ovens run either a little hot or a little cool. Instead of trying to recalibrate your oven (expensive!), buy a simple, cheap oven thermometer and adjust the temperature gauge accordingly. Always better to be safe than sorry here. For baking, it is extremely important to have an accurate oven temperature as cakes, brownies, and cookies can bomb spectacularly if the oven is off by as little as 25 degrees F.

- **Instant read thermometer:** This is one of those thermometers that resemble a large nail—the head of the nail being the readout or gauge—and it is great for taking the inside temperature of cheesecake and panettone (and turkey).

- **Candy thermometer:** We recommend using an old-school, inexpensive clip-on candy thermometer. It should have gradations of 2 to 5 degrees F and a range of 100 to 400 degrees F. Also, many basic candy thermometers mark all the stages of candy (hard ball, soft ball, and so on), so your life is even easier. They should cost no more than twenty dollars.

- **Chocolate thermometer:** We don't temper chocolate for any recipes in this book, but if you are an avid choco-holic, you should buy one. Look for 1-degree gradations (for truly accurate tempering).

Tube pans: We use a tube pan in this book to make the beautiful, tall, light Lime Angel Food Cake with Lime Glaze on page 41. Our pan has little feet that support it when it is turned upside down (an essential step in most angel food cake recipes). Don't worry—if your pan does not have feet, you can support the upturned pan with a large bottle. Unfortunately, we cannot recommend any substitutions for a tube pan. While similar to a Bundt, the tube pan is generally lighter, taller, and honed for these super-light cakes. Many testers have tried to reproduce our angel food cakes in a Bundt, but often the cakes are done on the outside and undercooked on the inside, and they do not rise properly.

Whisk: Home chefs need only one or two whisks (one small and one large or just one medium-size one) for all their whisking needs. We recommend a basic wire whisk with a wooden handle. Simple whisks—avoid all the extraneous, newfangled whisks—are great tools for combining dry ingredients, beating egg whites and yolks, and stirring together melted butter and chocolate. That said, do not use your whisk as an all-purpose stirring device; a silicone spatula works better, and using a whisk can cause you to accidentally incorporate too much air into your batter.

INGREDIENTS, TECHNIQUES, AND RECOMMENDED BRANDS

THE BAKING BASICS—at least the basics you will need for this book—are located below. We like to keep things simple and fun, and we think the best way to become a better baker is to start baking. You don't need an encyclopedic knowledge of ingredients or techniques or tips (your proficiency will grow with time)—just breathe deeply, read the recipe all the way through, prep your ingredients, and dive in.

Booze

This is simple: If you are baking with booze, use what is already in your liquor cabinet. Bake with the stuff you would normally drink. There is a rather puzzling and common misconception that you should bake with lesser-quality alcohol, but all you will end up with is a lesser-quality baked good. As far as bourbon brands go, we feel like we make up excuses to bake with Blanton's or Knob Creek (two must-haves). If you are going to make our Triple Rum Black Pepper Cake on page 82 (and you should), we are currently romanticizing Gosling's, and there is always a place in our hearts for Smith & Cross.

Butter

All of the recipes in this book were tested using unsalted butter. Salted butter is terrific—we love it on toast—but it is a bit heavy-handed in some baking recipes, a bit too pronounced. Ultimately, unsalted butter gives you more control of the final recipe.

We also often suggest using cool but not cold butter. More specifically, remove your butter from the refrigerator 15 to 20 minutes prior to using it in a recipe, and cut it into cubes if directed. The butter should be slightly malleable and cool to the touch—this will keep your cookies from spreading during baking.

Chocolate

We eat an absurd amount of chocolate, and we bake with an obscene amount of chocolate. Chocolate has become a part of us, and we have a lot to say about it.

- **Buy the good stuff**: This may seem bizarre to state, but if you are making a chocolate-based dessert, use the best you can find and afford.

- **Buy in bulk**: If you plan on making even just a few chocolate desserts throughout the year, you should buy chocolate in bulk—the savings is considerable, and there is something satisfying about chopping up a hefty brick of chocolate. (See Sources on page 215 for a complete list of places to purchase bulk chocolate.)

- **Chocolate percentages**: The percentage label on a bar of chocolate is referring to the cocoa mass in the bar itself. But even if the cocoa percentage is the same, the proportions of sugar, milk solids, and any other ingredients can be wildly different. Simply put, the content (and therefore taste) of chocolate bars varies widely from brand to brand.

- **Melting chocolate**: We are forever melting chocolate for various recipes, and lately we have been doing so via the microwave method (it's quick and requires less forward thinking), though either of the following methods will work perfectly. Regardless of the

---

There are many wonderful brands of chocolate in the world, and more seem to be coming out each year. As you get more familiar with them, you will start to align yourself with a few favorites. Here are a few brands that we recommend (see Sources on page 215):

IF A RECIPE CALLS FOR A DARK CHOCOLATE, 60 TO 72 PERCENT, USE ANY OF THE FOLLOWING:	IF A RECIPE CALLS FOR A MILK CHOCOLATE, USE ANY OF THE FOLLOWING:
• Scharffen Berger's Home Baking Bar 62% (found in most supermarkets)	• Jacques Torres Milk Chocolate Bar (found in specialty markets and online)
• Scharffen Berger's Home Baking Bar 70% (found in most supermarkets)	• TCHO Cacao Dark Milk Chocolate Bar 53% (found in specialty markets and online)
• Callebaut Chocolate Block 60% (found in specialty markets—often chopped and repackaged by the market)	• Scharffen Berger Milk Chocolate Bar 41% (found in most supermarkets)
• Callebaut Chocolate Block 70% (found in specialty markets—often chopped and repackaged by the market)	

method, make sure you melt the chocolate in a clean, absolutely dry bowl. Even a few drops of water can cause your chocolate to seize.

Microwave method: Place the chocolate chunks or chips (not whole slabs or bars—they won't melt evenly) in a microwave-safe bowl in the middle of the microwave. Microwave at 100% power (high) for 30 seconds. Remove the bowl (warning: the outside of the bowl may be very hot to the touch) and stir the chocolate. Continue microwaving in 15-second intervals, stirring in between, until the chocolate is completely melted. Do not overheat.

Double-boiler method: Fill a medium-size pot or saucepan with water and place it on the stove over medium heat, bringing the water to a slow simmer. Place the chocolate chunks or chips in a medium heatproof bowl that will sit partially in the pan without the bottom of the bowl touching the water. Stir the chocolate every minute or so, until it is completely melted, shiny, and smooth. Do not overheat.

Cocoa Powder

We tested every recipe in this book with Valrhona cocoa powder. We are enamored, and have always been, with Valrhona's deep, dark deliciousness. Don't overcomplicate your life with the Dutched (cocoa powder treated with alkali) versus natural debate. Instead, pay more attention to the color, smell, and taste of each cocoa powder you try. Lastly, we always recommend unsweetened cocoa powder and never use the sweetened versions. When you find one you like, buy it in bulk.

Crumb Coat

Essentially, a crumb coat is a very thin layer of frosting applied to a cake to keep the light crumbs suspended so they won't appear in the final layer of frosting. It also keeps the delicate cake from tearing apart when applying a thick frosting. It's like the first coat of paint; it lays the foundation for the next and final coat. A crumb-coated cake should be refrigerated for at least 15 minutes prior to applying the next frosting layer.

Folding

Folding is an often-used baking technique, employed when you want to gently mix two parts of a batter together. Use a very large rubber spatula to turn the bottom part of one batter (often the heavier one) onto the top of the other batter (often the lighter one) by scraping the sides of the bowl, then sweeping and twisting inward. Be gentle, be slow, and certainly don't use a whisk.

Malted Milk Powder

Malted milk powder, once a staple of soda fountain drinks, is a great and necessary baking ingredient (certainly for this book!). It imparts a tangy, nutty flavor in vanilla- and chocolate-based desserts alike. Carnation makes a readily available malted milk powder (usually carried near the coffee and tea section in grocery stores), but Ovaltine chocolate malt drink mix can be used as well.

Measuring Dry Ingredients

All the recipes using flour in this book were tested by the spoon-and-sweep method: spooning the flour into the measuring cup, then leveling the top of the cup with a straight-edged knife. All light and dark brown sugars should be firmly packed and leveled to the top of the cup.

When using measuring spoons, level to the rim of the spoon with a straight-edged knife.

Salt, Sea Salt, Fleur de Sel

Unless otherwise stated, whenever we refer to salt in this book, we mean (and tested all recipes with) your ordinary, average kosher salt. More than likely, you can substitute table or iodized salt without fear of ruining any recipe—just reduce the amount by about one-third (or to taste).

On the occasions when we don't use kosher salt, we use sea salt or fleur de sel. We recommend using a fine-grained to slightly chunky fleur de sel like the sort made by Le Saunier de Camargue (easily found on the Internet or at gourmet markets; see Sources, page 215).

Sifting

Sifting is the act of adding air to the dry ingredients to produce lighter cakes and baked goods. Sifting also does a great job of mixing and combining ingredients and removing lumps. Do not buy a special sifting knickknack; they are expensive and impossible to clean. Instead, just sift (or shake) your ingredients through a large, fine-mesh sieve; sieves are inexpensive and also multipurpose.

Superfine Sugar

Superfine sugar is basically a pulverized granulated sugar prized for its quick-dissolving properties. It also creates beautiful-looking, fine-grained cakes, and it is an essential ingredient in our Lime Angel Food Cake with Lime Glaze on page 41. If you can't find superfine sugar, you can make your own by running regular sugar through a food processor or spice grinder. Superfine sugar is a one-to-one substitution for granulated sugar.

ESTIMATED BAKING TEMPERATURES AND TIMES FOR DIFFERENT TYPES OF NUTS

pine nuts (pignoli)	5 minutes	300 degrees F
almonds, walnuts,* and pecans	10 minutes	300 degrees F
hazelnuts and macadamias	12 minutes	300 degrees F
shelled peanuts	15–17 minutes	350 degrees F
peanuts in their shells	20–22 minutes	350 degrees F

*We actually toast our walnuts for a slightly longer period (a) because we like them really dark and smoky and (b) because we are weird like that.

Toasting Nuts

It is incredibly easy and incredibly aromatic to toast nuts. Spread the required amount of nuts (we like to toast them for each recipe, not in huge batches) on a rimmed baking sheet and toast until they are fragrant and a shade darker. Use the chart above for estimated toasting times, but since most ovens vary widely, you should check the nuts early and often—nuts are often expensive, and you don't want to burn them. You should toss and flip the nuts halfway through the baking process. Cool them completely before eating or adding to a recipe.

Vanilla Bean Paste

We use Nielsen-Massey Madagascar Bourbon Pure Vanilla Bean Paste nearly as much as we use pure vanilla extract (see Sources, page 215). The paste is thick and fragrant and contains real vanilla bean seeds that give light-colored frostings, fillings, icings, and sponges a fun, speckled appearance. Generally speaking, vanilla bean paste is slightly more concentrated than extract, but it can be substituted for pure vanilla extract in a one-to-one ratio. Or you could also use slightly less paste than extract (but we don't).

Yeast

We use both instant and active dry yeast in this book. Instant dry yeast can be mixed in with your dry ingredients (flour, sugar, salt, etc.) directly, while active dry yeast needs to be "activated"—stirred separately into a warm liquid, usually water or milk—before being added to a recipe. Technically, you can substitute one for the other; however, the substitution is slightly complicated. If you are subbing active for instant, you have to first activate the active dry yeast with ¼ cup water, then you have to remove that same amount of liquid (¼ cup) from the existing recipe.

"PEANUT BUTTER" SOLD IN THE UNITED STATES MUST CONTAIN AT LEAST 90% PEANUTS IT'S THE LAW

approximately **540** PEANUTS EQUALS *one* 12-OUNCE JAR OF PEANUT BUTTER

GEORGIA *(the so-called peach state)* PRODUCES 49% OF THE USA'S PEANUTS

JANUARY **24TH** IS NATIONAL PEANUT BUTTER DAY

PEANUT BUTTER WAS REPORTEDLY USED TO MAKE MISTER ED'S MOUTH MOVE IN A WAY THAT WOULD LOOK LIKE HE WAS TALKING

a horse is a horse . . .

AMERICANS SPEND < < < < < < *nearly* < < < < < < $800 *million* A YEAR ON PEANUT BUTTER, THE SAME AMOUNT WE SPEND ON CHRISTMAS TREES

ONE ACRE OF PEANUTS EQUALS 30,000 PEANUT BUTTER SANDWICHES

ARACHIBUTYROPHOBIA: THE FEAR OF GETTING PEANUT BUTTER STUCK TO THE ROOF OF ONE'S MOUTH

Chapter 1

PEANUT BUTTER

If you have ever woken up with a slight hangover and a dubious, half-remembered, half-eaten jar of peanut butter at your side, we can empathize. We have lived this shame. Peanut butter is a surprisingly nimble comfort food, able to combine with almost any form of dessert (cakes, cookies, icings, macaroons, ice cream) in a beautiful all-encompassing embrace. We take its comfort often. Of course, there are naysayers, and we ignore them. If you dislike peanut butter, chances are you also dislike angels and puppies and we pity you. We are fans of both the nostalgia brands like Skippy and Peter Pan and the all-natural stuff (we are finally getting used to stirring the oil back into the paste). Slow, restful weekends were virtually invented for peanut butter snack time—whether directly from the jar or as part of a cookie—and in our lazy daydreams, the rivers are alive with smooth, crunchy, and toasty peanut butter.

6	cups crunchy, plain cereal (Rice Chex or something similar works best)
1¼	cups salted peanuts, coarsely chopped
1	cup firmly packed dark brown sugar
1	cup light corn syrup
1	cup smooth peanut butter (see page 26)
1	tablespoon pure vanilla extract
1½	teaspoons salt
6	ounces good-quality milk chocolate, chopped

GOOD MORNING SUNSHINE BARS

WE RARELY IDENTIFY our "favorite" recipes for the simple reason that they change all the time based on mood, environment, and time of year. Therefore, we consider it a slightly big deal to induct this recipe into the rarefied kingdom of "Matt and Renato's All-Time Favorite Recipes," which is neither a book nor a file nor a thing, but just a place in our collective minds. The recipe itself is embarrassingly simple—really, just cereal (therefore making these bars a perfectly plausible breakfast solution), peanut butter, peanuts, and chocolate. Combined, these ingredients make a bar that is absurdly transcendental—salty, sweet, crunchy, and addictive, with nods to some purer form of childhood nostalgia (think bake sales and campfire tales)—yet uniquely current, like an Eames chair. We make them for afternoon snacks, for parties, for romantic dates, for large events. In fact, there is rarely an occasion not to make these bars. We actually prefer them in the morning, with a hearty cup of coffee. The world just seems like a better place when you wake up with our Good Morning Sunshine Bars.

/// *Yield: 24 bars* ///

BAKED NOTE: *Though it might be tempting to cover the entire surface of the bar in chocolate as opposed to making just a few chocolate stripes or zigzags, we encourage you to refrain. Too much chocolate obscures some of the peanut flavor and crunch, thereby diluting the whole Good Morning Sunshine Bar experience.*

//

Butter the bottom and sides of a 9-by-13- inch baking pan. Line the pan with parchment paper so that the paper overhangs the pan on two sides. Butter the parchment.

Place the cereal and peanuts in a large bowl and use your hands to toss together until mixed well.

In a medium saucepan over medium heat, stir together the sugar and corn syrup. Bring the mixture to a boil for one full minute. Remove from the heat and stir in the peanut butter, vanilla, and salt. Stir until the mixture is combined.

Pour the sugar mixture over the cereal mixture and use a spoon or well-greased hands (be careful as the liquid may still be very hot) to toss until the cereal is completely coated with the sugar mixture.

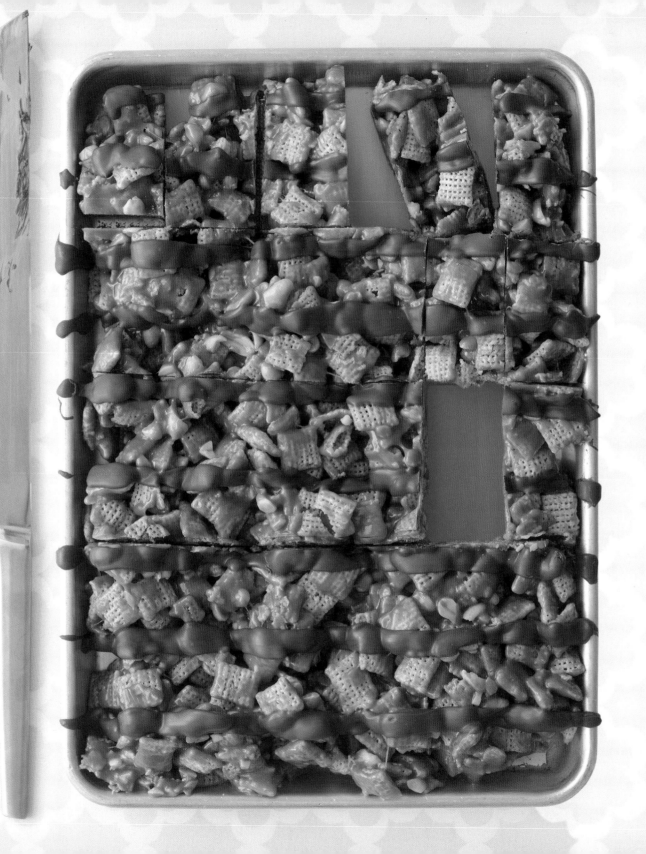

Turn the mixture out into the prepared pan. Grease your hands and press the mixture into the bottom of the pan, being careful not to crush the cereal. Allow the mixture to cool to room temperature (if you wish to speed this process, you may place the entire pan in the refrigerator for 15 to 20 minutes).

Melt the chocolate in a microwave or double boiler. Use a spoon or piping bag to decorate the tops of the bars in a stripe or zigzag pattern. Allow the chocolate to set.

Lift the bars out of the pan using the parchment paper overhang, cut them into approximately 3-by-1½-inch rectangles (i.e., candy bars).

The bars can be stored at room temperature, in an airtight container, for up to 3 days. If the weather is hot and humid, you might want to keep them in the refrigerator instead.

CRUNCHY PEANUT BUTTER BANANA BREAD

ALL THINGS CONSIDERED, we are still waiting for a loaf craze to take hold. We think the simple yet versatile loaf cake or bread (as in "banana bread," "zucchini bread," etc.) deserves the same kind of mania usually reserved for cupcakes and French macaroons. Though not as naturally attractive as some of the other more popular baked goods, loaf cakes have a lot going for them. They are almost always easy to prepare, simple enough to scale up for multiples, and effortless to cart around (have you ever tried to drive a three-layer buttercream-filled cake forty-three miles in an un-air-conditioned car?). This loaf is really the culmination of our favorite things: peanut butter, bananas, and chocolate. It's moist and nicely textured and we think it is one of those anytime, anywhere snacks that make life seem a little kinder.

/////////////////////////////////// *Yield: One 9-by-5-inch loaf* ///////////////////////////////////

> **BAKED NOTE**: *We suppose you could substitute smooth peanut butter for the crunchy peanut butter in this recipe, but we would rather you stick with the crunchy. It provides a lovely texture. In fact, if you crave even more texture, we suggest adding about ¼ cup chopped and salted peanuts to the batter.*

///

1½	cups plus 1 tablespoon all-purpose flour, divided
1	cup plus 1 tablespoon sugar
1	teaspoon salt
1	teaspoon baking soda
1	rounded cup mashed bananas (2½ to 3 bananas)
½	cup vegetable oil
2	large eggs
¼	cup whole milk
1	cup crunchy peanut butter (see page 26)
4	ounces (about ⅔ cup) semisweet chocolate chips

Preheat the oven to 350 degrees F and position the rack in the center. Butter a 9-by-5-inch loaf pan, dust it with flour, and knock out the excess flour.

In a large bowl, whisk together 1½ cups flour, the sugar, salt, and baking soda.

In another large bowl, whisk together the bananas, oil, eggs, milk, and peanut butter. Toss the chocolate chips in the remaining 1 tablespoon of flour, then stir the chocolate chips into the banana mixture.

Make a well in the center of the dry ingredients and pour the wet mixture into it. Fold the dry ingredients into the wet ever so gently until just combined. Pour the batter into the prepared pan and bake for 1 hour to 1 hour and 10 minutes, or until a toothpick inserted into the center comes out with a few moist crumbs.

Let the loaf cool in the pan for 15 minutes, then turn out onto a rack to cool completely.

The loaf can be stored at room temperature, in an airtight container or wrapped tightly, for up to 3 days.

2½	cups (about 14 ounces) home-roasted or store-bought roasted peanuts (see Note)
½	teaspoon salt
2	teaspoons honey
1 to 3	teaspoons peanut oil, as needed
¼ to ½	teaspoon fleur de sel, to taste (optional)

HOMEMADE PEANUT BUTTER

HOMEMADE PEANUT BUTTER is delightful. It is uncomplicated in a way that feels charming and wholesome without seeming precious or twee. It is also quick, requiring just a few spins around the food processor, and exceedingly adaptable—smooth or chunky, salty or subtle, skins or no skins. And lastly, of course, it makes a great base that plays well with others like cayenne, cocoa powder, and chocolate (white, milk, or dark). Of course, homemade peanut butter is only going to be as good as the peanuts you start with, so taste test with gusto. Great-tasting peanuts make great-tasting peanut butter, with a brightness and zing that most jarred varieties cannot match.

/////////////////////////////////////// *Yield: Approximately 2 cups* ///////////////////////////////////////

BAKED NOTE: *We like our homemade peanut butter a multitude of ways, but we highly recommend a "skins-on" approach. The skins add a subtle flavor, are visually appealing (to us anyway), and are supposedly healthier.*

///

Place the peanuts in a food processor. Sprinkle the salt and drizzle the honey over the peanuts. Pulse in 30-second bursts 4 to 5 times until the peanuts are reduced to a thick, pastelike consistency. Scrape down the sides and bottom of the bowl, replace the lid, and process while slowly adding 1 teaspoon of the peanut oil through the feed tube. Continue processing for another minute or two until you reach the desired consistency. If the peanut butter is too thick, slowly add more peanut oil while pulsing. Once the preferred consistency is reached, sprinkle ¼ teaspoon fleur de sel (if using) over the peanut butter and process again for 5 seconds. Taste, and add more fleur de sel if necessary.

Homemade peanut butter can be stored in the refrigerator, tightly covered, for up to 45 days.

VARIATION: For chunky peanut butter, reserve ¼ cup of the nuts, chop them very coarsely, and fold them into the smooth peanut butter after you've added and processed the fleur de sel.

BAKING BETTER WITH PEANUT BUTTER

The peanut butter aisle at your local grocery store is probably awash in choices—a lot more choices than we were confronted with during our formative (read: high school) years. This is a good thing. But it also means you need to make some difficult decisions and you need to read a lot of labels very closely. Though we remain loyal to our nostalgia brands, we also try to avoid anything with either added sugar (a bit of molasses is okay) or trans fats. Thankfully, a lot of less-expensive mass-market brands make trans fat–free or "natural" versions.

You can use homemade (we fancy our own version, opposite) or natural peanut butter for every peanut butter recipe in this book. That said, you need to make sure it is stirred together extremely well (not oily or runny) before adding it to the recipe. Also, you should be aware that these homemade and natural peanut butters differ greatly when it comes to salt—some are extremely salty and others are salt free. Saltier peanut butter makes for a saltier dessert. If you are using a heavily salted peanut butter, you might want to decrease the amount of salt per recipe, as we wrote each recipe in this book for a medium-salted peanut butter. If you are using an unsalted or salt-free peanut butter, you might want to increase the salt just a tad, but that is entirely up to you.

Ultimately, peanut butters taste vastly different from brand to brand. We've found that price is not a great indicator of a great peanut butter, as some really inexpensive brands taste much better than their pricey competitors. So if you have the wherewithal, we suggest taste testing across the crowded field. If the peanut butter is delicious to eat, it will be perfect for your baked goods.

For the Milk Chocolate Layers

- 2 ounces good-quality milk chocolate, coarsely chopped
- ½ cup dark unsweetened cocoa powder (like Valrhona)
- ⅔ cup hot coffee
- ⅓ cup whole milk
- 1⅓ cups all-purpose flour
- 1 teaspoon baking soda
- ½ teaspoon salt
- 5 ounces (1¼ sticks) unsalted butter, softened, cut into ½-inch cubes
- 1 cup firmly packed dark brown sugar
- ½ cup granulated sugar
- 3 large eggs
- 1 teaspoon pure vanilla extract

For the Peanut Butter Filling

- 2 ounces (½ stick) unsalted butter, softened, cut into ½-inch cubes
- ½ cup smooth peanut butter (see page 26)
- ½ cup plus 2 tablespoons confectioners' sugar, sifted
- 1 teaspoon pure vanilla extract

For the Vanilla Peanut Butter Frosting

- 1 cup granulated sugar
- ¼ cup all-purpose flour
- 1 cup whole milk
- ¼ cup heavy cream
- 8 ounces (2 sticks) unsalted butter, cool but not cold, cut into ½-inch cubes
- 1 tablespoon plus 1 teaspoon Peanut Butter Filling
- 1 teaspoon pure vanilla extract

For the Assembly

- ¼ cup roasted salted peanuts, chopped
- 2 ounces good-quality dark chocolate (60 to 72%), shaved

OOPSY DAISY CAKE

AT OUR BAKERY, the staff churns through many tons of butter, eggs, flour, chocolate, and sugar. They are nimble, efficient, and focused, and they always—even under extreme pressure—produce spectacular and bountiful baked goods. Occasionally, in the midst of so many ingredients and recipes passing so quickly through so many skilled hands, errors occur. On even rarer occasions, these errors produce something worth preserving. Our Oopsy Daisy Cake began life as one of those odd kitchen accidents—when Blair Van Sant mistakenly swapped milk chocolate for dark chocolate. Not only did the "accident" work, it became a signature cake. The Oopsy sponge is paler and sweeter than its dark chocolate cousin and is practically engineered (even if accidentally) to be filled with a sweet dose of peanut butter filling and swathed in our light and fluffy vanilla peanut butter frosting. It is the kind of cake you want for your birthday and hope that there are many leftovers for late-night snacking.

//////////////////////////////// *Yield: One 8-inch, 2-layer cake* ////////////////////////////////

BAKED NOTE: *Milk chocolate is sexy all of a sudden, and the selection and quality keep improving. We wholly encourage you to try some of the newer, more exciting brands available (we currently love TCHO)—taste testing is fun. Please do avoid using a run-of-the-mill, chalky, overly sweet milk chocolate in this cake. Aim for something without any artificial ingredients and a high cocoa liquor content.*

//

MAKE THE CAKE

Preheat the oven to 325 degrees F. Butter two 8-inch round cake pans, line the bottoms with parchment paper, and butter the parchment. Dust with flour and knock out the excess flour.

Place the chocolate and cocoa powder in a medium-size heatproof bowl. Pour the hot coffee directly over the chocolate and cocoa and whisk until combined. Add the milk and whisk until smooth.

In another bowl, sift together the flour, baking soda, and salt. Set aside.

In the bowl of a standing mixer fitted with the paddle attachment, beat the butter and both sugars on medium speed until light and fluffy, about 3 minutes. Add the eggs, one at a time, beating well after each addition, then add the vanilla and beat until incorporated. Scrape down the sides and bottom of the bowl and mix again for 30 seconds.

Add the flour mixture in three parts, alternating with the chocolate mixture, beginning and ending with the flour mixture.

Divide the batter between the prepared pans and smooth the tops. Bake for 35 to 40 minutes, rotating the pans halfway through the baking time, until a toothpick inserted in the center of each cake comes out clean. Transfer the pans to a wire rack and let cool for 20 minutes. Invert the cakes onto the rack, remove the pans, and let cool completely. Remove the parchment.

MAKE THE PEANUT BUTTER FILLING

In the bowl of a standing mixer fitted with the paddle attachment, beat the butter on high speed until smooth. Add the peanut butter and beat on medium-low speed until just combined. Add the confectioners' sugar and the vanilla and beat until smooth. Set aside.

MAKE THE VANILLA PEANUT BUTTER FROSTING

In a medium, heavy-bottomed saucepan, whisk the sugar and flour together. Add the milk and cream and cook over medium heat, whisking occasionally, until the mixture comes to a boil and has thickened, 10 to 15 minutes.

Transfer the mixture to the bowl of a standing mixer fitted with the paddle attachment. Beat on high speed until cool, at least 7 minutes. (You can speed up the process by pressing bags of frozen berries or frozen corn against the sides and bottom of the mixing bowl.) Reduce the speed to low and add the butter; mix until thoroughly incorporated. Increase the speed to medium-high and beat until the frosting is light and fluffy, 1 to 2 minutes.

Add 1 tablespoon plus 1 teaspoon of reserved peanut butter filling and the vanilla and continue mixing until combined. If the frosting is too soft, put the bowl in the refrigerator to chill slightly, then beat again until it is the proper consistency. If the frosting is too firm, set the bowl over a pot of simmering water and beat with a wooden spoon until it is the proper consistency.

ASSEMBLE THE CAKE

Place one cake layer on a serving platter. Trim the top to create a flat surface and evenly spread with the peanut butter filling, then spread about ¼ cup vanilla peanut butter frosting on top of the filling. Add the next layer, trim it, and frost the top and sides with the remaining vanilla peanut butter frosting. Sprinkle peanuts and shaved chocolate around the perimeter of the cake.

The cake can be stored at room temperature, covered with a cake dome or in a cake saver, for up to 3 days.

OATMEAL PEANUT BUTTER CHOCOLATE CHIP SCONES

WE HAVE NOTHING against dainty scones—the sort you might find on pricey china in quaint, library-quiet tearooms. We believe every dessert (as long as it's tasty) has a purpose—even small, tiny, crumbly scones. We just happen to like large, dense, intensely flavored scones much, much better. Actually, we really go crazy for the idea of a scone masquerading as an oatmeal peanut butter chocolate chip cookie. The following recipe is our preferred breakfast scone/cookie hybrid. As with most scone recipes, the dough comes together quickly and does not require a mixer—perfect for hassle-free morning pastry—and it pairs extremely well with coffee. Our only request: make sure to use a crunchy peanut butter—it is essential for texture.

// *Yield: 8 scones* //

BAKED NOTE: *This scone has the makings for the perfect peanut butter and jelly sandwich. Simply omit the chocolate chips, bake per the regular directions, cool completely, and slice horizontally through the middle of each scone to create the "bread" slices. Fill each "sandwich" with jam or jelly and serve.*

//

2	cups all-purpose flour
⅓	cup firmly packed dark brown sugar
1	teaspoon baking soda
1	teaspoon baking powder
¼	teaspoon salt
1	cup rolled oats
3	ounces (¾ stick) cold unsalted butter, cut into ½-inch cubes
¾	cup well-shaken buttermilk
1	large egg, separated
½	cup chunky peanut butter (see page 26)
6	ounces (about 1 cup) semisweet or milk chocolate chips
2	tablespoons raw sugar (optional)

Preheat the oven to 400 degrees F and position the rack in the center. Line a baking sheet with parchment paper.

In a large bowl, whisk together the flour, brown sugar, baking soda, baking powder, salt, and oats. Add the butter and use your fingertips (or a pastry cutter) to rub (or cut) the butter into the flour mixture until the butter is pea-size and the mixture looks like chunky, coarse sand.

In a glass measuring cup or small bowl, whisk together the buttermilk and egg yolk until combined.

Make a well in the dry ingredients and pour the buttermilk mixture into the center of the well. Add the peanut butter. Using clean, dry, lightly floured hands, gently mix and knead the dough in the bowl until it starts to come together. Add the chocolate chips and knead until just incorporated. Do not overwork the dough.

Turn the dough out directly onto the prepared baking sheet and shape it into a disk 7½ to 8 inches in diameter and about 1½ inches high. Beat the egg white slightly, brush the top of the dough with the egg white, and sprinkle with the raw sugar, if you wish.

Cut the dough into 8 wedges—but do not separate the wedges—and bake for 18 to 22 minutes, or until the scones start to brown, rotating the baking sheet halfway through. Alternatively, check for doneness by inserting a toothpick into the center of the scone. If the toothpick comes out clean or with just a few crumbs clinging to it, the scones are done. (Make sure these are fully cooked—an underbaked scone is not nearly as good as a slightly underbaked brownie.)

Remove from the oven, let cool for 5 minutes and re-slice and separate the scones. Serve slightly warm or transfer to a wire rack to cool completely. Scones taste best when consumed within 24 hours of baking, but you could store these scones in an air-tight container for up to 2 days.

For the Peanut Butter Dough

2¼	cups all-purpose flour
¾	teaspoon baking powder
½	teaspoon baking soda
1	teaspoon salt
6	ounces (1½ sticks) unsalted butter, cool but not cold
1	cup firmly packed dark brown sugar
½	cup granulated sugar
3	tablespoons vegetable oil (preferably canola)
¾	cup smooth peanut butter (see page 26)
1	large egg, plus 1 large egg yolk
2	teaspoons pure vanilla extract

For the Chocolate Filling

12	ounces good-quality dark chocolate (60 to 72%), coarsely chopped
½	teaspoon light corn syrup

PEANUT BUTTER CHOCOLATE WHIRLIGIGS

HALF THE THRILL of making these whirligig cookies is just enjoying (or abusing) the name "whirligig." The word, however nonsensical, implies a sense of fun and whimsy, and that is perhaps the best way to describe these cookies—fun and whimsical. Essentially, the cookie is a rich peanut buttery layer slathered with a liberal amount of dark chocolate, then the entire thing is rolled up into a log and sliced into generously portioned cookies. The end result: a cookie with overlapping layers of peanut butter and dark chocolate nirvana. Our Peanut Butter Chocolate Whirligigs are plenty delicious at room temperature alongside a tall glass of milk; however, served warm, these are the most dangerously addictive cookies around.

///////////////////////////////////// *Yield: 25 to 30* /////////////////////////////////////

BAKED NOTE: *Whirligig cookies are supposed to have personality. This means every slice might be different—like snowflakes—with some swirls misbehaving and acting out. You can absolutely use our suggestion in the directions below (to use your fingers to reshape some of the slices) but you shouldn't be too obsessed with making the Most Beautiful Cookie on Earth. Remember, whirligigs are fun and whimsical.*

///

MAKE THE PEANUT BUTTER DOUGH

In a large bowl, whisk together the flour, baking powder, baking soda, and salt. Set aside.

In the bowl of a standing mixer fitted with the paddle attachment, beat the butter, sugars, oil, and peanut butter on medium-high speed until fluffy, about 5 minutes. Scrape down the sides and bottom of the bowl and add the egg, egg yolk, and vanilla, beating until incorporated.

Scrape down the sides and bottom of the bowl and add half of the flour mixture. Beat until just incorporated; do not overmix. Add the remaining flour mixture and beat until just incorporated.

Transfer the dough to a cool, lightly floured work surface and shape into a disk. Wrap the dough in parchment paper, then in plastic wrap, and refrigerate until the dough is firm, about 3 hours. The dough can be made a day ahead and refrigerated for up to 24 hours.

Flour a rolling pin. Line a work surface with a piece of parchment paper about 14 inches long, dust the parchment with a sprinkling of flour, divide the disk of dough in half, and roll out one half directly on the parchment into a rectangle about 9½ inches long by 7½ inches wide and just under ½ inch thick. If the dough is too thin, it will be extremely difficult to roll up. Transfer the dough, keeping it on the parchment, to the refrigerator to firm up. Repeat the rolling process for the second half of the disk and refrigerate.

MAKE THE CHOCOLATE FILLING

While the dough is chilling, melt the chocolate and corn syrup in a microwave or double boiler. Whisk until smooth, then set aside to cool for a few minutes.

ASSEMBLE THE ROLL

Remove 1 sheet of dough from the refrigerator. Dip a pastry brush in the chocolate and brush the top surface of the dough almost to the edge. Make sure the chocolate coverage is good and hearty, but leave a ½-inch strip with no chocolate on one of the long sides of the rectangle and double up the chocolate on the opposite long side—this will be the center of the cookie. (Alternatively, drizzle some of the chocolate mixture on the dough and use the back of a spoon to spread into an even layer.) Using the parchment paper to help you, slowly roll the dough into a log, starting from the long side of the rectangle that has double chocolate. (The paper should not be inside the log but used as a tool to help create the log.) Once the dough is rolled, keep it wrapped in the paper, then wrap tightly in plastic and refrigerate. Repeat this process with the second sheet of dough.

Chill the logs for at least 3 hours, or up to 24 hours, until the logs feel very solid; if they do not feel solid, they probably need to be refrigerated for a few hours longer.

MAKE THE COOKIES

Preheat the oven to 350 degrees F. Line two baking sheets with parchment paper.

Unwrap the logs and place on a cutting surface. Dip a knife in very hot water and cut the log into individual cookies, ½ to ¾ inch thick, and place on the prepared baking sheets. If they get a tiny bit disfigured in the cutting process, you can use your fingers to reshape the cookies slightly; if the chocolate breaks or spills out, you can gently push it back in place.

Bake for 11 to 13 minutes, rotating the baking sheets halfway through the baking time. Do not overbake these cookies—remove them from the oven the second they start to brown.

Place the baking sheets on wire racks to cool for 5 minutes. Then use a spatula to transfer the cookies to the racks to cool completely.

Whirligigs can be stored at room temperature, tightly covered, for up to 2 days.

BALE BARS

RENATO IS EXTREMELY pretzel conscious. He not only loves pretzels and is thinking about them often, but if he is imagining a recipe that calls for crushed pretzels, he doesn't think of just *any* crushed pretzels, he thinks of a very particular crushed pretzel (thick rods versus thin sticks versus classic pretzel style, salted versus unsalted, flavored versus unflavored). So it should not be a surprise that pretzels make frequent appearances in our recipes. The crunch and salt provided by the pretzel is often a welcome addition to the world of sweet, and the overall taste and texture work beautifully in our Bale Bars. The bars are quite simple to put together, and there is something delightful about them that transports you back to the many grade-school birthday parties of yore (or at least our birthday parties of the late '70s). We know you and your guests, whatever age, will enjoy these sweet, crunchy, nutty, peanut buttery bars—just be sure to use the pretzels specified in the ingredients. It's a Renato thing.

// **Yield: 24 bars** //

BAKED NOTE: *If you are not a white chocolate fan, we suppose you could substitute good-quality milk chocolate, though it should be noted that many of our friends and family who consider white chocolate to be an unnecessary evil really enjoy it in this bar.*

1½	ounces (3 tablespoons) unsalted butter
⅓	cup firmly packed dark brown sugar
⅓	cup heavy cream
1	teaspoon fleur de sel, divided
8	ounces good-quality white chocolate, chopped
1	tablespoon plus 1½ teaspoons pure vanilla extract, divided
¾	cup crunchy peanut butter (see page 26)
¾	cup (about 4 ounces) salted peanuts, coarsely chopped
3	cups (about 8½ ounces) salted thin pretzel sticks, crushed into small pieces

Lightly spray a 9-by-13-by-2-inch baking pan with nonstick cooking spray and line it with parchment paper, allowing the parchment to overhang on two sides.

In a medium saucepan over low heat, melt the butter. Stir in the sugar, cream, and ½ teaspoon fleur de sel. Increase the heat to medium and bring the mixture to a low boil for about 4 minutes. Remove the pan from the heat and add the white chocolate and 1 tablespoon of the vanilla. Stir until the mixture is smooth and the chocolate is melted. Add the remaining ½ teaspoon fleur de sel, remaining 1¼ teaspoons vanilla, and the peanut butter and stir until the mixture is completely smooth and uniform.

Place the peanuts and pretzels in a large bowl and use your hands to toss together until mixed well. Pour the white chocolate mixture over the peanut mixture and stir to coat all of the pieces. Pour the mixture into the prepared pan, then, using lightly oiled hands, press the mixture into an even layer. Refrigerate until hard, about 90 minutes.

Lift the bars out of the pan using the parchment paper overhang and cut them into squares. Bars can be served at room temperature, though we like them best directly from the refrigerator (or even the freezer). The bars can be stored in the refrigerator, tightly covered, for up to 3 days.

95% OF AMERICAN LEMONS ARE PRODUCED IN **CALIFORNIA AND ARIZONA**

YOU CAN USE A LEMON, A COPPER PENNY, AND A GALVANIZED NAIL TO POWER A SMALL LED LIGHT, AND MAYBE AN ALARM CLOCK

LEMON JUICE CONTAINS *about* **5% CITRIC ACID** WHICH CAN BE USED TO PRESERVE OTHER FRESH PRODUCE, SUCH AS APPLES, AVOCADOES, AND BANANAS

hello! **1908** FRANK N. MEYER INTRODUCES THE MEYER LEMON TO THE U.S.

WEIGHT *of the* WORLD'S HEAVIEST LEMON

11 LBS ✡ **9.7 OZ.**

GROWN IN ISRAEL

FLORIDA'S OFFICIAL STATE PIE: **KEY LIME PIE**

KEY LIMES WERE NAMED AFTER THE FLORIDA KEYS, HAVING BEEN FIRST COMMERCIALLY GROWN AND DISTRIBUTED THERE

FOR 100% of your daily serving of Vitamin C consume...

 OR

1 WHOLE LEMON   THE JUICE OF 3 LEMONS

Chapter 2

LEMON & LIME

Lemon and lime are the brightest and shiniest flavors in our bakery. They both have an unmatched purity—pure puckery sunshine— that permeates layers of secondary flavors and ingredients without being obnoxious. Citrusy cakes and curds and cookies are the things of summer breezes, pool parties, and picnics—probably due to their perceived lighter quality. However, we are fond of lemon and lime desserts anytime of the year. Lemon cake in June is delightful. Lemon cake during a cold, gray New York January is essential, therapeutic, and transportive and should be prescribed for Seasonal Affective Disorder. Oddly, the more sour and acidic the lemon (or lime) flavored dessert, the happier we are.

LIME ANGEL FOOD CAKE
with
LIME GLAZE

I SPENT MANY dark days and nights tinkering with myriad angel food cake recipes. It was an inescapable rabbit hole of the too-sweet and too-spongy—overall too precious to become a common guest on my home dessert rotation. Recipes, red-lined and tear-stained, piled up like locusts in the corner of my drawer—each one more fantastically bizarre and un-angel-food-like than the next. I was trying to reinvent the wheel. Then I stopped trying so hard. I relaxed. I went back to a bare-bones angel food cake formula and boosted the flavor with just the right amount of lime zing to cut the sweetness. Suddenly I was swimming in angel food nirvana. The lime glaze might seem audacious, but it is a lively and perfect companion to the billowy cake.

//////////////////////////////////// **Yield: One tube cake** ////////////////////////////////////

> **BAKED NOTE**: *As with most angel food cakes, this cake should be cooled upside down over a funnel or bottle (unless you are lucky enough to own one of those fancy angel food cake pans with feet): this keeps the cake tall (so it won't collapse in on itself). However tempting it may be, do not grease your pan or use a nonstick pan, as the cake will just plop out before it has cooled. It will appear as though your cake is stuck, but I promise it will free itself quite naturally with a little gentle coaxing.*

MAKE THE LIME ANGEL FOOD CAKE

Preheat the oven to 350 degrees F and position a rack in the center.

In a medium bowl, sift together ½ cup superfine sugar, the flour, and the salt. Repeat the sifting process two more times.

In the bowl of a standing mixer fitted with the whisk attachment, beat the egg whites, lime zest, and vanilla on medium speed until frothy (do not let the greenish hue of the batter scare you, it will return to normal after the remaining ingredients are added). Sprinkle the cream of tartar over the mixture and beat on medium-high until soft peaks form.

Gradually (in a stream or a few tablespoons at a time) add the remaining 1 cup of superfine sugar and beat just until stiff peaks form. Remove the bowl from the mixer and sprinkle one-third of the flour mixture over the egg whites. Gently—really gently—fold in the flour. Add half of the remaining flour and fold in gently. Add the remaining flour and fold in until just incorporated.

For the Lime Angel Food Cake

1½	cups superfine sugar, divided
1	cup cake flour
¼	teaspoon salt
10	large egg whites, at room temperature
2	teaspoons finely grated lime zest (from the lime used below)
1	teaspoon pure vanilla extract
1	teaspoon cream of tartar

For the Lime Glaze

½	cup granulated sugar
4	tablespoons fresh lime juice, divided (about 2 limes)
½	cup unsalted raw pistachios, finely chopped
½	cup confectioners' sugar
1	tablespoon tequila (optional, but delicious)

Transfer the batter to an ungreased 10-cup tube pan with removable bottom (do not use a nonstick pan). Use an offset spatula to smooth the top of the batter.

Bake the cake for 35 to 38 minutes, rotating the pan halfway through the baking time, until it is pale golden in color and a toothpick or skewer inserted near the center of the cake comes out clean. Immediately invert the pan onto a work surface if the pan has feet, or place the center of the tube pan onto the neck of a bottle or metal funnel, and cool the cake completely.

Using a long, thin knife, cut around the sides of the cake and the center tube to loosen. Lift out the center tube with the cake still attached; run the knife between the cake and the bottom of the pan to loosen. Remove the cake from the center tube and invert it onto a wire rack. Set the rack with cake onto a rimmed baking sheet.

MAKE THE LIME GLAZE

In a small saucepan over medium heat, stir together the granulated sugar and 3 tablespoons of the lime juice until the sugar dissolves. Brush the lime syrup over the top and sides of the cake and immediately press the finely chopped pistachios over the syrup so they adhere.

In a small bowl, whisk together the confectioners' sugar, the remaining tablespoon of lime juice, and the tequila until smooth. Drizzle the glaze over the top of the cake in a zigzag pattern. Let the glaze set, about 10 minutes, before serving.

The cake can be stored at room temperature, tightly covered, for up to 3 days, though angel food cake is generally best served within 48 hours.

SUNRISE KEY LIME TARTS

BOTH OF US spent a portion of our formative years in the Sunshine State (a.k.a. Florida)—Renato on the Atlantic side, myself on the Gulf—and we can attest, true to stereotype, the state is awash in Key lime pies. They were everywhere, and we took them for granted. Only after we left the state, and outgrew the arrogance of youth, did we understand the true beauty of this dessert—we had to leave it to love it. Our Sunrise Key Lime Tarts are Key lime tarts reinterpreted with bits and pieces of our favorite things. Renato thought a pretzel crust was snazzier and saltier than the traditional graham cracker crust, and I thought a splash of tequila seemed predestined. Thus we added a tiny bit of Brooklyn sentiment to what otherwise closely resembled a Florida classic—a creamy, tart, refreshing filling on a snappy crust.

/////////////////////////////////// *Yield: Eight 4-inch tarts* ///////////////////////////////////

> **BAKED NOTE**: *Key limes, smaller and more tart than the traditional, ubiquitous Persian lime, are quite obviously associated with the Florida Keys. They have a thinner rind, more seeds, and are less juicy (i.e., you will need many more Key limes than you would Persians to get the requisite amount of juice in this recipe). Outside of Florida, Key limes can be difficult to track down, and expensive. You can substitute Persian limes (their juice and their zest) in this recipe without worry: the amount of juice and zest is a one-to-one substitution, though you will need fewer Persian limes overall to get there.*

MAKE THE PRETZEL CRUST

Preheat the oven to 325 degrees F. Lightly spray a paper towel with vegetable oil and use it to apply the oil to the sides and bottom of eight 4-inch tart pans with removable bottoms. Place the tart pans on a baking sheet.

In a medium saucepan over low heat, melt the butter. Whisk in the brown sugar and remove from the heat. Add the pretzel crumbs and stir until combined—the mixture should look like wet sand. Place about 3 tablespoons of the crumb mixture in each prepared tart pan. Using your fingers or the bottom of a small metal measuring cup, press the mixture into the bottom and up the sides of each tart pan.

Bake the tarts on the baking sheet for about 10 minutes (the tops will appear set), then set them aside to cool completely.

Increase the oven temperature to 350 degrees F.

MAKE THE KEY LIME FILLING

In a large bowl, whisk the egg yolks with the sweetened condensed milk until

For the Pretzel Crust

5	ounces (1¼ sticks) unsalted butter
2	tablespoons firmly packed dark brown sugar
1½	generous cups (about 6 ounces) salted thin pretzel sticks, ground

For the Key Lime Filling

3	large egg yolks, at room temperature
14	ounces (1 can) sweetened condensed milk
¼	cup plus 2 tablespoons fresh Key lime juice (about 12 to 15 Key limes)
	Zest of 2 Key limes or 1 regular Persian lime (about 1 tablespoon)
2	tablespoons good-quality tequila
1	tablespoon triple sec or orange juice

For the Topping

1	cup heavy cream
2	tablespoons granulated sugar
	Zest of 4 Key limes or 2 regular Persian limes (about 2 tablespoons)
8	thin slices of Key lime (optional)

well blended. Add the lime juice, lime zest, tequila, and triple sec and whisk until combined and slightly thickened. Divide the filling among the prepared tart pans and bake on the baking sheet for 10 to 12 minutes, until the filling appears set. Transfer the baking sheet to a wire rack to cool completely, then refrigerate the tarts until the tops are cool to the touch, about 2 hours.

MAKE THE TOPPING

Pour the cream into a chilled metal bowl and beat it with a chilled whisk for about 1 minute. Sprinkle the granulated sugar and zest on top and continue whisking vigorously until soft peaks form.

To serve, gently push up on the tart bottoms to release the tarts from their pans. Top with the whipped topping and a thinly sliced lime pinwheel, if desired.

These tarts taste best if eaten within 24 hours but can be stored in the refrigerator (without the whipped topping), tightly covered, for up to 2 days.

⅔	cup sugar
1½	cups champagne (see Note)
	Zest and juice of 2 lemons
	Zest and juice of 1 lime
5	fresh mint leaves, plus more for garnish (optional, but perfect for summer)

LEMON LIME CHAMPAGNE GRANITA

MY FIRST GRANITA attempt was an effort to recapture a moment in time. I wanted to make an icy, sweet, fruity concoction that mimicked (or at least so I thought) the product I had made from my favorite childhood toy, the Snoopy Sno-cone Machine. The machine, compact and in the shape of Snoopy's doghouse, somehow elevated the process of making a snow cone into a nearly religious act (I suppose this is the power of character marketing to kids), though I am somehow certain the fogginess of my memories masks a chemically sweet aftertaste—fruit by way of science lab. Unfortunately, or fortunately, my first granita ventures didn't quite resemble the kind churned by Snoopy, but I was bitten nonetheless. I continued dabbling in granitas—mixing fruits, adding alcohol, removing sugar—and eventually, this sweet and sour and bubbly ice dream appeared. Our Lemon Lime Champagne Granita is like a perfect frozen lemonade dressed in black tie. It's refreshing and giddy. It's also incredibly easy (though it does require some freezer time), and I have yet to serve it to someone who didn't request a second helping.

/// *Yield: 4 servings* ///

BAKED NOTE: *We rarely recommend using inexpensive booze, but cheap (or inexpensive) champagne will work just as well as expensive champagne in this recipe. Lemon and lime are the real stars of this mix. The champagne is more like background music—it provides a nice bubbly essential sensation—but you (and, more important, your guests) most likely won't be able to tell if it is the no-name discount stuff or a premium couture brand.*

///

In a small saucepan over medium-low heat, stir together the sugar and ⅔ cup water until the sugar dissolves. This is your simple syrup base. Allow the simple syrup to cool completely.

In a separate bowl, whisk together the champagne, the zest and juice of the lemons and the lime, and the mint leaves (you are either a fresh mint person or not—if you like it, you will love it in this recipe). Whisk in the simple syrup and pour the mixture directly into an 8-inch square metal baking pan. Cover tightly with aluminum foil and put in the freezer.

Every hour, use a fork to scrape or stir the mixture, breaking up any large pieces of ice; continue checking and scraping until the granita is completely frozen, about 6 hours. Use the tines of the fork to scrape the granita into fluffy flakes. Divide it among 4 glasses, discarding the mint leaves. Garnish with new mint leaves and serve immediately with small spoons. The effect should be snow cone–like.

GOING GRANITA

We've tried many granita variations and like them all. It's hard to beat fresh fruit, pureed and frozen, with a little bit of alcohol and sugar. We wholeheartedly encourage you to experiment with the confidence that almost any slushy granita will be delicious and refreshing. But changes to each component will produce quite different results. Different alcohol will change the frozen texture, as will different fruit purees, and other fruits will require different amounts of sugar than the lemon and lime juice used in our granita recipe. Our only caveats:

Taste the mixture before you freeze it.
Remember that your liquid mix is utterly forgiving—it can be altered on the fly before you place it in the freezer. Freezing rarely improves overall taste (only texture)—so add more simple syrup or fruit (or flavor) as needed, then freeze.

Fluffy is generally better (in our opinion).
In our Lemon Lime Champagne Granita recipe (page 46) we provide a guideline for scraping the mixture as it freezes. Scrape more often for a looser, fluffier consistency (our preference); scrape less often for a denser concoction.

Freeze and combine anything.
We make almond granitas with almonds, cinnamon, and coffee (the exact recipe appears in our first book *Baked: New Frontiers in Baking*). And we like mixing and matching various fruits with various liquors (orange juice, white wine and Cointreau is a popular option). We are currently working on a sweet Long Island iced tea version. Don't be afraid to dream up your own creation.

8	ounces (2 sticks) unsalted butter, softened
⅔	cup confectioners' sugar
⅓	cup firmly packed light brown sugar
I	teaspoon salt
I	teaspoon minced fresh tarragon
I	tablespoon lime zest (about I lime)
2	teaspoons fresh lime juice
2	cups all-purpose flour

For the White Chocolate Lime Topping

3	ounces good-quality white chocolate, coarsely chopped
	Strips of zest of I lime (about I tablespoon)

LIME TARRAGON COOKIES

with

WHITE CHOCOLATE LIME TOPPING

THE ORIGINAL IDEA behind this recipe was to create a giant lime cookie—something the size of a small UFO—to satiate a very peculiar craving for a large, buttery, lime cookie. This craving would overtake me at inopportune moments (in the middle of a movie, on the phone with a business associate, during a long plane ride), and I couldn't shake the feeling that my lime craving was in direct proportion to the amount of chocolate I had consumed. I needed some tart to combat the sweet rumbling through my veins. Needless to say, the oversized lime cookie experiment went awry. It was like grocery shopping on an empty stomach—too much of everything. The cookie was too extreme: too large, the lime flavor too pronounced, and overall too one-note. In a less hallucinatory state, I reworked the cookie a few times, and the end result is this soul-satisfying recipe. The final cookies are back to normal-ish size. I added a bit of tarragon for an almost imperceptible anise taste (a surprising and welcome addendum), and the white chocolate and lime zest topping acts as both the perfect playful decor and a subtly sweet counterbalance.

////////////////////////////////// *Yield: 12 cookies* //////////////////////////////////

BAKED NOTE: *Tarragon is a funny herb. Some testers wanted more of a tarragon-y taste, and others were somewhat terrified to add it to the batter. I think the 1 teaspoon called for in the recipe is just enough—and it adds a dimension without being overpowering. However, if you are crazy about the herb, go ahead and add another teaspoon—just don't leave it out altogether.*

//

MAKE THE LIME TARRAGON COOKIES

In the bowl of a standing mixer fitted with the paddle attachment, beat the butter and sugars together until smooth and creamy. Add the salt, tarragon, lime zest, and lime juice and beat on high speed for 30 to 45 seconds, until the zest appears to separate and speckles the dough. Add the flour and beat on low speed until incorporated. Scrape down the sides and bottom of the bowl and beat again for 10 seconds. Scrape down the bowl again and use a spatula to mound the dough in the center. Cover the bowl and refrigerate for at least 1 hour.

Preheat the oven to 350 degrees F. Line two baking sheets with parchment paper.

Using a small ice cream scoop with a release mechanism, scoop out the dough into 2 tablespoon–size balls. (Alternatively, measure the dough using a tablespoon and use your hands to form it into balls.) Place the dough balls about 1 inch apart on the

prepared baking sheets. Bake for 13 to 15 minutes, until the edges of the cookies are golden brown and just start to darken.

Remove the baking sheets from the oven and place on wire racks to cool for 10 minutes. Use a spatula to transfer the cookies to the racks to cool completely.

MAKE THE WHITE CHOCOLATE LIME TOPPING

Place the chocolate in a glass measuring cup (or small microwave-safe bowl). In 10-second bursts, microwave the chocolate at 100% power (high), stirring in between, until the chocolate is completely melted and smooth, about 3 bursts. (Alternatively, the chocolate can be melted using the double-boiler method.)

Using an offset spatula, spread a dollop of white chocolate on the top of each cookie, then sprinkle the white chocolate with a little bit of lime zest (less is more here—you are trying to achieve a nice, minimal decoration, not lime zest overload). Allow the chocolate to set completely before serving.

The cookies can be stored at room temperature, in an airtight container, for up to 3 days.

LEMON SHAKER PIE

WE IMAGINE LEMON must always feel like the runner-up, the silver medalist. It is a bright and shiny and popular dessert flavor, but not as popular as the more loved, more ubiquitous chocolate. Alas, lemon desserts are tempered by an imagined seasonality that chocolate does not have to contend with: a lemon bar in January feels fundamentally doubly awkward, like an uninvited party guest dressed in improper attire. It doesn't have to be that way. We think our Lemon Shaker Pie is a great way to extoll the virtues of lemon year round. This pie is a lemon lover's dream. We didn't add any distracting nuances (herbs, caramel, or vanilla); it is just a straight-up lemon injection—pure and distinguished. It is homey in a way that is specific to pie and sweet and sour in a way that is specific to lemon, and we are certain that you will enjoy it almost any time of year.

// *Yield: One 9-inch pie* //

BAKED NOTE: *We adore this pie as is; however, we recognize that it is on the sweeter (but very tasty) side. Feel free to temper the sweetness with mounds of whipped cream or a side of black coffee.*

I	recipe Classic Pie Dough (page 161)
I	recipe Sugared Lemons (page 52)
4	large eggs, plus I large egg white, divided
3	tablespoons all-purpose flour
I	tablespoon cornstarch
¼	teaspoon salt
2	ounces (½ stick) unsalted butter, melted and cooled
I	tablespoon raw sugar

Dust a work surface with a sprinkling of flour. Roll out the first dough ball into a 12-inch round. Transfer it to a 9-inch pie plate and carefully work it into place, leaving a slight overhang. Using your floured work surface, roll out the second ball of dough into a 12-inch round, cover with plastic wrap, and reserve on a large plate in the refrigerator.

Remove the sugared lemon slices from the sugar and spread them out over the bottom of the prepared pie crust. Set aside the lemon sugar.

In a separate bowl, whisk the 4 eggs slightly. Add the flour, cornstarch, salt, and butter and whisk again until combined. Add the reserved lemon sugar and whisk until combined. Pour the mixture into the pie crust, directly over the lemon slices, and top with the chilled dough round. Trim the dough, leaving a ½ inch overhang. Crimp the edges together, cut 3 steam vents into the top crust, cover lightly with plastic wrap, and refrigerate for 1 hour.

Preheat the oven to 425 degrees F.

Remove the pie from the refrigerator. Whisk the egg white, brush it over the top crust of the pie, and sprinkle with the raw sugar.

Bake for 20 minutes, then reduce the oven temperature to 350 degrees F and continue baking for another 25 to 30 minutes, or until the pie is golden brown and a paring knife inserted into the center of the pie comes out relatively clean.

Place the pie on a wire rack to cool completely. Serve at room temperature or cover the pie and refrigerate for about 2 hours and serve chilled (a very popular method with a lot of our taste testers).

The pie can be stored in the refrigerator, tightly covered, for up to 2 days. Serve while still slightly cool.

SUGARED LEMONS

NORMALLY, WE WOULD INSIST on blanching the lemons for this recipe, as the process of submerging them in boiling water for a minute or two really tempers the bitterness and chewiness of the lemon peel. However, we found that many of our taste testers preferred a pure, bitter, and chewy lemon. We realize that blanching is an extra step, so to that end, we decided to write the recipe without the blanching step. If you decide to blanch (and we think it might be worth the extra step, we really do), then just bring a pot of water to a boil, remove the pot from the heat, drop in the lemon slices, stir for 1 minute, then transfer the slices to a bowl of ice water. Drain immediately and continue with the recipe.

Yield: 1 cup

2	cups sugar
2	lemons

Place the sugar in a large shallow bowl. Wash the lemons thoroughly, pat dry, and place in the freezer for about 30 minutes (this will make them easier to slice). Zest one of the lemons and place the zest in the bowl with the sugar. Slice the ends off of the zested lemon and remove the pith (the white interior under the skin). Use a mandolin to slice the zested lemon into paper-thin slices. Make sure the lemon slices are as thin as possible, or they will be too chewy (for us at least, though we know some of you prefer a chewier texture). Cut the ends off the second lemon, but do not zest and do not remove the pith. Again, use a mandolin to slice the lemon into paper-thin slices. Place both sets of lemon slices in the bowl of sugar (or blanch and drain the slices before adding to the sugar, if desired). Use your hands to gently toss them in the sugar to cover completely. Cover the bowl with plastic wrap. Let sit at room temperature for 48 hours, stirring the mixture with your hands about every 12 hours, to macerate.

½	cup shelled pistachios, divided
2	large eggs
¾	cup sour cream
2	teaspoons lemon juice
	Zest of ½ lemon
3	ounces (¾ stick) unsalted butter, melted and cooled
¾	cup all-purpose flour
1¼	cups yellow cornmeal
1	cup granulated sugar
1	teaspoon salt
2	teaspoons baking powder

LEMON PISTACHIO CORNMEAL MUFFINS

WE BELIEVE THAT in the same bizarre way some people start to resemble their pets over many years of bonding, we are starting to resemble our desserts. Whereas some people see the Virgin Mary in their morning buns, we see just an odd exaggerated reflection of ourselves. It is odder still then that a baked good could approximate exactly half of each of us—that a muffin could be our hybrid love child. I could subsist nearly forever on nothing more than lemon poppy seed muffins. Renato is deeply committed to a strict corn variation. This recipe, our Lemon Pistachio Cornmeal Muffin, is a little bit of both with a coarse topping of pistachio for flavor and textural oomph. The muffin crumb is probably closer to a corn muffin—flakier versus tight and moist. The flavor is very much "lemon," but with a salty finish. We are still not sure if it is a breakfast muffin or predinner treat, but we suppose it doesn't really matter when you make and eat them. Just make and eat them.

// *Yield: 12 to 15 muffins* //

BAKED NOTE: *How do you improve upon a muffin? We once watched, mouths agape, as a line cook sliced a large (head-of-cabbage size) muffin vertically, than basically pan-fried it (cut side down) in some browned butter for about 30 seconds. Should you do this to every muffin? Maybe. Should you do this to our Lemon Pistachio Cornmeal Muffin? Absolutely!*

//

In the bowl of a food processor, pulse the pistachios until they are coarsely chopped. Remove ¼ cup of the coarse pistachios and set aside. Continue to process the rest of the pistachios until they are almost powdery but not a superfine dust.

Preheat the oven to 400 degrees F. Lightly spray each cup of a standard 12-cup muffin pan with a little bit of vegetable spray and use a paper towel to spread the oil evenly along the bottom and up the sides of each cup.

In a medium bowl, lightly whisk the eggs. Add the sour cream, lemon juice, lemon zest, and butter and whisk again until combined. Set aside.

In a large bowl whisk together the flour, cornmeal, sugar, salt, the powdery (not the coarse) pistachios, salt, and baking powder. Make a well in the middle of the dry ingredients, pour the wet ingredients into the well, and fold the dry into the wet until just mixed.

Fill each muffin cup about three-quarters full. Sprinkle the tops with the coarse pistachios and tap the bottom of the pan against the counter to level the batter. Bake for 12 to 15 minutes, or until the tops are golden brown and a toothpick inserted in the center comes out clean. Transfer the pan to a wire rack to cool for 10 to 15 minutes. Pop the muffins out while they're still warm and serve immediately.

Leftover muffins will keep, wrapped tightly in plastic wrap, for up to 36 hours.

1886 MILTON HERSHEY

OPENS THE

LANCASTER CARAMEL COMPANY

HE LATER LEARNED ABOUT CHOCOLATE-MAKING BECAUSE HE WAS LOOKING FOR NEW WAYS TO COAT HIS CARAMELS.

SALTED CARAMEL

WENT FROM A FRENCH OBSCURITY *to an ubiquitous* MAINSTREAM U.S. PRODUCT OVER THE LAST FIFTEEN YEARS, POPULARIZED BY COMPANIES SUCH AS STARBUCKS, WAL-MART, AND HAAGEN-DAZS. IT'S FAMOUSLY BELOVED BY PRESIDENT OBAMA

1950s: CARAMEL APPLES

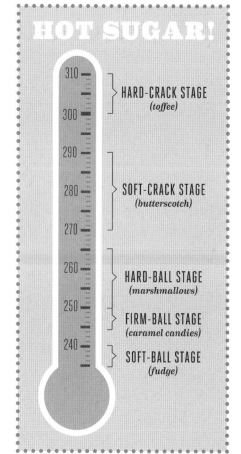

ARE INVENTED

BY A SALES REP FOR KRAFT FOODS; THE COMPANY STILL PRINTS THE RECIPE ON THE BACKS OF THEIR CARAMEL PACKAGES

HOT SUGAR!

310

HARD-CRACK STAGE
(toffee)

300

290

SOFT-CRACK STAGE
(butterscotch)

280

270

260

HARD-BALL STAGE
(marshmallows)

250

FIRM-BALL STAGE
(caramel candies)

240

SOFT-BALL STAGE
(fudge)

1,000

APPROXIMATE NUMBER OF BAGS OF

CRACKER JACK

(famous caramel-coated popcorn-peanut mix)

SOLD PER BASEBALL GAME AT

BOSTON'S
FENWAY PARK

Chapter 3
CARAMEL

Our bakery in Brooklyn is a tasting lab of sorts. We can produce a few samples of new product, sample them out to consumers, and immediately gather feedback. Our data collection is robust (according to us), though it would probably wither if held to the normal scientific precedents. Regardless, our findings are consistent: caramel is king. If you put caramel in or on something, people will like it better than the same item sans caramel. Caramel makes people, including us, crazy, wild eyed, and euphoric. Lately, caramel is experiencing a resurgence—one of many it has had and will have—though this time seems slightly loftier than previous incarnations. Lemon verbena–infused caramel is suddenly a thing and salty caramel is ubiquitous. We wholeheartedly embrace each and every take on caramel, but we are just as happy with the classic, simple, concoction of sugar, butter, and cream. It is, after all, the stuff of a million memories. Alas, some of the memories include shameful moments of lost willpower—moments where caramel on pasta seemed like a reasonable dinner—but they are our memories and they persevere.

CARAMEL

VARIATIONS ON A THEME

THE CATALYST IS IMPOSSIBLE to remember. Perhaps there wasn't one. Regardless, one day I woke up and made a jar of basic homemade caramel—not for a specific recipe, not in anticipation of a late-night ice cream sundae binge, not for any other reason except that it seemed like a great time to make a jar of home-made caramel—and I haven't stopped since. The fascination is partly fueled by both my chemistry geek wannabe side (see how the soupy sugar mixture turns to caramel?) and my overall love for the taste of burnt sugar (a little caramel on almost anything makes it taste better). I make jars for friends and even not-so-friendly friends. It's a simple DIY gift that is hard to dislike (I call "Scrooge!" to anyone who dislikes caramel).

The three recipes that follow are only the beginning of the endless riffs on caramel, and we embrace them all (though we are partial to the Sweet and Salty Caramel recipe—always have been). Some of the caramel recipes here are referenced throughout the book as parts of other recipes. However, we believe you don't need an excuse to make a jar of caramel. In fact, we think you should have a jar of caramel in your refrigerator just like you have a jug of milk or a bottle of ketchup—you never know when you'll need it.

The act of making caramel is not scary. We promise. It is easier than you might believe. First and foremost, gather all your ingredients prior to starting. Make sure you clear the room of distractions (i.e., telephone, television, guests) and make sure the area where you will be cooking is well lit. We almost always eyeball the caramel—we think a lot of caramel beginners get hung up and lost on thermometers—and you will need a clear, bright view as the syrup turns from translucent to nut brown (or darker in some cases).

DULCE DE LECHE

//////////////////////// **Yield: About 3 cups** ////////////////////////

28	ounces (2 cans) sweetened condensed milk
½	teaspoon salt

Stovetop method: Stir together the sweetened condensed milk and salt in a medium heatproof bowl and set it over a saucepan of boiling water over medium heat. Cook for 1 to 1½ hours, checking the water occasionally and adding more water as necessary, until the mixture is thick and dark-caramel colored. Remove the bowl from the pan and beat until smooth. Set aside to cool.

Microwave method: Stir together the sweetened condensed milk and salt in a large microwave-safe bowl. Cook at 50% power (medium) for 4 minutes, stirring briskly halfway through until smooth. Cook at 30% power (medium-low) for 12 to 18 minutes, until very thick and caramel colored, stirring briskly every 2 minutes until smooth. Set aside to cool.

Oven method: Preheat the oven to 425 degrees F. Stir together the sweetened condensed milk and salt in a 9-inch glass pie plate. Wrap the entire plate very tightly in aluminum foil and place the plate in a roasting pan. Fill the roasting pan with enough water so that it is level with the sweetened condensed milk (make sure the water does not leak into the pie plate, though). Bake for 60 minutes, checking the water level in the roasting pan every 20 minutes or so to ensure that it is level with the sweetened condensed milk. After 60 minutes, remove the foil. If the mixture is thick and dark-caramel colored, remove from the oven. If it is not quite dark enough, continue to cook for another 10 minutes or until done. Set aside to cool.

Dulce de Leche can be made ahead of time and stored in the refrigerator, tightly covered, for up to 3 weeks.

CLASSIC
CARAMEL SAUCE

/////////////// **Yield: About 3 cups** ///////////////

1½   cups sugar

¼   cup light corn syrup

4   ounces (1 stick) unsalted butter, softened, cut into ½-inch cubes

1½   cups heavy cream

In a medium saucepan with high sides, combine the sugar and corn syrup with ½ cup water. Stir the mixture gently so you don't splash any of it up on the sides of the pan. Cook over medium-high heat, stirring until the sugar dissolves. Increase the heat to high and, without stirring, allow the mixture to boil. Once it beings to turn a rich caramel color (300 degrees F on a candy thermometer), remove it from the heat. Add the butter and cream, and stir until combined. Set aside to cool.

The caramel sauce can be stored in the refrigerator, tightly covered, for up to 1 week. Let it come to room temperature before using it on cakes, ice creams, or quick breads. If you want a warm topping, heat the sauce in short bursts in a microwave or in a double boiler.

SWEET AND SALTY
CARAMEL SAUCE

/////////////// **Yield: 1⅓ cups** ///////////////

1   cup sugar

2   tablespoons light corn syrup

½   cup heavy cream

1   teaspoon fleur de sel

¼   cup sour cream

In a medium saucepan, combine the sugar and corn syrup with ¼ cup water. Stir the mixture gently so you don't splash any of it up on the sides of the pan. Cook over medium-high heat, stirring until the sugar dissolves. Increase the heat to high and, without stirring, cook over high heat until the mixture is dark amber in color (keep a close eye on the caramel at all times, as it goes from golden brown to black and burnt very quickly) or just shy of 350 degrees F on a candy thermometer, 6 to 8 minutes. Remove from the heat, and slowly add the cream (be careful, as it will bubble up) and then the fleur de sel. Whisk in the sour cream. Set aside to cool.

The sauce can be stored in the refrigerator, tightly covered, for up to 10 days.

ANTIQUE CARAMEL CAKE

For the Caramel Cake

- 4 ounces (I stick) unsalted butter, softened, cut into ½-inch cubes
- 1¼ cups granulated sugar
- ½ cup firmly packed light brown sugar
- 3 large eggs
- 2 cups all-purpose flour, sifted
- I cup well-shaken buttermilk
- I teaspoon baking soda
- I tablespoon white vinegar

For the Caramel Frosting

- ¼ cup firmly packed dark brown sugar
- 5 ounces (1¼ sticks) unsalted butter, at room temperature, cut into ½-inch cubes, divided
- ⅓ cup heavy cream
- 8 ounces cream cheese, softened
- ¼ teaspoon salt
- 2 cups confectioners' sugar, sifted

For the Assembly

- ¼ cup Sweet and Salty Caramel Sauce (optional, page 59)

THIS IS ONE of those recipes that has been kicking around my periphery ever since my University of Alabama days. I am fairly certain I ate many a caramel cake during those years, but honestly, I just remember eating many a cake—caramel, red velvet, coconut, lemon, chocolate, praline—it was like a big fluffy Southern dream. I decided to revisit caramel cake via an old college friend, Gerald, from Fulton, Mississippi. His mom, Terrisa, gave us her treasured recipe—her antique or vintage recipe—and we toyed with it ever so gently. The layers by themselves were beautiful as is—a sturdy, tasty, yellow crumb—but we dialed down (only a few notches) the sweetness of the frosting by adding cream cheese. We imagine this cake was invented for large picnic tables and Southern breezes, but we will eat it just about any time.

/////////////////////////////////////// *Yield: One 8-inch, 2-layer cake* ///////////////////////////////////////

BAKED NOTE: *If you want to ratchet the sweetness level up a bit (to approximate a true Southern delight), we suggest poking holes in the layers a few minutes after they come out of the oven and drizzling them with warm Classic Caramel Sauce (page 59)—it will seep into the cake.*

MAKE THE CARAMEL CAKE

Preheat the oven to 350 degrees F.

Butter two 8-inch round cake pans, line them with parchment paper, and butter the parchment. Dust the parchment with flour and knock out the excess flour.

In the bowl of a standing mixer fitted with the paddle attachment, beat the butter on medium speed until creamy, about 1 minute. Add both sugars and beat until fluffy, about 3 minutes. Scrape down the sides and bottom of the bowl and add the eggs, one at a time, beating well after each addition. Scrape down the bowl again and add the flour in three parts, alternating with the buttermilk, beginning and ending with the flour.

In a small bowl or cup, dissolve the baking soda in the vinegar and beat it into the batter until just combined.

Divide the batter between the prepared pans and smooth the tops. Bake for 32 to 37 minutes, rotating the pans halfway through the baking time, until the cake tops are slightly browned and a toothpick inserted in the center of the cake comes out clean. Transfer the pans to wire racks and let cool for 20 minutes. Turn the cakes out onto the racks and let cool completely. Remove the parchment.

MAKE THE CARAMEL FROSTING

In a medium saucepan over medium heat, stir together the brown sugar and 2 ounces (½ stick) of the butter until melted and combined. Bring the mixture to a boil and boil for 10 to 15 seconds. Remove from the heat, whisk in the cream, and transfer the mixture to a bowl to cool completely. (Note: To cool the mixture quickly for immediate use, you can stir or whisk the mixture vigorously to release excess heat or you can nestle the bowl with the mixture in a larger bowl filled halfway with ice.)

Once the brown sugar mixture is nearly cool, place the remaining 3 ounces of butter in the bowl of a standing mixer fitted with the paddle attachment and beat until it is lump free. Add the cream cheese and salt and continue beating until mixture is smooth. Scrape down the sides and bottom of the bowl and beat again for 15 seconds. Turn the mixer to low and stream in the brown sugar mixture. Scrape down the bowl again, add the confectioners' sugar, and beat until smooth. If the mixture feels too loose, refrigerate it for 5 to 10 minutes until it firms up.

ASSEMBLE THE CAKE

Place one cake layer on a serving platter. Trim the top to create a flat surface and evenly spread about ¾ cup frosting on top. Place the next layer on top, then trim and frost it the same way. Frost the sides of the cake with the remaining frosting, drizzle with the caramel sauce (either in a zigzag or circular pattern), and refrigerate the cake for 15 minutes to set before serving.

The cake can be stored in the refrigerator, covered with a cake dome or in a cake saver, for up to 3 days. Allow it to come to almost room temperature before serving.

For the Toasted Coconut

- 3 cups shredded sweetened coconut, divided

For the Cookie Base

- 2 cups all-purpose flour
- ½ teaspoon salt
- 8 ounces (2 sticks) unsalted butter, softened, cut into ½-inch cubes
- ½ cup granulated sugar
- ½ teaspoon pure vanilla extract

For the Caramel Layer

- 1 cup light corn syrup
- ½ cup granulated sugar
- ½ cup firmly packed light brown sugar
- 1 cup heavy cream
- ⅓ cup sweetened condensed milk
- 2 ounces (½ stick) unsalted butter, at room temperature, cut into ½-inch cubes
- 1 teaspoon pure vanilla extract

For the Assembly

- 6 ounces good-quality dark chocolate (60 to 72%), coarsely chopped
- 2 ounces good-quality milk chocolate, coarsely chopped

CARAMEL COCONUT CLUSTER BARS

THE LIST OF compulsive Girl Scout Cookie hoarders is both long and varied. It is full of people, like Renato, whose happiness is dictated by a meticulous cookie production and distribution schedule—a life that is ordered by the rhythms and whims of Girl Scout Cookies with happy-sounding names like Do-si-dos and Trefoils. Renato's obsessive compulsive about placing his frequent cookie order: two boxes of Samoas, one box of Thin Mints (always eaten directly from the freezer), and one box of Tagalongs (peanut butter patties usually reserved for me). Samoas, the doughnut-shaped caramel and toasted coconut cookies, are his favorites (thus the two boxes). In fact, he constructed this recipe as a tribute to the Samoa in bar form. The bottom layer is a solid, buttery short-bread and is topped with an old-school candylike coconut caramel. After the bars are cut, the base of each one is individually dipped in a mix of chocolate, then the top is drizzled in even more chocolate. In short, it's double the cookie quotient and triple the caramel quotient with tons of chocolate, and it really hits the Girl Scout Cookie sweet spot.

// *Yield: 24 bars* //

BAKED NOTE: *A Samoa homage without coconut is hardly a true homage. We think you should try this recipe with the recommended coconut; however, a few anti-coconut testers swapped the coconut in the recipe with 2 cups of toasted nuts (any kind will work) and have been raving about the results ever since. We can't deny that shortbread + caramel + nuts + chocolate is a winning combo as well.*

//

MAKE THE TOASTED COCONUT

Preheat the oven to 300 degrees F. Line a baking sheet with parchment paper.

Spread the coconut in an even layer on the baking sheet and toast, tossing and turning every 4 minutes or so, until the coconut just starts to turn golden, about 12 minutes total. Remove the coconut from the oven and set aside to cool.

MAKE THE COOKIE BASE

Increase the oven temperature to 350 degrees F. Lightly spray a 9-by-13-inch baking pan with nonstick cooking spray and line it with parchment paper, allowing the parchment to overhang on two sides. Lightly spray the parchment paper.

In a medium bowl, whisk together the flour and salt.

In the bowl of a standing mixer fitted with the paddle attachment, beat the butter and sugar on medium speed until fluffy, approximately 2 minutes. Add the vanilla and the flour mixture and beat just until combined.

Turn the dough out into the prepared baking pan and, with lightly floured hands, press it into an even layer on the bottom of the pan (do not press up the sides). Prick the top of the dough with the tines of a fork and bake the crust for 25 to 30 minutes, rotating the pan halfway through the baking time, until golden. Remove the pan from the oven and place on a wire rack to cool.

MAKE THE CARAMEL LAYER

In a medium saucepan, combine the corn syrup, both sugars, and 2 tablespoons of water and stir gently so you don't splash any of it up on the sides of the pan. Set the saucepan over low heat and continue to stir gently until the sugar dissolves. Clip a candy thermometer to the side of the pan, making sure the bulb of the thermometer is immersed in the syrup. Turn the heat up to medium-high and wait without stirring for the mixture to reach 240 to 245 degrees F, about 7 minutes. Keep a watchful eye on the temperature while you proceed with the next step—you do not want the mixture to exceed 250 degrees F.

Meanwhile, in a small saucepan over medium heat, stir together the cream and sweetened condensed milk. Gently warm the mixture while stirring; do not let it boil.

Once the sugar mixture turns amber, remove it from the heat and stir in the butter and the warm cream mixture until completely combined (be careful, as it will bubble up when you add the cream mixture). Place the pan back over medium heat, stop stirring, and bring the mixture back to 245 to 250 degrees F.

Remove the pan from the heat, stir in the vanilla, and fold in 2 cups of the toasted coconut.

Pour the caramel directly onto the cookie base and, working quickly, use an offset spatula to spread it into an even layer. Sprinkle the remaining 1 cup toasted coconut over the caramel and press lightly to adhere. Let cool to room temperature, about 2 hours, then place in the refrigerator to chill for at least 1 hour.

Line a baking sheet with parchment paper. Use a knife to loosen the chilled bars from the sides of the pan, then lift the bars out using the parchment paper overhang. Spray a sharp knife with nonstick cooking spray and cut the bars into twenty-four 3-by-1½-inch rectangles and place on the prepared baking sheet. Refrigerate until ready to assemble.

ASSEMBLE THE BARS

Melt both chocolates together in the bowl of a double boiler over medium heat or in the microwave (in a microwave-safe bowl, cook the chocolate at 50% power—medium—for 15-second bursts, stirring between each blast, until melted).

Dip half of each individual bar in the melted chocolate, scrape off the excess chocolate with an offset spatula, and place the bar back on the baking sheet. Repeat with the remaining bars.

Alternatively, dip the bottom of each bar into the chocolate, then scrape off the excess chocolate with an offset spatula. Return to the baking sheet to set. Once set, squeeze the chocolate into one corner of zippered plastic bag and twist the other end of the bag a few times to form a makeshift pastry bag. Use a kitchen scissor to snip off a small corner of the bag where the chocolate has collected (you don't want too large a snip or the chocolate will ooze out). Working quickly, drizzle the chocolate in a zigzag pattern across all of the bars.

Place the pan of bars back into the refrigerator for 15 minutes to let the chocolate set up. Serve immediately.

The bars can be stored in the refrigerator, tightly covered, for up to 4 days. They taste really good directly from the refrigerator as well as at room temperature—entirely up to you.

2 cups heavy cream

1 vanilla bean

6 large egg yolks

⅓ cup granulated sugar

⅛ teaspoon salt

3 tablespoons firmly packed dark brown sugar

CLASSIC CRÈME BRÛLÉE
with
CARAMELIZED BROWN SUGAR

IF YOU ARE going to fully embrace a dessert that has become somewhat of an ordinary staple—some would say boring—you have to really embrace it. You have to ignore the mediocre (or downright awful) versions that haunt restaurant menus and supermarket aisles and semidecent sweet shops. You have to assume that there is light at the end of the crème brûlée tunnel. We want to reintroduce you to crème brûlée here, because it deserves another chance. We like the versatility of a well-made crème brûlée—it's simple, unfussy, and the flavor profile is gentle enough to pair with any meal (or even just coffee or tea). This version adheres closely to a classic recipe, though we use dark brown sugar for the crackly, caramelized top (everyone's favorite part of eating the brûlée is breaking through the top) to bring out a hint of molasses flavor. Don't be afraid to bring back the brûlée, just bring it back with good, fresh ingredients (the vanilla bean is imperative) and a little flair.

/// *Yield: 4 servings* ///

BAKED NOTE: *We don't normally encourage buying kitchen equipment that has a limited use, but we wholeheartedly believe that owning a kitchen torch (crème brûlée torch) is worth the splurge. We use our torches to add color to meringue, gently re-warm chilled frosting (by torching the outside of a metal bowl), and, of course, create the perfect glasslike top on crème brûlée.*

//

Preheat the oven to 325 degrees F. Place four 6-ounce ramekins in a small roasting pan or large, high-sided baking pan.

Pour the heavy cream into a medium saucepan. Cut the vanilla bean in half lengthwise and, using the tip of a knife or a small spoon, scrape the seeds into the cream. Add the split vanilla bean pod and stir. Heat the cream to just below a boil (bubbles will form around the perimeter of the pan), turn off the heat, and let the mixture steep for 10 minutes.

In another bowl, whisk together the egg yolks, granulated sugar, and salt. Keep whisking until the mixture is well combined and begins to lighten in color, but do not overmix. Pour a small amount of the heavy cream into the egg yolk mixture while stirring (not whisking). Continue to add the cream, a little at a time, until it is incorporated. Push the mixture through a fine-mesh sieve into a pourable glass measuring cup or bowl.

Divide the mixture equally among the ramekins, filling almost to the top. Carefully pour boiling water into the roasting pan until the water reaches about halfway up the sides of the ramekins. Bake for 30 to 35 minutes, until the custards are set on the edge but still wobbly in the middle. Remove the ramekins from the water, let cool to room temperature, cover, and refrigerate least 4 hours or overnight.

Remove the ramekins from the refrigerator at least 15 minutes prior to serving. Sprinkle each ramekin with the brown sugar and use a kitchen torch to caramelize the sugar and create a smooth top. Wait a few minutes for the sugar to become crisp, and serve.

2 cups all-purpose flour

¾ teaspoon baking powder

¾ teaspoon baking soda

½ teaspoon salt

1 cup cornstarch

6 ounces (1½ sticks) unsalted butter, cool but not cold, cut into ½-inch cubes

⅔ cup granulated sugar

Zest of 1 lemon (about 1 tablespoon)

3 large egg yolks, plus 1 large egg

2 tablespoons good-quality light rum

1 teaspoon pure vanilla extract

2 to 2½ cups Dulce de Leche (page 58) or prepared dulce de leche

2 tablespoons confectioners' sugar for dusting (optional)

ALFAJORES

THE ALFAJOR HAS been interpreted many times for many palates on many continents, but the one we are most familiar with is the version that is popular in Argentina: two lovely shortbreadlike cookies sandwiching a beautiful, creamy dulce de leche filling. Even in Argentina, variations on this cookie abound. Some are enrobed in chocolate, some are dusted with confectioners' sugar, and some are filled with less traditional fillings like jam, peanut butter, or chocolate mousse. We are quite happy with the most basic alfajor—the snap and crumble of the cookie is more than the perfect complement to the thick caramel filling. As with all great sandwich cookies, we occasionally find ourselves dissecting this one with a wild-eyed pleasure—twisting off the top and eating it separately, scraping out the filling for a caramel fix—but usually, we just eat the cookie as it is meant to be eaten, as a simple, sweet sandwich.

/////////////////////////////////// *Yield: 24 to 28 sandwich cookies* ///////////////////////////////////

BAKED NOTE: *As home baking enthusiasts, we almost always make our own dulce de leche with sweetened condensed milk, but we would be remiss not to tell you that there are several all-natural brands available for purchase at your specialty grocer. Recently we became enamored with the La Salamandra brand—it tastes bright and uncomplicated—and we guard our individual jars with serious intention.*

In a large bowl, whisk together the flour, baking powder, baking soda, and salt. Sift the cornstarch over the flour mixture and whisk again to combine. Set aside.

In the bowl of a standing mixer fitted with the paddle attachment, beat the butter and granulated sugar together on medium-high speed until smooth and creamy. Scrape down the sides and bottom of the bowl, add the zest, and beat for 15 seconds. Add the egg yolks and egg, one at a time, beating until the mixture is light and fluffy. Scrape down the bowl again, add the rum and vanilla, and beat for 10 seconds.

Add half of the flour mixture and beat for 15 seconds. Add the remaining flour mixture and beat until just incorporated. Transfer the dough to a sheet of plastic wrap and pat it into a disk; wrap and refrigerate it for at least 1½ hours.

Preheat the oven to 350 degrees F. Line two baking sheets with parchment paper.

Unwrap the dough and divide it into 2 equal portions. Place the first portion on a work surface lightly dusted with flour (or, for extra ease, roll it out on a flour-dusted piece of parchment) and return the other portion to the refrigerator.

Form the dough into a small disk and roll it to ⅛ inch thick (or just a bit thicker). Use a 2-inch round cookie cutter to create your tops and bottoms, and transfer them to the prepared baking sheets, leaving about 1 inch of space around each cookie. Continue the process with the second piece of dough. Extra dough scraps can be refrigerated for about 10 minutes to firm them up so they can be rerolled, if desired.

Refrigerate the cookie-filled sheet pans for 5 minutes before baking. Bake for 8 to 11 minutes, rotating the sheets halfway through the baking time. The cookies will be done when they just begin to color (they won't "brown" necessarily). Place the baking sheets on wire racks to cool for 5 minutes. Use a spatula to transfer the cookies to the racks to cool completely before filling them.

Using a pastry bag with a medium tip, or a small spoon, apply about 2 tablespoons of dulce de leche to the flat side of a cookie (and don't feel shy about adding slightly more filling if you are in the mood—we often do). Place another cookie, flat side down, on top. Press slightly so that the filling spreads to the edges of the cookie. Repeat until all the sandwich cookies are made. Sift some confectioners' sugar over each cookie, if desired, and let them set up for about 15 minutes before serving.

The cookies can be stored at room temperature, tightly covered, for up to 3 days. Let it be known that some people think these cookies taste their best on day 2.

EASY CANDY BAR TART

WE ARE CANDY BAR fan boys. We swoon over American classics (Snickers, Kit Kats), stockpile European imports (Aero, Bounty, Twirl, Toffee Crisp), and embrace (er, hoard) the mini or fun-size versions of everything in the candy bar category. Naturally then, a candy bar rendered in tart form just seems like part of our lifeblood—an essential part of our day-to-day functionality—and this recipe is one of our favorite interpretations. First, it is impossibly tasty—like a gigantic, chewy, handmade candy bar. It has bite and texture and sates the hunger that lingers between lunch and dinner. Second, it is ridiculously easy to make. Tarts can be fussy, but this one is easy (made more so by the cookie crust) and can be thrown together with minimal ingredients and effort, though it will impress and shine in almost any dessert environment. The final effect is an attractive, grown-up elegance without arrogance—and it is irresistible.

/////////////////////////////////// *Yield: One 9-inch tart* ///////////////////////////////////

BAKED NOTE: *For whatever reason, this tart tastes even more candy bar–like with really dark (slightly overtoasted) walnuts. Regularly toasted walnuts are great, but something about the smoky, dark walnuts really brings out an unusual and warm flavor. Just use caution and let your taste buds guide you: blackened and blistered is not the same as dark—blackened and blistered is bad.*

///

MAKE THE CHOCOLATE COOKIE CRUST

Preheat the oven to 300 degrees F. Lightly coat a 9-inch springform pan with nonstick cooking spray.

In a food processor, pulse the cookies into a very fine powder. You should have about 1½ cups. Place the crumbs in a medium bowl and stir in the sugar.

Pour the butter over the crumb mixture and mix until well combined. The mixture will feel wet. Turn the crumb mixture out into the prepared pan and press it into the bottom and up the sides (just shy of 1 inch high). You can use the back of a large spoon or the bottom of a glass to even out the crust. Put it in the refrigerator while you make the filling.

MAKE THE CARAMEL WALNUT FILLING

In a medium saucepan with high sides, combine the sugar with ¼ cup water. Stir the mixture gently so you don't splash any of it up on the sides of the pan. Cook over medium-high heat, stirring until the sugar dissolves. Increase the heat to high, and, without stirring, allow the mixture to boil. Once it begins to turn a rich amber color, remove it from the heat and slowly stream in the cream. After the mixture stops

For the Chocolate Cookie Crust

- 30 chocolate wafer cookies (about 6 ounces)
- 1 tablespoon sugar
- 3 ounces (¾ stick) unsalted butter, melted

For the Caramel Walnut Filling

- 1 cup sugar
- ⅓ cup heavy cream
- 2½ ounces (5 tablespoons) unsalted butter, softened, cut into ½-inch cubes
- ½ teaspoon pure vanilla extract
- ½ teaspoon fleur de sel
- 2 cups walnuts, toasted (see Note and page 19)

For the Chocolate Glaze

- 4 ounces good-quality dark chocolate (60 to 72%), coarsely chopped
- 3 ounces (¾ stick) unsalted butter, softened, cut into ½-inch cubes
- 1 teaspoon light corn syrup

bubbling, return the pan to very low heat and whisk in the butter. Continue whisking gently until the caramel is uniform and slightly thickened, about 2 minutes. Stir in the vanilla and fleur de sel.

Remove the pan from the heat and stir in the walnuts. Pour the filling into the prepared crust and chill the tart for at least 1 hour.

MAKE THE CHOCOLATE GLAZE

Place the chocolate, butter, and corn syrup in the bowl of a double boiler over medium heat. Using a rubber spatula, stir the mixture until the chocolate and butter are completely melted and smooth. Remove the bowl from the water and stir the glaze to release excess heat.

Pour the glaze over the tart and use an offset spatula to smooth it out to the edges—try to cover the entire surface of the tart. Refrigerate the tart for 1 hour to set the glaze before slicing and serving.

Serve slightly chilled or at room temperature. The tart can be stored, tightly covered, in the refrigerator for up to 3 days.

For the Thumbprint Cookies

2	cups all-purpose flour
I	cup dark unsweetened cocoa powder (like Valrhona)
1½	teaspoons salt
8	ounces (2 sticks) unsalted butter, softened, cut into ½-inch cubes
I	cup firmly packed dark brown sugar
¼	cup granulated sugar
2	large eggs, plus I large egg white, divided
2	tablespoons whole milk
I	tablespoon pure vanilla extract
3	cups pecans, toasted (page 19), finely chopped

For the Caramel Filling

14	ounces (I can) sweetened condensed milk
½	cup firmly packed light brown sugar
3½	ounces (7 tablespoons) unsalted butter
3	tablespoons light corn syrup
I	tablespoon heavy cream
2	teaspoons pure vanilla extract
I	teaspoon salt
24 to 30	whole pecans, toasted (optional, page 19)

TURTLE THUMBPRINT COOKIES

WE ARE, AT HEART, easily smitten with anything turtle. The concept of a turtle dessert—usually some combination of chocolate, caramel, and pecans—is easy to love, and the variation on the turtle theme is endless. We have made turtle cakes (chocolate cake with caramel pecan filling), turtle sundaes (caramel ice cream flooded with chocolate chunks and pecans), turtle bars (more caramel, more chocolate, in a pecan crust), and of course Turtle Thumbprint Cookies. These cookies are rich and chocolaty—like all good turtle-y things— and the nuts and the caramel filling round out the serious chocolate flavor in a perfectly Zen way. They're fun to make (kids love making the thumbprint) and fun to eat (we suggest eating them chilled, directly from the refrigerator). Turtle worship has never felt so good.

/////////////////////////////////////// *Yield: 24 to 30 cookies* ///////////////////////////////////////

BAKED NOTE: *More than likely, this recipe will make slightly more filling than you will need, depending on the size of your cookie and the size of your thumbprint—this is not a bad thing. The extra caramel can be stored in the refrigerator, tightly covered, for up to 3 days. Warm the caramel before using it as an ice cream topping or pound cake accompaniment, or spoon it directly from the cold jar into your mouth.*

///

MAKE THE THUMBPRINT COOKIES

In a large bowl, whisk together the flour, cocoa powder, and salt. Set aside.

In the bowl of a standing mixer fitted with the paddle attachment, beat the butter and both sugars together until light and fluffy, about 3 minutes. Scrape down the sides and bottom of the bowl, add 1 whole egg, 1 egg yolk, the milk, and vanilla and beat until incorporated. Scrape down the bowl again and beat for 10 seconds. Add half of the dry ingredients and beat for 15 seconds. Add the remaining dry ingredients and beat until just incorporated. Do not overmix. Scrape the dough into a ball, wrap the bowl tightly and refrigerate until the dough is chilled and firm, at least 1 hour. The dough can be made a day ahead and refrigerated for up to 24 hours.

Preheat the oven to 350 degrees F. Line two baking sheets with parchment paper.

In a small bowl, whisk the 2 egg whites until frothy. Place the pecans in a separate wide-mouthed, shallow bowl.

With clean hands, form the dough into tablespoon-size balls, taking care that they have no lumps or cracks. Dip each ball in the egg white mixture, then roll in the pecans to cover completely and place on the prepared baking sheets (if the dough starts to become too soft, refrigerate it briefly to firm it up).

Use your thumb or a small dowel to make an indentation in the center of each cookie, rocking your thumb or the dowel ever so slightly back and forth to create a larger thumbprint (to hold more caramel). Bake for 8 minutes, remove the baking sheets from the oven, and use your thumb (careful—the cookies will be hot) or the dowel to make the indentation more visible. Return the sheets to the oven and bake for another 4 to 5 minutes, until the cookies appear set. (These are the type of cookie that can over-bake very quickly—pull them out at the first sign of cracking.)

Remove the pans from the oven, set the baking sheets on wire racks, and make one last impression using your thumb (again, careful—the cookies will be hot) or the dowel to make a larger thumbprint. Cool for 5 minutes. Use a spatula to transfer the cookies to the racks to cool completely before filling them.

MAKE THE CARAMEL FILLING

In a medium saucepan over medium heat, stir together all the filling ingredients except the pecans. Increase the heat to medium-high and bring the mixture to a boil while stirring very occasionally. Once the mixture reaches a consistent boil, stir gently and continuously until the mixture starts to thicken and darken, about 10 minutes. Remove from the heat and strain through a fine-mesh sieve (to remove any unsightly brown bits) into a pourable glass measuring cup or bowl.

Fill the thumbprint indendations with the caramel filling using a spoon, a glass measuring cup, or pastry bag. Allow them to set until the caramel filling is room temperature, about 45 minutes. About halfway through the set-up time, drop a pecan in the center of the caramel filling in each cookie. These cookies taste great at room temperature or directly from the refrigerator.

They can be stored in the refrigerator, tightly covered, for up to 3 days.

BARREL MADE OF WHITE OAK + CHARRING OF THE INTERIOR OF THE BARREL + 131 PROOF WHISKEY = KENTUCKY BOURBON

1854

SAMUEL KIEL BEGINS DISTILLING CRUDE OIL IN OLD WHISKEY STILLS. CRUDE OIL WAS CHEAPER AND MORE EFFECTIVE THAN THE WHALE OIL USED IN THEN-UBIQUITOUS OIL LAMPS. AFTER THIS DISCOVERY, WHALE OIL WAS NO LONGER USED.

AHOY MATEY!

WATER WAS OFTEN UNDRINKABLE ON SHIPS, SO PIRATES DRANK RUM TO SURVIVE LONG SAILS

"RUM-RUNNING"
ILLEGALLY CARRYING RUM ASHORE OR ACROSS A BORDER

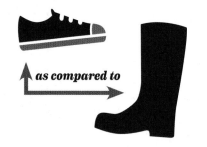

as compared to

"BOOTLEGGING"
SIMPLY CARRYING, PRODUCING, OR DISTRIBUTING ANY ALCOHOL ILLEGALLY

WHISKEY WAS BROUGHT TO THE NEW WORLD BY IRISH SETTLERS IN THE 18th CENTURY

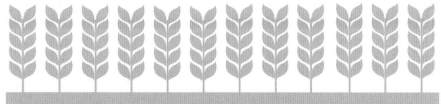

"SINGLE-MALT WHISKEY"
REFERS TO WHISKEY THAT IS MADE WITH EXPENSIVE BARLEY THAT IS MALTED BEFORE FERMENTATION AND DISTILLATION. IN SINGLE-MALTS, MALTED BARLEY IS THE ONLY GRAIN INGREDIENT.

Chapter 4

BOOZE

In the dark days before I discovered NyQuil, my dad (who was DIY before DIY was cool) used to create various homemade natural cold remedies. From the time I was eleven years old, he used to treat my cough and congestion with a shot of whiskey in hot water (or cider) and a quick squeeze of lemon or a spoonful of honey or both. It worked wonders. It also led me to believe that booze makes everything better (dangerous, I know, but I never dallied too close to the devil). Baking with booze is as natural to us as baking with vanilla or mint. It adds a back-of-the-throat heat (like a chile, but less aggressive) and it rescues a few pastries from the dangerous threshold of monotony. Whiskey is the most versatile ingredient (sub it for a splash of vanilla), but essentially anything in your liquor cabinet will work—rum, flavored liqueurs, brandy—except vodka and gins for obvious reasons. We also don't believe that you should bake with substandard hooch because you are concerned about cutting the "good stuff" with too much chocolate, fruit, sugar, or the like. Cheap booze will create cheap-tasting desserts. If you wouldn't drink it, you shouldn't use it.

3 to 3½	cups premium vanilla ice cream, to taste
1½	cups whole milk
3 or 4	ice cubes
¼	cup good-quality bourbon
6	tablespoons Simple Chocolate Syrup (page 192), cooled, divided

BOURBON, VANILLA, AND CHOCOLATE MILK SHAKES

I'D LIKE TO THINK that my introduction to the bourbon milk shake was pure destiny: that we met at a bar, a happy accident. In truth, I stalked this concoction from almost 2,000 miles away. I was living in the East Village in New York City, and the mythical shake (going by the name "Aspen Crud") was being served at the Hotel Jerome in Aspen, Colorado. Though the hotel recipe was readily available (5 scoops of vanilla ice cream and 3 shots of bourbon), I decided to make my own pilgrimage and taste the recipe in its proper environs. It was well worth the trip. The milk shake was exactly as boozy and as thick as I'd imagined—perfect for après ski or a sunny afternoon. Our version of this recipe is the result of many, many tests (think bourbon at 10 A.M.) and we think of it as soda jerk meets rumpled barfly. The chocolate syrup adds a fun dimension and the bourbon portion is pumped up enough to be brash—great for almost any occasion, but preferably a wintry one.

/////////////////////////////////////// *Yield: 4 milk shakes* ///////////////////////////////////////

BAKED NOTE: *Plainly and simply, use a good-quality bourbon for this milk shake (heck, you can always nip away at what's left in the bottle). We tested with Blanton's and Knob Creek, but almost any complex, earthy, caramel-y bourbon will work.*

///

Place 4 heavy (12-ounce or larger) glasses in the freezer to chill for 30 minutes.

Place 3 cups of the ice cream, the milk, ice cubes, bourbon, and 4 tablespoons of the chocolate syrup in a powerful blender. Blend until smooth. A good milk shake should be eaten with a spoon—so if the milk shake seems too thin, add another ¼ to ½ cup ice cream and blend again. Divide the shake evenly among the chilled glasses and top each with ½ tablespoon of the remaining chocolate syrup. Serve immediately.

For the Whiskey Sauce

2	ounces (½ stick) unsalted butter, cut into ½-inch cubes
1	cup firmly packed light brown sugar
¼	cup good-quality whiskey
½	cup heavy cream

For the Lacy Panty Cakes

4	large eggs
½	cup all-purpose flour
½	cup firmly packed light brown sugar
¼	cup granulated sugar
1	teaspoon baking soda
1	teaspoon baking powder
½	teaspoon salt
1	cup graham cracker crumbs (about 14 whole graham crackers)
1	cup sour cream
3	tablespoons good-quality whiskey
1	ounce (¼ stick) unsalted butter, cut into ½-inch cubes
	Confectioners' sugar for dusting

LACY PANTY CAKES

with
WHISKEY SAUCE

SOMETIMES YOU COME across a recipe name that is so unbelievably bad—a name so reckless it borders on camp—that you feel compelled to make it in order to conceptualize the implied vision. Obviously, Lacy Panty Cakes is one such poorly named recipe. Renato unearthed the original version of Lacy Panty Cakes from a 1950s cookbook, *The Complete Book of Home Baking* by Ann Seranne, and it has remained imprinted, ever so delicately, phantomlike, on his subconscious ever since. Our methodical (er, Internet-based) research into the world of Lacy Panty Cakes was futile. No pictures of said recipe. No mentions of said recipe. No critiques of said recipe. This left a lot of room for interpretation. Essentially, the recipe is supposed to produce a pancake-like treat that texturally resembles the lace in lace panties (yes, it hurts to think about), but we were more interested in the taste. It's actually a delicious, though skewed, take on your standard breakfast fare, combining the reassuring flavor and texture of graham with just enough whiskey (well, this was wholeheartedly our addition) to enhance the entire recipe. It's pancakes gone rogue. It's Lacy Panty Cakes. It's love.

/////////////////////////////////// *Yield: 12 to 14 panty cakes* ///////////////////////////////////

BAKED NOTE: *We are rather fond of making these pancakes for breakfast, though the whiskey in both the pancakes and the sauce is quite a wake-up (the effect is similar to having a Bloody Mary for breakfast after a long night out). You could serve them with maple syrup instead of the whiskey sauce. However, these cakes are also great as a dinner side dish (trust us), and the extra whiskey sauce tastes perfect on just about anything, but especially on ice cream.*

MAKE THE WHISKEY SAUCE

In a small saucepan over medium heat, stir together the butter and sugar until the mixture is smooth and the sugar is completely melted.

Add whiskey and cook for 3 minutes, stirring constantly. Add cream and cook an additional 3 to 5 minutes. Remove from heat and set aside. (You can also refrigerate—the sauce will thicken into a caramel-sauce-like syrup.)

MAKE THE LACY PANTY CAKES

Place a large heatproof plate or serving dish in the oven. Preheat the oven to 225 degrees F. Place a skillet or griddle over medium heat.

In a medium bowl, beat the eggs vigorously with a whisk until they are pale and thick, 1 to 2 minutes.

In a large bowl, sift together the flour, sugars, baking soda, baking powder, and salt. Stir in the graham cracker crumbs. Make a well in the center of the dry ingredients and pour the eggs into it. Gently fold the eggs into the dry mixture until just combined. Add the sour cream and whiskey and stir again until combined.

Add the butter to the hot skillet or griddle and swirl it around so it covers the entire cooking surface. Once the butter is completely melted and starts to sizzle, drop batter by scant ¼-cup measures onto the cooking surface and cook until dark brown, 1 to 2 minutes, then flip the cakes over and cook for 1 to 2 minutes, or until dark brown. Transfer the cakes to the heated plate and return it to the warm oven while you make the rest. Serve immediately with a sprinkling of confectioners' sugar and a hearty drizzle of the warm or cooled sauce.

For the Rum Cake

3	cups all-purpose flour
1	teaspoon baking powder
1	teaspoon baking soda
2	teaspoons freshly ground black pepper
¼	teaspoon salt
8	ounces (2 sticks) unsalted butter, at room temperature, cut into ½-inch cubes
1	cup granulated sugar
1	cup firmly packed dark brown sugar
3	large eggs, plus 1 large egg yolk
1	cup well-shaken buttermilk
¾	cup good-quality dark rum
1	tablespoon pure vanilla extract

For the Rum Syrup

4	ounces (1 stick) unsalted butter, cut into ½-inch cubes
⅓	cup granulated sugar
¼	cup good-quality dark rum

For the Buttered Rum Drizzle

1	cup confectioners' sugar, sifted
2	ounces (½ stick) unsalted butter, melted
3	tablespoons good-quality dark or spiced rum

TRIPLE RUM BLACK PEPPER CAKE

THE TRADITIONAL HOMEMADE rum cake recipe (at least the one that is in mass circulation, passing from one handwritten recipe card to the Internet and back) is quite good. It's a boozy holiday treat with tropical leanings, though it is almost universally made using yellow cake mix and instant vanilla pudding. Neither of us is anti–cake mix. Betty Crocker was a virtual pinup during our teen years, and she remains a nostalgic patron saint. Our rum cake is a not so much a reinvention of the ever-present box-mix recipe, it is simply reinterpreted with a "from scratch" format. And we upped the rum quotient. If you are going to make a cake with rum, you might as well make a cake with a lot of rum. (Subtlety, though sometimes appreciated, is not always required with us.) That said, indulgence requires balance, and we think the ground black pepper adds a little bit of edge to the otherwise smooth rum flavor. The crumb is tender with a holiday heart. It's a party in a cake, though you most certainly don't have to wait until the end of the year to bake one.

//////////////////////////// *Yield: One 10- or 12-cup Bundt cake* ////////////////////////////

> **BAKED NOTE**: *Sorry, there are no real alcohol-free substitutions for this cake. However, if you want to cut down on the rum, you could probably skip the glaze altogether or change it to something chocolaty like a straightforward ganache (like the Chocolate Ganache Filling, page 202).*

//

MAKE THE RUM CAKE

Preheat the oven to 350 degrees F. Generously spray the inside of a 10- or 12-cup Bundt pan with nonstick cooking spray; alternatively, butter it thoroughly, dust it with flour, and knock out the excess flour.

In a medium bowl, whisk together the flour, baking powder, baking soda, black pepper, and salt and set aside.

In the bowl of a standing mixer fitted with the paddle attachment, beat the butter and both sugars together on medium speed until light and fluffy, 3 to 4 minutes. Add the eggs and egg yolk one at a time, beating for 10 to 15 seconds after each addition, until incorporated. Scrape down the sides and bottom of the bowl with a rubber spatula and mix again for 10 seconds.

Pour the buttermilk into a glass measuring cup, add the rum and vanilla, and whisk or stir vigorously until combined.

Add the flour mixture to the mixer bowl in three parts, alternating with the buttermilk mixture, beginning and ending with the flour mixture. Beat for 10 to 15 seconds after each addition, or until incorporated. Scrape down the sides and bottom of the bowl and mix again for 10 seconds.

Pour the batter into the prepared pan, smooth the top, and bake for 1 hour, rotating the pan halfway through the baking time, until a toothpick inserted in the center comes out clean. Transfer the pan to a wire rack to cool for about 30 minutes. Use a small knife or a very small offset spatula to loosen the sides of the cake from the pan. Turn the cake out onto the rack and let it cool completely. Wash and dry the Bundt pan.

MAKE THE RUM SYRUP

In a medium saucepan with high sides, gently stir together the butter, sugar, and 3 tablespoons of water. Turn the heat to medium-high and continue stirring until the sugar dissolves and the butter is melted. Stop stirring, increase the heat to high, and allow the mixture to gently boil for about 3 minutes (if the bubbling mixture starts to reach the top of the pan, reduce the heat). Remove the pan from heat, transfer the mixture to a pourable glass measuring cup or bowl, stir vigorously to reduce excess heat, and stir in the rum.

Place the cake back into the Bundt pan and use a toothpick or skewer to poke the bottom several times. Use a spoon to slowly drizzle a little bit of the rum syrup over the cake (you might not want to use all of it, but you certainly can—if you don't use it all, leftover syrup tastes great on French toast and ice cream). Let the cake stand bottom side up in the pan for at least 3 hours, then invert it onto a serving platter and remove the pan.

MAKE THE BUTTERED RUM DRIZZLE

Place the confectioners' sugar in a small bowl. Pour the butter over the sugar and whisk until combined. Add the rum and keep whisking until glossy and almost pourable. Drizzle the glaze along the crown of the cake, allowing it to drip down the sides. Allow the glaze to set for 10 to 15 minutes before serving.

The cake can be stored at room temperature, tightly covered, for up to 3 days.

SIMPLE CHOCOLATE WHISKEY TART

with

WHISKEY WHIPPED CREAM

PRIOR TO THE electronic age, I used to clip or transcribe recipes and stuff them into various folders and three-ring binders. Often organization was haphazard and pages were loose, fragile, torn, and in danger of falling out, but the end result was a library of well-loved recipes. The recipes that appeared at the front of each folder or section (yes, set up by ingredient) were the favorites, the most cherished, the stuff I made all the time. Undoubtedly, there was a chocolate cake recipe, a few chocolate chip cookie recipes, cornbread, macaroni and cheese, and, of course, a simple chocolate tart. I would not venture out into this world without having a simple chocolate tart recipe, and this one is a favorite. It's versatile enough for both picnics and fancy dinner parties and everything in between. It's incredibly quick and easy: the shortbread crust is just a bed of cookies and the filling consists of common pantry items. Only a well-loved recipe can be this complete.

//////////////////////////////////// **Yield: One 9-inch tart** ////////////////////////////////////

BAKED NOTE: *Debate abounds about the best way to serve this tart. We like it both directly from the refrigerator and at room temperature (funny, we feel the same way about pizza). But many taste testers have a distinct preference for either the room temperature version (whose fans claim the effect is more melt-in-your-mouth) or the directly-from-the-fridge version (whose fans are simply loud and adamant). We suggest you try it both ways.*

//

MAKE THE SHORTBREAD CRUST

Preheat the oven to 300 degrees F and position the rack in the center. Lightly spray a 9-inch springform pan with nonstick cooking spray.

In a food processor, pulse the cookies into very fine crumbs. You should have approximately 1¾ cups. Place the crumbs into a bowl, add the sugar and salt, and stir until combined.

Pour the butter over the crumbs and use a fork to mix until combined. Turn the mixture out into the prepared pan and press it into the bottom and up the sides of the

For the Shortbread Crust

8	ounces shortbread cookies
1	tablespoon sugar
½	teaspoon salt
2	ounces (½ stick) unsalted butter, melted

For the Chocolate Whiskey Filling

¾	cup heavy cream
⅓	cup whole milk
5	ounces good-quality dark chocolate (60 to 72%), coarsely chopped
4	ounces good-quality milk chocolate, coarsely chopped
1	large egg, plus 1 large egg yolk
1	tablespoon all-purpose flour
2	tablespoons good-quality whiskey

For Serving

Whiskey Whipped Cream (page 86) and good-quality cocoa powder, or ice cream pan (using your fingers or the bottom of a metal measuring cup). Place the pan in the freezer for about 5 minutes.

Place the pan on a baking sheet, and bake the crust until it is just dry to the touch, about 12 minutes (you do not want it to brown). Remove the baking sheet from the oven and place on a wire rack to cool.

Increase the oven temperature to 325 degrees F.

MAKE THE CHOCOLATE WHISKEY FILLING

In a medium saucepan over medium-low heat, stir together the cream and milk. Bring the mixture just to a low simmer (bubbles will start to form around the edge of the pan) but do not scald or boil. Remove the pan from the heat. Add the chopped chocolates and whisk very gently until the mixture is completely smooth. Continue stirring to release excess heat. Set aside for 5 to 10 minutes, or until the mixture is only slightly warm or has cooled to room temperature.

In a small bowl, use a fork to lightly beat the egg, egg yolk, flour, and whiskey. Use the tip of your finger to make sure the chocolate mixture is only slightly warm or has cooled to room temperature (not too hot or the eggs will cook). Add the egg mixture and whisk until completely blended.

Pour the filling into the tart shell, place the baking sheet in the oven, and bake for 20 to 25 minutes, until the edges are slightly set, but the middle is still slightly jiggly. Remove the baking sheet from the oven and transfer the tart pan to a wire rack to cool for at least 15 minutes. Gently push up on the tart bottom to release the tart from the pan and cool completely.

Serve the tart either at room temperature or directly from the fridge (see Note) with a big dollop of whiskey whipped cream and a dusting of cocoa powder, or a scoop of ice cream.

WHISKEY WHIPPED CREAM

IN OUR OPINION, Whiskey Whipped Cream is much tastier than regular whipped cream—booze wins out yet again. However, if you want a boozeless but flavorful whipped cream, feel free to replace the whiskey with extracts, powders, or spices. Mint extract, coffee extract, cinnamon, and all manner of florals really enhance a basic whipped cream. However, these variations are all more strongly flavored and more highly concentrated than whiskey, so they can't be substituted in a one-to-one ratio—you only need 1 to 2 teaspoons, to taste. If you want to use pure vanilla extract in place of the whiskey, however, we suggest using 1 tablespoon, as we are pushovers for super rich vanilla flavor in our whipped cream.

///////////////////////////////////// **Yield: 2½ cups** /////////////////////////////////////

1¼	cups heavy cream
2	tablespoons superfine sugar
1 to 2	tablespoons good-quality whiskey, to taste

Pour the cream into a chilled metal bowl and beat vigorously with a chilled whisk for about 1 minute or until soft peaks form. Sprinkle the sugar and whiskey over the cream and continue whisking vigorously until stiff peaks form. Serve immediately.

WHISKEY PEACH UPSIDE-DOWN CAKE

LATELY, MY GRANDMOTHER has a thing about peaches. She has always been generous with her trove of recipes—beautifully transcribing her favorites onto small slips of paper for me to repurpose—but the last few batches have been extraordinarily peach-centric. This is odd because prior to my 37th(-ish) birthday, I remember hardly ever seeing a peach in her kitchen. The optimist in me believes that Grandma's recent peach conversion is about the ability to find new experiences (and tastes) later in life, her own private peach revolution. Our Whiskey Peach Upside-Down Cake is Grandma approved—one full pound of fresh peaches is nestled between a caramel whiskey topping and hearty cake. It's the rare cake that is both substantial and light at the same time, and even the whiskey averse tend to enjoy the subtle hint of smoky notes that linger on the tongue.

/////////////////////////// **Yield: One 9-inch, single-layer cake** ///////////////////////////

> **BAKED NOTE**: *This cake tastes great with a multitude of accompaniments—confectioners' sugar, ice cream, Whiskey Whipped Cream (page 86). However, as a few caramel-loving taste testers pointed out, another worthy option is to make a second batch of the Whiskey Cake Topping sans peaches (basically a whiskey caramel) to pour over the top of the cake after it is done baking.*

///

MAKE THE WHISKEY CAKE TOPPING

Preheat the oven to 350 degrees F and position the rack in the center. Butter the bottom and sides of a 9-inch round cake pan, line the bottom with parchment, and butter the parchment.

In a small saucepan over medium-low heat, melt the butter. Whisk in the brown sugar and whiskey and cook until the sugar is melted and the mixture is foamy. Remove from the heat, pour into the prepared pan, and swirl the mixture to coat the bottom of the pan.

Arrange the peach slices in a circle directly on top of the sugar mixture to cover the bottom of the pan. Do not try to overload the pan with peaches and do not be concerned if you have a few peaches left over. Set the pan aside.

For the Whiskey Cake Topping

- 3   ounces (¾ stick) unsalted butter, cut into ½-inch cubes
- 1   cup firmly packed dark brown sugar
- 2   tablespoons good-quality whiskey
- 1   pound fresh peaches, cut into ¼- or ½-inch slices, or frozen sliced peaches, defrosted on paper towels

For the Whiskey Cake

- ¾   cup cake flour
- ¾   cup all-purpose flour
- 1½   teaspoons baking powder
- ½   teaspoon baking soda
- ½   teaspoon salt
- 3   ounces (¾ stick) unsalted butter, at room temperature
- 1   cup granulated sugar
- 3   large egg yolks, plus 2 large egg whites, divided
- 3   tablespoons vegetable oil
- ¾   teaspoon pure vanilla extract
- ¼   teaspoon pure almond extract
- ¾   cup well-shaken buttermilk
- 2   tablespoons good-quality whiskey
- ½   teaspoon cream of tartar

For Serving

Whiskey Whipped Cream (optional, page 86)

MAKE THE WHISKEY CAKE

In a large bowl, sift together the flours, baking powder, baking soda, and salt. Set aside.

In the bowl of a standing mixer fitted with the paddle attachment, beat the butter until creamy, about 2 minutes. Add the granulated sugar and beat until light and fluffy, about 2 minutes. Add the egg yolks, oil, vanilla, and almond extract and beat until just combined.

In a small bowl or glass measuring cup, whisk together the buttermilk and the whiskey. Add the flour mixture to the mixer bowl in three parts, alternating with the buttermilk mixture, beginning and ending with the flour mixture. Scrape down the sides and bottom of the bowl, then mix on low speed for a few more seconds.

In a medium bowl (or in the bowl of a standing mixer fitted with the whisk attachment), whisk the egg whites vigorously for 1 minute. Sprinkle the cream of tartar over the whites and continue beating until soft peaks form.

Gently fold one-quarter of the egg white mixture into the cake batter until almost combined. The mixture will begin to lighten. Fold another quarter of the egg white mixture into the cake batter until nearly combined. Finally, add the remaining egg white mixture to the cake batter and fold in gently until completely combined.

Pour the batter over the peaches (since this is an upside-down cake, the peaches will become the topping when you flip the cake over later). Bake for 45 to 50 minutes, rotating the pan halfway through the baking time, until the cake is very brown (but not burnt) and a toothpick inserted into the center of the cake (not all the way through to the sticky topping) comes out clean. Transfer the pan to a wire rack to cool for at least 15 minutes. Run a paring knife around the edge of the cake and carefully invert onto a serving platter. Let the cake cool to almost room temperature and serve with a dollop of whiskey whipped cream, if desired.

The cake tastes best the day it is made; however, it can be stored in the refrigerator, covered with a cake dome or in a cake saver, for up to 2 days. Bring the cake to room temperature before serving.

S'MORE-STYLE CHOCOLATE WHISKEY PUDDING

with

WHISKEY MARSHMALLOW TOPPING

NOBODY MAKES PUDDING as often as they should. Between us, we have scoured many bakeries (both in and out of the grand old US of A) and invited ourselves to the homes of many friends and acquaintances, and our wayward research strongly reinforces our theory: pudding is a rare bird indeed. It's as scarce as snow in Florida. There are numerous reasons for the shortage of this dessert (it's not quite an "event" dessert, it is frequently thought of as a lunchbox snack and nothing more, it doesn't always look appealing), but there also numerous reasons for its inevitable comeback (it's fairly easy to make, it's adaptable to so many flavors, it's delicious). We are convinced that a pudding obsessive is lurking in the subconscious of every sweet tooth. Perhaps our S'more-Style Chocolate Whiskey Pudding will unlock the floodgates... or at least give you a good reason to revisit pudding more often. This treat is pudding at its best: a layered affair providing both visual flair and impeccable flavor through multiple textures—smooth and rich (the pudding), crunchy and toasty (the graham), fluffy and gooey (the marshmallow topping). It's the kind of dessert you will suddenly think about at 3 A.M., so be sure to keep a supply handy.

//////////////////////////////// *Yield: 6 to 8 servings* ////////////////////////////////

BAKED NOTE: *The best part about pudding: you can compose it and serve it in virtually any serving piece you want. True, this pudding looks great in glass (so you can view the multiple layers), but it also looks fantastic in vintage and found ceramics and all manner of interesting individual porcelain pieces—and it even works as one large, buffet-style, giant-bowl dessert.*

///

MAKE THE GRAHAM CRACKER CRUST

Preheat the oven to 300 degrees F. Line a baking sheet with parchment paper.

Place the graham crackers, butter, sugar, and cinnamon in a food processor and pulse until coarse crumbs form. Turn the crumbs out onto the prepared baking sheet, spread to form an even layer (if necessary, break up any large pieces with your fingertips), and bake, stirring once, until the crumbs are crisp, about 10 minutes. Remove from the oven and cool completely.

MAKE THE CHOCOLATE WHISKEY PUDDING

In a medium, heavy-bottomed saucepan, whisk together the sugar, cornstarch, cocoa powder, espresso powder, and salt. Add the egg yolks and whisk to blend (the mixture will resemble wet sand). Gradually whisk in the milk, then the cream. Place the saucepan over medium heat, and cook the mixture, whisking constantly, until it comes to a boil. Boil for 30 seconds, remove from the heat, and continue to whisk for 15 seconds to release excess heat. Add the chocolate, whiskey, and butter; whisk until the chocolate and butter are melted and the mixture is smooth. Let the pudding cool slightly, about 10 minutes, whisking occasionally.

Spoon ⅓ cup pudding into each of six (small and wide or sundae-like) 1-cup glasses; smooth out the tops. Divide the graham cracker mixture equally among the glasses, sprinkling it on top of the pudding. Top each glass with another ⅓ cup pudding; smooth out the tops. Cover each glass with plastic wrap, pressing the plastic directly onto the pudding. Chill at least 2 hours, until ready to serve.

MAKE THE WHISKEY MARSHMALLOW TOPPING

In the heatproof bowl of a standing mixer fitted with the whisk attachment, whisk the egg whites, sugar, ¼ cup water, corn syrup, and whiskey. Set the mixer bowl with the egg white mixture over a saucepan of simmering water. Using a hand whisk, whisk the mixture constantly until an instant read thermometer inserted into the mixture registers 160 degrees F, about 6 minutes. Return the bowl to the standing mixer (still fitted with the whisk attachment) and beat on high speed until the marshmallow topping forms stiff peaks, 6 to 8 minutes.

Top each chilled pudding with 2 large spoonfuls of marshmallow topping, covering the top of the pudding completely and creating peaks, if desired.

Use a kitchen torch to lightly toast the topping to your liking. Serve immediately.

 PUMPKINS ARE **90%** WATER

IN COLONIAL TIMES PUMPKINS WERE *used to make* PIECRUSTS **NOT** PIE FILLING

 PUMPKINS CAN GROW *on* EVERY CONTINENT **EXCEPT** ANTARCTICA

GREEN GOBLIN CINDERELLA GLADIATOR & SORCERER

NOT NEW COMIC BOOK CHARACTERS, BUT VARIETIES OF PUMPKIN

4483.51 ft. THE FARTHEST A PUMPKIN

 HAS EVER BEEN "CHUNKED" *(i.e., launched)*

ON OCTOBER 27, 1966 **"IT'S THE GREAT PUMPKIN, CHARLIE BROWN"** AIRED FOR THE FIRST TIME

THAT'S ABOUT 12.5 FOOTBALL FIELDS

1818.5 POUNDS CURRENT RECORD FOR  WORLD'S LARGEST PUMPKIN

 APPROXIMATELY HALF OF ALL TELEVISIONS IN THE UNITED STATES WERE TUNED IN

Chapter 5
PUMPKIN

When the authorities knock down my door and drag me from my apartment on hoarding charges (a recurring nightmare with no basis in reality), they will inexplicably find a bizarre and rather embarrassing number of pumpkin curios. My fall from grace will be paved in gourds. Our love of all things baked and pumpkin-y obviously dovetails with our deep devotion to fall. Once the leaves start their dramatic turn, we turn to pumpkin scones, cakes, breads, pies, and a bevy of savory pumpkin dishes. Baking with pumpkin is forgiving, and you can adjust your spice ratio (cinnamon, clove, allspice, nutmeg) according to your own palette: don't let anyone tell you to go easy on the cloves unless you want to go easy on the cloves. Lastly, if you want to extend the traditional pumpkin season past Thanksgiving, we certainly wouldn't say a word. Sometimes a pumpkin loaf in March is exactly what you need.

2	tablespoons olive or canola oil
2	cups raw, hulled pumpkin seeds
2½	teaspoons salt, divided
2	cups sugar
¼	cup light corn syrup
2	tablespoons honey
3	ounces (¾ stick) unsalted butter, cut into ½-inch cubes
¾	teaspoon baking soda
I	teaspoon cinnamon

TOASTED PUMPKIN SEED BRITTLE

OUR ENJOYMENT OF PUMPKIN extends far beyond the pumpkin flesh. I suppose we fancy ourselves "nose-to-tail" pumpkin people in that we use the whole pumpkin in the same way a hunter might utilize a whole animal. It's a concept (less waste) that works, especially if you have an affinity for Halloween; after you use the fleshy insides for untold amounts of puree to make soups, pies, muffins, and quick breads, you can use the shell for your garden compost. We save the seeds for a salty (or salty and cinnamon-y) snack. Our brittle recipe is just an extension of our heightened pumpkin awareness. It is a classic brittle—no fussy interpretations except for a hint of cinnamon—holding the salty pumpkin seeds in splendid suspension and providing a perfect, snappy bite. We like to imagine that we make this recipe for the singular purpose of gifting away the results (wrap the large pieces in parchment and tie the whole thing up with string for a great present), but we are always surprised how much we end up eating ourselves.

/////////////////////////// *Yield: Approximately 2 pounds* ///////////////////////////

BAKED NOTE: *If you want to add a chocolate shell layer to your brittle, coarsely chop 4 ounces of good-quality dark chocolate (60 to 72%) and set aside. Immediately after the brittle has been poured on the baking sheet and spread into an even layer, sprinkle the chocolate directly over the brittle, wait 2 minutes, then use an offset spatula to spread the softened chocolate into an even layer.*

///

Line a baking sheet with two layers of paper towels.

Place the oil in a medium, heavy-bottomed skillet over medium-high heat. Swirl the pan a few times to make sure the oil is completely covering the bottom of the skillet. When the oil is hot, after 1 to 2 minutes, add the raw pumpkin seeds and toss with a large spoon until they just start to brown (you want them lightly toasted), about 2 minutes. (Alternatively, toast the seeds in a 350-degree-F oven by tossing them with 1 tablespoon of oil and spreading them in an even layer in a baking pan. Bake for 10 minutes, stir the seeds, and bake for another 10 minutes, or until lightly toasted.) Transfer the seeds to the prepared baking sheet, sprinkle with 1 teaspoon of the salt, and let them cool.

Place the cooled pumpkin seeds in a small bowl. Remove the paper towels and line the baking sheet with parchment paper. Lightly coat the parchment paper with nonstick cooking spray.

In a medium saucepan over very low heat, gently stir together ¼ cup water, the sugar, corn syrup, and honey until the mixture is almost clear. Stir in the butter. Increase the heat to medium-high and continue gently stirring the mixture until it just begins to boil. Stop stirring and cook until the mixture is golden brown, 8 to 10 more minutes. Remove from the heat and gently stir in the baking soda, then the cinnamon and the remaining 1½ teaspoons of salt. After the mixture has stopped bubbling vigorously (light bubbling is fine), stir in the pumpkin seeds. Pour the mixture onto the prepared baking sheet and use a lightly greased offset spatula to spread it out in an even layer. Allow the brittle to cool completely, at least 3 hours.

Break the brittle into pieces with a sharp knife or your hands. It can be stored at room temperature, between layers of parchment in an airtight container, for up to 1 week.

PUMPKIN ALMOND CAKE

with
ALMOND BUTTER FROSTING

IT IS IMPORTANT to practice a certain amount of self-delusion when your entire world revolves around pastry and caffeine with nary a green vegetable in sight. For instance, we have rightly (or wrongly) convinced ourselves that single-layer cakes are both somehow better for you and possibly even more nutritious than their more indulgent three-layer cousins. This is obviously not true, but it is probably worth partaking in this mini fantasy if only for this cake. Our Pumpkin Almond Cake is all things a pumpkin cake should be, but better: it's moist without being oily, spicy enough to stand out, and easy to make. The Almond Butter Frosting is a slight departure from the more frequently used cream cheese frosting, but we like the unique understated flavor. We should also mention that it is completely agreeable any time of day (breakfast, afternoon or midnight snack, post-dinner indulgence, etc.), or in any season—no need to confine this "healthy" cake solely to your fall holiday baking schedule.

//////////////////////////// *Yield: One 9-inch, single-layer cake* ////////////////////////////

BAKED NOTE: *If you want to save a little money, and if you don't want to go searching for almond flour, you can make your own. Simply grind up some blanched almonds to a fine powder in a blender or food processor (be careful not to grind for too long or the nuts will turn to almond butter). By the by, a mini coffee grinder (sans coffee residue) does a fine job of processing almonds.*

//

MAKE THE PUMPKIN ALMOND CAKE

Preheat the oven to 350 degrees F. Butter one 9-inch round cake pan, line with parchment paper, and butter the parchment. Dust the parchment with flour and knock out the excess flour.

In a medium bowl, whisk together the flours, baking powder, baking soda, salt, cinnamon, ginger, nutmeg, and cloves. Set aside.

In the bowl of a standing mixer fitted with the paddle attachment, beat the butter and sugars together on medium speed until light and fluffy. Add the pumpkin puree and beat just until incorporated. Add the eggs one at a time, beating well after each addition. Scrape down the sides and bottom of the bowl and mix again for 30 seconds.

Add the flour mixture in three parts, alternating with the buttermilk, beginning and ending with the flour mixture. Scrape down the sides and bottom of the bowl and beat for a few more seconds.

For the Pumpkin Almond Cake

1½	cups all-purpose flour
¾	cup almond flour
1½	teaspoons baking powder
½	teaspoon baking soda
½	teaspoon salt
1	teaspoon cinnamon
1	teaspoon ground ginger
1	teaspoon freshly grated nutmeg
¼	teaspoon ground cloves
4	ounces (1 stick) unsalted butter, at room temperature
1	cup granulated sugar
¼	cup firmly packed dark brown sugar
1	cup pumpkin puree (see page 100)
2	large eggs
¾	cup well-shaken buttermilk

For the Almond Butter Frosting

½	cup almond butter
2	ounces (½ stick) unsalted butter, softened
2 to 4	tablespoons almond milk, to taste
1¼ to 1¾	cups confectioners' sugar, sifted, to taste
½	teaspoon salt
1	teaspoon vanilla bean paste

For the Assembly

¼	cup sliced almonds, toasted (page 19), or pumpkin seeds, raw or toasted (page 94)

Pour the batter into the prepared pan and bake for 40 to 50 minutes, or until a toothpick inserted in the center of the cake comes out clean. Set the pan on a wire rack to cool for at least 20 minutes. Loosen the sides of the cake from the pan, then turn the cake out onto the rack. Remove the parchment, flip the cake right side up, and let the cake cool completely.

MAKE THE ALMOND BUTTER FROSTING

Place the almond butter, butter, 2 tablespoons of almond milk, 1¼ cups confectioners' sugar, and salt in a food processor. Pulse in short bursts until the frosting comes together and is shiny and smooth. If you prefer a slightly looser frosting, add 1 to 2 additional tablespoons almond milk; if you prefer a thicker frosting, add ½ cup confectioners' sugar. Process again.

ASSEMBLE THE CAKE

Transfer the cake to a board or serving platter and use an offset spatula to spread the frosting evenly across the top. Sprinkle the perimeter with the almonds or pumpkin seeds.

The cake can be stored, tightly covered, at room temperature for up to 3 days.

2 to 4 pie pumpkins (on the smallish side)

HOMEMADE PUMPKIN PUREE

WITH SOME RESERVATIONS, I enjoy making pumpkin puree. The slicing and scooping feels very vintage high-school biology—at once anachronistic and scientific and a tiny bit strange—as if I were dissecting something rather than engaging in kitchen prep. The anthropomorphic aspect of pumpkins as jack-o'-lanterns is a hard idea to shake. The taste is not noticeably different from the canned variety, but it is near meditative to prepare and all you need is one ingredient. Besides, there is something eerily calming and relaxing about roasting pumpkin on a slow, overcast fall day.

/////////////////////////////////////// *Yield: 2 to 4 cups* ///////////////////////////////////////

> **BAKED NOTE**: *Pay special attention to the only ingredient listed in this recipe: pie pumpkins (also fine are cheese and sugar pumpkins). Pie pumpkins are NOT jack-o'-lantern pumpkins. Jack-o'-lantern pumpkins are usually grown to be carved, not roasted—their flesh is usually stringy and watery, and often they are chock-full of seeds.*

Preheat the oven to 350 degrees F. Line a rimmed baking sheet with parchment paper (it will make cleanup easier) and set aside.

Slice the top off of each pumpkin just below the stem, then slice each pumpkin in half from top to bottom. Use an ice cream scoop with a release mechanism or a very sturdy spoon to scoop out the innards, reserving the seeds for toasting or to make our Toasted Pumpkin Seed Brittle (page 94). Place the pumpkins cut side down on the baking sheet. I often add a little water to the rimmed baking sheet—just enough to create a perceptible, even layer (about ⅛ inch) in the pan—but it is not necessary.

Bake for 50 to 70 minutes, depending on the size and shape of your pumpkins. To determine doneness, I recommend testing at the 45-minute mark, and then every 5 minutes thereafter. When done, the flesh should give way to a fork without any effort.

Remove the pan from the oven and allow the pumpkins to cool for about 15 minutes, until you can handle them with bare hands. Using a small paring knife, separate the pumpkin skin from the flesh. Discard the skins, place all the flesh in a food processor, and pulse until smooth.

Oftentimes, homemade puree contains too much liquid, so I recommend you strain the puree in cheesecloth (a coffee filter will do in a pinch) for at least 1 hour. Use the puree immediately or freeze in an airtight container for up to 1 month. (Make sure you allow the puree to thaw completely before using.)

OVERFLOWING WITH PUMPKIN PUREE

Though my mom was not really a cook, we used to have one of those ubiquitous basement- or garage-type freezers (ours just happened to be located in a guest room in the basement—classy) for storing backup meats, ice cream, and all manner of either large or coupon-friendly foodstuffs. I often wish I still had that freezer (or one like it) to squeeze into my typical economy-size NYC apartment. I would cram it full with cookie doughs, cake layers, tubs of ice cream, and—of course—puree. Mountains and mountains of pumpkin (and banana) puree.

Freeze It

Inevitably, at one point, you will have extra pumpkin puree. You might only need half of a can for a recipe. You might use only 1 cup of the fresh variety. Do not throw out the remainder. Pumpkin puree freezes and thaws amazingly well. We freeze our puree in large plastic zip-top bags. Just fill with leftover puree, zip shut, press, and freeze flat (easier to stack and easier to thaw) and thaw overnight in your refrigerator before using.

Use It

Pumpkin puree is versatile. Maybe too versatile. We probably add it to too many things, too often, and we attribute this to a deep love and affection for all things pumpkin. We use pumpkin puree for more than just sweets (though it is hard to beat the Pumpkin Almond Cake on page 97). There are untold recipes floating about for pumpkin pasta, pumpkin lattes, pumpkin smoothies, pumpkin sauces, and pumpkin pancakes. Keep your eyes, and pumpkins, peeled.

For the Chocolate-Chunk Pumpkin Bread

1½	cups plus 2 tablespoons all-purpose flour
1	teaspoon baking soda
1	teaspoon salt
1	teaspoon cinnamon
¼	teaspoon freshly grated nutmeg
¼	teaspoon ground allspice
¼	teaspoon ground ginger
¾	cup plus 2 tablespoons pumpkin puree (see page 100)
½	cup vegetable oil
1¾	cups granulated sugar
2	large eggs
½	teaspoon pure vanilla extract
6	ounces good-quality dark chocolate (60 to 72%), coarsely chopped

For the Pumpkin Custard

2	large eggs, plus 4 large egg yolks, at room temperature
1	cup firmly packed dark brown sugar
3	cups half-and-half, at room temperature
1¾	cups pumpkin puree (see page 100)
4½	ounces (1 stick plus 1 tablespoon) unsalted butter, melted and cooled, divided
½	teaspoon salt
¼	teaspoon ground cloves
¼	teaspoon ground cayenne
½	teaspoon cinnamon
½	teaspoon ground allspice
½	teaspoon freshly grated nutmeg
1	tablespoon pure vanilla extract

CHOCOLATE-CHUNK PUMPKIN BREAD PUDDING

IT IS A RARE OCCURRENCE that I ever have enough leftover bread around to make bread pudding. I love bread too much and always seem to eat it before it goes off. It is an even rarer occurrence that I would just happen to have our signature Chocolate-Chunk Pumpkin Bread lounging about—it is usually consumed with an unnatural ferocity. As such, I typically bake two loaves and then I snack on one and reserve the other just for this bread pudding. (You can do the same if you want some bread for snacking—the recipe below doubles perfectly.) Our Chocolate-Chunk Pumpkin Bread Pudding is plenty pumpkin-y, rich without being insane, and tailor-made for the fall months. In my dreams, I would start every October morning with a cup of black coffee and a side of this pudding. If you wish to use canned pumpkin puree in this recipe, you will need two 15-ounce cans.

/////////////// *Yield: One 9-by-13-inch pudding (18 to 24 servings)* ///////////////

BAKED NOTE: *If you wish to fancy this recipe up a bit, you might want to serve individual puddings. Simply butter and flour individual 4-ounce ramekins or a couple of standard 12-cup muffin pans and fill three-quarters full with the custard. Adjust the bake time to 25 minutes (instead of 45 to 55 minutes), or until the custard is set and a toothpick inserted into the middle of a custard comes out clean. Unmold and serve. This will make about 18 muffin-size puddings.*

MAKE THE CHOCOLATE-CHUNK PUMPKIN BREAD

Preheat the oven to 350 degrees F and position the rack in the center. Butter a 9-by-5-by-3-inch loaf pan, dust it with flour, and knock out the excess flour.

In a large bowl, whisk together the flour, baking soda, salt, cinnamon, nutmeg, allspice, and ginger.

In another large bowl, whisk together the pumpkin puree and oil until combined. Add the sugar and whisk again. Whisk the eggs into the mixture, one at a time, followed by the vanilla. Add ⅔ cup room-temperature water and whisk until combined. Stir in the chocolate.

Fold the dry ingredients into the wet ingredients. Do not overmix. Pour the batter into the prepared pan and smooth the top. Bake for 65 to 85 minutes, rotating the pan halfway through the baking time, until a toothpick inserted into the center of the loaf comes out clean. Transfer the pan to a wire rack and cool for 15 minutes. Turn the loaf out onto a wire rack and cool completely, 30 to 45 minutes. The loaf can be stored at room temperature, tightly covered, for up to 2 days.

TOAST THE BREAD

Preheat the oven to 325 degrees F. Line a baking sheet with parchment paper.

Cut the loaf into 1-inch cubes (you should have approximately 7 cups of cubes). Spread the cubes out onto the prepared baking sheet and toast for 10 minutes. Remove the baking sheet from the oven, flip the cubes with a spatula, and return to the oven for another 10 to 15 minutes, or until the cubes are toasted. Place the baking sheet on a wire rack to cool, 15 to 25 minutes.

MAKE THE PUMPKIN CUSTARD

In a large bowl whisk together the eggs, egg yolks, and brown sugar until combined. Add the half-and-half, pumpkin puree, and 5 tablespoons of the butter and whisk until well combined. Add the salt, cloves, cayenne, cinnamon, allspice, nutmeg, and vanilla and whisk again. Stir in 6 cups of the toasted bread cubes until all the cubes are coated in the mixture. Let the mixture sit for 30 minutes, stirring every 10 minutes or so.

ASSEMBLE THE BREAD PUDDING

Preheat the oven to 325 degrees F. Butter the bottom and sides of a 9-by-13 glass or light-colored metal baking pan (glass is preferred).

Toss the reserved 1 cup of bread cubes with the remaining butter.

Pour the custard into the prepared pan. Scatter the buttered cubes over the custard. Bake for 45 to 55 minutes, or until the custard is set and a toothpick inserted into the center comes out clean.

Transfer the pan to a wire rack to cool for 30 minutes before serving warm. Feel free to serve as is, or with unsweetened whipped cream or caramel sauce (page 59), or simply sprinkle the top with sifted confectioners' sugar.

Bread pudding tastes best fresh from the oven, but you can refrigerate any leftover bread pudding, tightly covered, for up to 2 days. Slice and reheat it in a 225-degree-F oven until warm to the touch before serving.

For the Pumpkin Dough

3 ½	cups bread flour
¼	cup granulated sugar
¼	cup firmly packed dark brown sugar
1	tablespoon instant dry yeast
1	teaspoon salt
½	teaspoon cinnamon
¼	teaspoon ground ginger
¼	teaspoon ground cardamom
3	ounces (¾ stick) unsalted butter, softened, cut into ½-inch cubes
⅔	cup whole milk
1	large egg
⅔	cup pumpkin puree (see page 100)

For the Cinnamon Filling

¾	cup firmly packed light brown sugar
¼	cup granulated sugar
½	teaspoon cinnamon
¼	teaspoon ground cloves
¼	teaspoon freshly grated nutmeg
¼	teaspoon salt
1	ounce (¼ stick) unsalted butter, melted

For the Assembly

1	ounce (¼ stick) unsalted butter, melted

For the Cream Cheese Frosting

2	ounces cream cheese, softened
3	tablespoons well-shaken buttermilk
1¼	cups confectioners' sugar, sifted

PUMPKIN CINNAMON ROLLS

AMERICA'S FOOD COURTS and highway rest stops are filled with myriad oddities and vast collections of the absurd—bizarre and horrible fast food chains that wouldn't survive outside the protective womb of a mall or the glamless oasis of a roadside pit stop—but even in these locales, a shop dedicated to a single breakfast item (oversized cinnamon rolls) seems slightly alien. Yet we find ourselves transfixed by the store, its yeasty cinnamon aroma lulling its followers into a trancelike state. How is this a business concept? How many cinnamon rolls can one person eat in a given year? Why aren't there more flavors? None of these questions matter as we place our order, hearts beating erratically in anticipation. Our Pumpkin Cinnamon Rolls were created partly as an ode to this chain store, a chain store beloved by Renato. They are surprisingly simple to put together and highly impressive to serve for a Sunday brunch. They taste like delicate bites of coffee-klatsch heaven and, as they bake, your entire home will smell like the perfect fall day—pumpkin-y, cinnamon-y bliss.

// *Yield: 10 to 12 rolls* //

BAKED NOTE: *If you are hosting a brunch or breakfast and want to make your morning slightly easier, you can make the bulk of this recipe the night before. Once the rolls are sliced and in the pan, cover them with two tight layers of plastic wrap and refrigerate them. In the morning, remove the pan from the refrigerator and proceed with the recipe as normal; however, make sure you allow sufficient time for the dough to come to room temperature and rise properly.*

///

MAKE THE PUMPKIN DOUGH

Butter one 10-inch round cake pan, line the bottom with parchment paper, and butter the parchment. Dust the parchment with flour and knock out the excess flour.

In the bowl of a standing mixer fitted with the paddle attachment, mix the flour, sugars, yeast, salt, cinnamon, ginger, and cardamom on medium speed. Add the butter and mix until incorporated, about 1 minute. Add the milk and egg and mix on low speed until incorporated. Add the pumpkin puree and mix on medium speed for 3 minutes. The dough will be light orange in color and feel soft and sticky.

Remove the dough from the bowl, carefully form it into a large ball, smooth the top with your hands, and place it in a clean, lightly greased bowl. Cover with plastic wrap and let the dough rest for 30 minutes. Meanwhile, make the filling.

MAKE THE CINNAMON FILLING

In a small bowl, stir together the sugars, cinnamon, cloves, nutmeg, and salt. Add the melted butter and stir until combined.

ASSEMBLE THE ROLLS

Dust a work surface with a sprinkling of flour. Using a rolling pin, roll the dough into a large rectangle approximately 20 by 10 inches, brush the dough with half the melted butter, and sprinkle the filling over the butter, leaving a ¼-inch border around the edges. Use the palms of your hands to press the filling lightly into the dough.

Roll up the long side of the rectangle to form a tight log and place it seam side down. Slice the log into ten 2-inch rolls. Place one roll in the center of the cake pan, then fill in the rest of the pan with the other rolls. Brush the tops of the rolls with the remaining melted butter, cover with plastic wrap, and set aside until the rolls have almost doubled in size, about 45 minutes.

Preheat the oven to 350 degrees F and position the rack in the center.

Bake for 25 to 30 minutes, or until the tops of the rolls are browned. In order to pour your icing over still-warm rolls for the best effect, prep all the frosting ingredients while the rolls are baking and put together the frosting (this will only take about 5 minutes) immediately after the rolls come out of the oven.

MAKE THE FROSTING

In the bowl of a standing mixer fitted with the paddle attachment, beat the cream cheese and buttermilk on medium speed until the mixture is lump free. Add the confectioners' sugar and beat on medium-low speed until a smooth, fluid mixture forms.

SERVE THE ROLLS

Invert the pan of rolls onto a serving plate or leave them in the pan for a rustic look. Pour the frosting over the warm rolls. It's okay if a little bit of the frosting drips down the sides—it's even encouraged. (Alternatively, use an offset spatula to apply the icing.) Serve immediately.

PUMPKIN CHEESECAKE BARS

WE ARE CONVINCED that our Pumpkin Cheesecake Bars are infused with a little bit of witchcraft. Normally, we like to believe we have a certain dessert resolve—that we can casually split a cookie and easily avoid a second slice of cake. These bars, however, render us defenseless. Trancelike, we can eat one bar followed by another and maybe even another before waking from our pumpkin-voodoo-induced state. They are light—deceptively light—and not overly rich—more like a pumpkin kiss enveloped in a fluffy cream cheese cloud on top and a classic sweet dough on the bottom. You will want more than one. Our Pumpkin Cheesecake Bars are party-friendly (much easier to serve than hulking slices of pumpkin cheesecake), Thanksgiving approved, and quite impossible to put down.

/// **Yield: 24 bars** ///

> **BAKED NOTE**: *Everybody loves these bars as written—even anti-pumpkin people generally like them. That said, a group of hardy testers tried these bars with various toppings because it seemed appropriately thorough, in the name of good testing. Not surprisingly, toppings such as caramel (see pages 58–59), pecans (an option in the recipe), walnuts, and even chocolate chips taste great with these bars.*

///

MAKE THE SWEET PASTRY DOUGH

Butter the bottom and sides of a 9-by-13-inch glass or light-colored metal baking pan. Line the bottom with a sheet of parchment paper and butter the parchment.

Place the flour, sugar, and salt in a food processor and pulse until combined. Add the butter and pulse until sandy (6 to 10 quick pulses). In a small bowl, whisk the egg and add it to the food processor. Pulse just until the dough begins to hold together (if the dough seems exceedingly dry and crumbly, add a teaspoon of water and pulse again). Form the dough into a disk, wrap it tightly in plastic wrap, and refrigerate for at least 1 hour or overnight.

Dust a work surface with a sprinkling of flour. Using a rolling pin, roll the dough into a rectangle slightly larger than 9 by 13 inches (the size of the pan) and about ¼ inch thick. The dough might be sticky, so turn it with a bench knife or spatula as needed and keep the work surface floured. Some people find it easier to roll the dough between two layers of parchment paper—this can make it less messy and easier to transfer to the pan.

For the Sweet Pastry Dough

- 1½ cups all-purpose flour
- ¼ cup sugar
- ¼ teaspoon salt
- 4 ounces (1 stick) cold unsalted butter, cut into ½-inch cubes
- 1 large egg

For the Pumpkin Cheesecake Filling

- 16 ounces cream cheese, softened
- ½ cup sugar
- ¾ cup pumpkin puree (see page 100)
- 2 tablespoons maple syrup
- ½ teaspoon vanilla bean paste
- ½ teaspoon salt
- 1 teaspoon cinnamon
- ½ teaspoon freshly grated nutmeg
- ½ teaspoon ground ginger
- ½ teaspoon ground allspice
- 2 large eggs

For the Cream Cheese Frosting

- 4 ounces (1 stick) unsalted butter, softened
- 8 ounces cream cheese, softened
- 3 cups confectioners' sugar, sifted
- 1 tablespoon pure vanilla extract
- ½ teaspoon salt

For the Assembly

- ½ cup pecans, toasted (page 19), coarsely chopped (optional)

Ever so gently, guide the dough into the pan and lightly press it—without pulling—into the bottom; it is not necessary to bring the dough up the sides of the pan, only to completely cover the bottom of the pan. Trim off any excess. Place the pan in the freezer for 30 minutes.

Preheat the oven to 375 degrees F.

Remove the pan from the freezer, line it with aluminum foil, and fill it three-quarters full with pie weights or dried beans. Bake for 15 minutes, then remove the foil and weights and bake for another 10 minutes, until the crust is lightly browned. Transfer the pan to a wire rack to cool. Reduce the oven temperature to 300 degrees F.

MAKE THE PUMPKIN CHEESECAKE FILLING

In the bowl of a standing mixer fitted with the paddle attachment, beat the cream cheese on medium speed just until it is lump free and smooth. Do not overbeat or the tops of the bars may crack. Add the sugar and beat again until well combined, about 2 minutes.

In a large bowl, whisk together the pumpkin puree, maple syrup, vanilla bean paste, salt, cinnamon, nutmeg, ginger, and allspice. Add this mixture to the cream cheese mixture and beat on medium-low speed until completely combined. Scrape down the sides and bottom of the bowl and add the eggs, one at a time, beating well after each addition, then beat until the mixture is smooth. Note: This batter is slightly looser than the average cheesecake batter.

Pour the mixture over the crust and bake for 23 to 30 minutes, or until the bars are set and slightly puffy (if the tops start to crack, the bars are overbaked). Transfer the pan to a cooling rack and allow the bars to come to room temperature, then refrigerate until chilled, at least 2 hours.

MAKE THE CREAM CHEESE FROSTING

In the bowl of a standing mixer fitted with the paddle attachment, beat the butter until it is completely smooth. Add the cream cheese and beat until combined. Add the confectioners' sugar, vanilla, and salt and beat until smooth (be careful not to overbeat the frosting or it will lose its structure). The frosting can be made a day ahead: after mixing, cover the bowl tightly and refrigerate; let it soften to room temperature before using.

Use an offset spatula to spread the frosting evenly across the top of the filling layer. If you like, sprinkle the pecans evenly over the top of the frosting. Place the bars in the refrigerator for 30 minutes to set before cutting and serving.

The bars can be stored in the refrigerator, tightly covered, for up to 3 days.

2	cups all-purpose flour
2	cups rolled oats
1	teaspoon baking soda
1	teaspoon salt
2	teaspoons cinnamon
¼	teaspoon ground ginger
⅛	teaspoon freshly grated nutmeg
⅛	teaspoon ground cloves
8	ounces (2 sticks) unsalted butter, room temperature
1	cup firmly packed dark brown sugar
¾	cup granulated sugar
1	large egg
1	cup pumpkin puree (page 100)
1	teaspoon pure vanilla extract
5	ounces (1 cup) dried cranberries
6	ounces (about 1 cup) semisweet chocolate chips (optional)

PUMPKIN HARVEST DUNKING COOKIES

WE VIEW THE WORLD through highly caffeinated eyes—everything filtered via many, many cups of strong, muddy, invigorating coffee. Coffee is our constant companion and, often, our savior. We are also unapologetic dunkers. We dunk cookies, loaves, biscotti, bits of pie crust, brownies, and almost anything else we can rescue from neglect into our coffee without any regard for proper etiquette. So, it should come as no surprise that Renato created a new cookie expressly for dunking. His pumpkin harvest dunking cookie is a multipurpose, many wondered thing. It is soft yet durable, packed with fall flavors, properly textured (à la the cranberries and chocolate chips), and highly absorbent—it practically begs to take a dip in a hot beverage (coffee, tea, hot chocolate). Of course, if you are firmly on the anti-dunking team, this cookie is completely delicious as is—it just happens to be a great cookie made even greater via a hot coffee bath.

// *Yield: 36 cookies* //

BAKED NOTE: *Some cookies require a precise bake time—they have to be pulled from the oven within seconds of browning or they will be overbaked and inedible. Not these cookies. In fact, we encourage you to bake them slightly longer than you are comfortable with to make sure the cookies are hearty (really browned) on the outside, moist on the inside. They also hold up extremely well over a period of days (if they last that long).*

///

In a large bowl, whisk together the flour, oats, baking soda, salt, cinnamon, ginger, nutmeg, and cloves. Set aside.

In the bowl of a standing mixer fitted with a paddle attachment, beat the butter and sugars together until smooth and creamy, about 3 minutes. Scrape down the sides and bottom of the bowl and add the egg, pumpkin, and vanilla until incorporated.

Add half of the dry ingredients and mix for 15 seconds. Add the remaining dry ingredients and beat until just incorporated. Scrape down the sides and bottom of the bowl, and beat for 5 more seconds. Remove the bowl from the mixer and fold in the cranberries and chocolate chips. Cover the bowl tightly and refrigerate the dough for at least 4 hours.

Preheat oven to 350 degrees F. Line two baking sheets with parchment paper.

Use a small ice cream scoop with release mechanism to scoop out dough in 2 tablespoon–size balls (or use a tablespoon measure) and place the balls onto the prepared baking sheet about 1 inch apart. Bake for 14 to 18 minutes, rotating the pans halfway through the baking time, until the cookies begin to brown.

Remove the pan from the oven and cool on a wire rack for 5 minutes. Use a spatula to transfer the individual cookies to the rack to cool completely.

The cookies can be stored, in an airtight container, for up to 3 days.

9,000 FEET

THE HEIGHT OF THE MOUNTAIN RANGE THAT ADMIRAL RICHARD BYRD NAMED AFTER *malted milk patent-holder* WILLIAM HORLICK, WHILE ON AN EXPEDITION **TO THE** ANTARCTIC

FIVE-TIME "WORLD'S STRONGEST MAN" MARIUSZ PUDZIANOWSKI *sites* MALTED MILK AS HIS KEY STRENGTH SUPPLEMENT

1904

IN SWITZERLAND, DR. GEORGE WANDER CREATES OVALTINE, A DRINK MADE BY COMBINING MALTED BARLEY WITH COCOA, MILK, AND EGG.

144,000 THE APPROXIMATE HEIGHT OF THE MOUNTAIN RANGE IN TERMS OF NUMBER OF MALT BALLS

PIZZA AND BEER
—connected through malt—

MALT EXTRACT: THE SAME INGREDIENT THAT WOULD BE USED FOR BREWING A PILSNER CAN BE USED IN PIZZA DOUGH TO CREATE A CRUST THAT IS BOTH CRISPY AND CHEWY

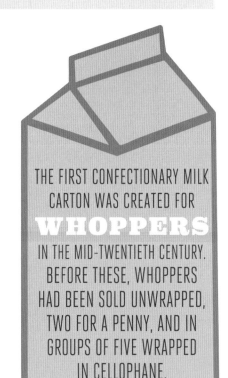

THE FIRST CONFECTIONARY MILK CARTON WAS CREATED FOR **WHOPPERS** IN THE MID-TWENTIETH CENTURY. BEFORE THESE, WHOPPERS HAD BEEN SOLD UNWRAPPED, TWO FOR A PENNY, AND IN GROUPS OF FIVE WRAPPED IN CELLOPHANE.

Chapter 6

MALTED MILK POWDER

The difference between a milk shake and a malted milk shake is like the difference between Paris, Texas, and Paris, France—there is no comparison. We will always prefer the nutty, creamy, yeasty, multi-dimensional taste of a malted milk shake, and if we are on a plane to Paris, it better be headed toward Europe. Malted milk powder, usually made from barley malt, wheat, and milk (sometimes salt) is like magic dust—it can add a hint of soda fountain or candy reminiscence (think Whoppers or Maltesers; see Sources, page 215) to almost any baked good. If you want to transform a cocoa-based dessert into chocolate malt–based dessert, swap out a portion of the cocoa with an equal portion of malted-milk powder. Changing vanilla-based desserts into malted vanilla–based desserts requires a little more trial and error (usually it means you have to dissolve some malt powder in a liquid and then sneak the liquid into the recipe), but at least you can nibble the errors en route.

For the Devil Dogs

- ½ cup dark unsweetened cocoa powder (like Valrhona)
- 2 cups all-purpose flour
- 1 teaspoon baking soda
- 1 teaspoon instant espresso powder
- ½ teaspoon baking powder
- ½ teaspoon salt
- 2 ounces (½ stick) unsalted butter, at room temperature, cut into ½-inch cubes
- ¼ cup vegetable shortening, at room temperature
- 1 cup firmly packed dark brown sugar
- 2 teaspoons pure vanilla extract
- 1½ ounces good-quality dark chocolate (60 to 72%), melted and cooled
- 1 large egg yolk
- 1 cup well-shaken buttermilk

For the Malted Buttercream Filling

- ¼ cup malted milk powder
- 2 tablespoons boiling water
- ¼ cup plus 2 tablespoons whole milk
- ½ cup heavy cream
- ¼ cup all-purpose flour
- 8 ounces (2 sticks) unsalted butter, softened, cut into ½-inch cubes
- 1 cup confectioners' sugar, sifted

DEVIL DOGS

with

MALTED BUTTERCREAM FILLING

IT IS A STRANGE THING to be haunted by a childhood snack, especially a snack you are fairly certain was mass-produced in a large, impersonal factory, a snack that is chock-full of impossible-to-pronounce ingredients. Yet we still possess a slavish devotion to these snacks, if only because they informed our sweet obsession. We may not eat as many Hostess (or Drake's or Little Debbie) cakes as we used to, but we still think they deserve homage. The genius of these snack cakes is that they always managed to include an icing shot (think Hostess CupCakes) or icing layer (think Drake's Devil Dogs or Hostess Ho Hos) encased in a moist chocolate (on occasion, vanilla) cake while still remaining packaged and portable (an inverse cupcake before the cupcake craze). Our Devil Dogs do the same and are less sticky-sweet than the cellophane-wrapped original. The cakes themselves are rich without reaching into decadent territory, and the filling is sweet but tempered by a bit of malt nuttiness. Mostly though, we recommend you make these because they will make you smile—it's difficult to suppress a grin when eating a bone-shaped dessert with "dog" in the name. And sometimes that is reason enough.

/// *Yield: 12 devil dogs* ///

BAKED NOTE: *You can bump up the malt quotient and add a pleasant texture to the Devil Dogs by rolling the edges of the filled dogs in coarsely chopped or crushed malted milk balls (they will stick to the filling)—just ¼ cup Whoppers or Maltesers should be plenty to coat all 12 dogs.*

///

MAKE THE DEVIL DOGS

Sift the cocoa powder into a medium bowl. Add the flour, baking soda, espresso powder, baking powder, and salt and whisk to combine.

In the bowl of a standing mixer fitted with the paddle attachment, beat the butter and shortening together on medium speed until creamy, 2 to 3 minutes. Add the brown sugar and vanilla and beat until fluffy, about 3 minutes. Scrape down the sides and bottom of the bowl, add the chocolate and egg yolk, and beat until just combined. Scrape down the bowl again, then turn the mixer to low. Add the flour mixture in three parts, alternating with the buttermilk, beginning and ending with the flour mixture. Scrape down the bowl again, then mix for a few more seconds. Remove the bowl from the mixer and use a spatula to scrape down the bowl one last time and gather the batter into the middle. Place the bowl in the refrigerator for 10 minutes.

Preheat the oven to 400 degrees F. Line two baking sheets with parchment paper.

Scrape the chilled batter into a pastry bag fitted with the largest plain tip (usually about ½ inch in diameter). Slowly pipe twenty-four 4-inch-long "bones" (strips side by side with flares on the top and bottom; 2 to 2½ tablespoons of batter in each, but no more) directly onto the parchment, about 1½ inches apart.

Bake the cakes for 5 to 8 minutes, rotating the pans halfway through the baking time, until they are just dry to the touch and spring back ever so slightly when gently pressed. Do not overbake.

Place the baking sheets on wire racks to cool for 10 minutes. Then use a spatula to transfer the cakes to the racks to cool completely.

MAKE THE MALTED BUTTERCREAM FILLING

In a small bowl, dissolve the malted milk powder in the boiling water. In a medium saucepan over medium heat, stir together the milk, cream, and malted milk mixture. Whisk in the flour and stir constantly until the mixture comes to a boil and has thickened, 2 to 4 minutes. Transfer the mixture to a medium bowl (to hasten the cooling process). Whisk vigorously for about 1 minute to release excess heat and set aside to cool to nearly room temperature.

In the bowl of a standing mixer fitted with the paddle attachment, beat the butter and confectioners' sugar on medium speed until pale and fluffy, about 3 minutes. Turn the mixer to low and stream in the cooled milk mixture. Increase the speed to medium and continue beating until the filling is fluffy and stiff peaks start to form.

ASSEMBLE THE DEVIL DOGS

Turn half of the cooled cakes flat side up. Using a pastry bag, or a small spoon and offset spatula, pipe or spread about 3 tablespoons of filling onto the flat side of a cake, place another cake flat side down on top of the filling and press slightly so that the filling just spreads to the edges of the cakes. Repeat until all the cakes are used. Put the Devil Dogs in the refrigerator for 5 to 7 minutes to firm up before serving.

Devil Dogs are meant to be eaten the day they are made. If you really want to save a few, they can be stored at room temperature, in an airtight container, for up to 24 hours.

MALTED VANILLA MILK SHAKES

WHEN WE WERE both younger and distinctly greener around the edges (that is naive, not eco-conscious), we took it upon ourselves to participate in a large food festival to spread the Baked gospel. Our wide-eyed enthusiasm carried us to a strange, enormous kitchen, and we worked several days, nearly round the clock, to produce approximately 1,200 samples of our multitiered Cookie and Cream Tower—a recipe that did not easily translate into the "sample format." In a moment of inspired 2:00 A.M. kitchen delirium, we also decided to serve each sample with a shot glass of Malted Vanilla Milk Shake. Good ideas rarely come to the temporarily insane. The festival opened and hundreds of people ran, in filmlike "slo-mo," toward our booth. Everyone enjoyed the dessert, but it was the milk shake they wanted more of, the milk shake that people fought over. A simple, no-brainer treat (at least no-brainer for a book with a malted milk powder section), Malted Vanilla Milk Shakes need very little introduction other than that they are one of those rare items that is much better than you remember—rich, vanilla-y, nutty malted bliss. Just a few spoonfuls (we like them extra thick) will provide a portal to 1950s America.

/////////////////////// *Yield: 2 large milk shakes or 6 mini milk shakes* ///////////////////////

BAKED NOTE: *A good malted is only as good as the ice cream you use. Make sure to use a premium brand of vanilla ice cream or to make your own. And yes, you can substitute different ice cream flavors—just stay away from anything fruity or minty.*

¼ cup malted milk balls (such as Whoppers or Maltesers)

¾ cup very cold whole milk

1 vanilla bean

2¼ to 2¾ cups premium vanilla ice cream, to taste

2 tablespoons malted milk powder

Freeze 2 large (12-ounce or larger) or 6 small (4-ounce) glasses for at least 30 minutes.

Crush the malted milk balls with a mortar and pestle until they are a chunky powder.

Pour the milk into a blender. Cut the vanilla bean in half lengthwise and, using the tip of a knife or a small spoon, scrape the seeds into the milk. Discard the vanilla bean pod or reserve it for another use. Cover and blend for about 15 seconds. Add 2¼ cups of the ice cream and the malted milk powder and blend until thick and creamy. A good milk shake should be eaten with a spoon—so if the milk shake seems too thin, add another ¼ cup to ½ cup ice cream and blend again. Divide the shake between the chilled glasses, garnish with the crushed malted milk balls, and serve immediately.

4	ounces good-quality milk chocolate, coarsely chopped
2¼	cups heavy cream
¼	cup malted milk powder
5	large egg yolks
¼	cup sugar
I	teaspoon fleur de sel
¼	cup malted milk balls (such as Whoppers or Maltesers), whole or crushed, for garnish

MALTED MILK CHOCOLATE POTS DE CRÈME

IT JUST SO HAPPENED that my pots de crème addiction coincided with my madeleine addiction (see page 123). Though I do not generally consider myself a Francophile, I couldn't help but recognize that I might be going through a French-inspired dessert phase by focusing solely on two of the country's most recognized sweets for an inordinate period of time. I also recognized that this sole focus might be borderline obsessive—how else to explain the wormhole of lost money and time that went into my madeleine pan and vintage ramekin/soufflé dish collection, but I suppose there are worse addictions in life. Pots de crème are really just heavenly custards: dense, velvety, and rich. This version, befitting of the malted milk powder chapter, is of course bursting with malt powder and milk chocolate, providing a playful American riff on the classic French dessert. They also happen to be great for those fancy sit-down dinner parties as they are easy to make ahead and they look very regal served in individual teacups.

/////////////////////////////////////// *Yield: 8 servings* ///////////////////////////////////////

BAKED NOTE: *A good-quality milk chocolate is imperative for this dessert. The flavor is reminiscent of a very rich, very grown-up malted milk ball. However, we tested this recipe with 2 ounces each of good-quality milk and dark chocolate and enjoyed it almost as much as the original milk chocolate–only version.*

///

Preheat the oven to 325 degrees F. Place eight 4-ounce ramekins or soufflé dishes in a roasting pan and set aside.

Place the chocolate in a heatproof bowl.

In a medium saucepan over medium-high heat, whisk together the cream and malted milk powder (don't worry if the malted milk powder is lumpy or clumps at this point). Cook the mixture until it just begins to boil, stirring occasionally. Pour the hot cream mixture over the chocolate, let the mixture sit for 30 seconds, then whisk until the chocolate is melted and the mixture is smooth.

In another bowl whisk together the egg yolks, sugar, and fleur de sel until blended. Whisking constantly, slowly stream the chocolate mixture into the egg mixture until combined. (If you want a super-smooth texture, push the combined mixture through a fine-mesh sieve into another bowl. If you aren't in the mood to use the sieve and you don't want to mess up another bowl, you can forgo this step.)

Divide the custard equally among the ramekins. Carefully pour hot tap water into the roasting pan until the water reaches about halfway up the sides of the ramekins. Bake for 20 to 30 minutes, until the custards are set around the edge but still wobbly in the middle. Remove the ramekins from the water, let cool for 10 minutes, and refrigerate, uncovered, for at least 3 hours. Top with the malted milk balls before serving.

Pots de crème generally taste best if eaten within 24 hours; however, they still taste dandy as leftovers and can be stored in the refrigerator, tightly covered after the initial chilling period, for up to 2 days.

MILK CHOCOLATE MALT SEMIFREDDO

with

CHOCOLATE SYRUP

10	ounces (about 1¾ cups) malted milk balls (such as Whoppers or Maltesers)
½	cup sugar, divided
⅓	cup malted milk powder
5	large eggs, separated*
2	cups heavy cream
I	tablespoon pure vanilla extract
½	teaspoon salt
	Simple Chocolate Syrup, warmed (optional, page 192)

WE ARE FAIRLY CERTAIN that *semifreddo* means "lazy man's ice cream" in Italian. If you are not in the mood to wrangle with your ice cream machine (or if you don't own one), then semifreddo is the way to Zen. This semifreddo tastes as though you poured the perfect melty malted milk shake into a loaf pan and froze it for a few hours to firm it up in anticipation of a hot summer night. The texture of this semifreddo is like ice cream, and the malt flavor packs a serious punch (most likely attributed to the lack of applied heat to any component in the recipe). We are also kind of in love with the presentation of this treat. The layers of the dessert are very visible when sliced, so it has a retro ice cream cake quality about it but with a surprisingly sophisticated look and taste.

//////////////// *Yield: Two 9-by-5-inch semifreddi (about 18 servings)* ////////////////

BAKED NOTE: *You do not have to serve this recipe with the Simple Chocolate Syrup (page 192), but we really like the interplay of the warm sauce on a cold dessert (oh, and we really love chocolate). Feel free to serve the syrup in a ramekin on the side in case anyone wants to enjoy the semifreddo in its purest state, or offer an assortment of toppings such as Classic Caramel Sauce (page 59), whipped cream, crushed chocolate wafer cookies, and additional crushed malted milk balls. The semifreddo can become the base of a marvelous sundae.*

///

Line two 9-by-5-inch loaf pans with plastic wrap and allow a generous overhang on all sides. Spray a paper towel with nonstick cooking spray and wipe the plastic wrap with it so that the plastic wrap is nonstick but not oily.

In a food processor, pulse the malted milk balls until they are coarsely chopped. (Do not process until powdery—you want some decent-size chunks.) Sprinkle the bottom of each loaf pan with approximately one-quarter of the chopped malted milk balls.

In a large bowl, whisk together ¼ cup plus 1 tablespoon of the sugar, the malted milk powder, and the egg yolks fairly vigorously until the mixture turns pale, 1 to 2 minutes.

In a chilled medium bowl, vigorously whisk the cream for 1 minute, sprinkle the remaining 3 tablespoons of sugar and the vanilla over top of the cream, then continue

* The eggs in this recipe are not cooked, which may be of concern if salmonella is a problem in your area.

beating until soft peaks form. Fold the whipped cream into the egg yolk mixture. Set aside.

In the bowl of a standing mixer fitted with the whisk attachment, beat the egg whites with the salt just until stiff peaks form. Do not whip past the stiff peak stage or the whites will become dry and unusable.

Fold one-third of the egg white mixture into the egg yolk base. Add half of the remaining egg whites and gently fold until almost incorporated. Fold in the remaining egg whites.

Use a large spoon to fill each loaf pan halfway with the semifreddo. Smooth out the surface with the back of the spoon and place in the freezer for 10 minutes.

Remove the loaf pans from the freezer and sprinkle the remaining chopped malted milk balls over the semifreddo in each pan. Then cover the malted milk ball layer with the remaining semifreddo. Smooth out the top with the back of the spoon. Cover the pans tightly with the plastic wrap overhang and freeze until firm, about 6 hours.

To serve, invert the semifreddi onto a platter and remove the plastic wrap. Drizzle some of the chocolate syrup over the tops. Using a knife dipped in hot water (and dried thoroughly), slice the semifreddi into 1-inch slices. Serve the remaining chocolate syrup on the side.

MALTED MADELEINES

I SUPPOSE I was unaware (perhaps blissfully so) of the mystique and rarefied history associated with the madeleine when I purchased my first madeleine pan. I simply liked the shape of the molds, so I bought the pan. Only after researching recipes for my new pan did I realize two important things. First, the madeleine has a long, rich, romantic background (see Marcel Proust). Second, madeleine opinions run deep and are very personal—and madeleine purists distrust any deviation in flavor and method. Well, the purists are wrong. Madeleines are fun, and they can be explored without being exploited. Yes, a good madeleine should have a crisp, crunchy exterior and a light and tender interior, and should always be consumed within 6 hours of baking (preferably with a good coffee or tea standing by), but I do think different flavors should be explored. Though my first few years of madeleine experimentation consisted solely of the lemon-flavored variety, I have since branched out and can highly recommend this malted riff on the hallowed treat. The malt flavor is subtle in this recipe, but it provides a nice nutty taste. I wouldn't be averse to dipping these in some melted chocolate, but then again, I wouldn't be averse to dipping almost anything in chocolate.

///////////////////////////////////// *Yield: 24 madeleines* /////////////////////////////////////

BAKED NOTE: *Though madeleine protocol would suggest otherwise, I sometimes cheat a crunchy exterior by heavily buttering the molds and heating the pan in the oven for about 3 minutes (until the butter melts and sizzles) right before adding the batter. The only drawback to this method is that some people might have trouble unmolding the cakes when cooled—it really depends on your pan (we recommend a heavy nonstick or cast-iron pan)—but I still think you should try it at least once.*

//

Butter the madeleine pans, dust with flour, and knock out the excess flour.

Whisk together the flour, 3 tablespoons of the malted milk powder, 2 tablespoons of the cocoa powder, and the baking powder.

In the bowl of a standing mixer fitted with the whisk attachment, beat the eggs, sugar, and salt on high speed until frothy, about 3 minutes. Drizzle in the butter on low speed until just blended.

Remove the bowl from the mixer and sift the dry ingredients over the top of the egg mixture. Gently fold the dry ingredients into the wet ingredients. Cover the bowl with a dry cloth and set aside for 1 hour.

½	cup plus 2 tablespoons all-purpose flour
3	tablespoons plus I teaspoon malted milk powder, divided
2	tablespoons plus I teaspoon dark unsweetened cocoa powder (like Valrhona), divided
I	teaspoon baking powder
2	large eggs, at room temperature
½	cup sugar
¼	teaspoon salt
2½	ounces (5 tablespoons) unsalted butter, melted and nearly at room temperature

Preheat the oven to 375 degrees F.

Give the batter a quick stir, then spoon the batter gently into the pans, filling the molds about three-quarters full. Bake for 10 to 12 minutes, rotating the pans halfway through the baking time.

Remove the pans to wire racks to cool for 1 minute, then carefully unmold the madeleines onto the cooling rack. In a small bowl, stir together the remaining cocoa powder and malted milk powder until blended and sift over the madeleines.

I think madeleines taste best if eaten within a few hours of baking, but they can be stored at room temperature, tightly covered, for up to 2 days.

VANILLA BEAN MALT CAKE

For the Vanilla Bean Malt Cake

I	teaspoon good-quality bourbon
I	vanilla bean or 2 teaspoons vanilla bean paste
1½	cups all-purpose flour
¼	cup plus I tablespoon malted milk powder
2	teaspoons baking powder
¼	teaspoon salt
7	ounces (1¾ sticks) unsalted butter, softened, cut into ½-inch cubes
¾	cup granulated sugar
¼	cup firmly packed dark brown sugar
2	large eggs, plus I large egg yolk
½	cup well-shaken buttermilk

For the Vanilla Glaze

⅔	cup confectioners' sugar, plus more if needed
2	tablespoons whole milk, plus more if needed
I	teaspoon pure vanilla extract

I'D THINK THE best time to make this cake would be late at night, half watching some campy horror film—this is how I make many of my cakes. For me, chocolate cake and Godzilla go hand in hand at I A.M. But in fact, I have only made this cake in the early morning hours—usually from 7 A.M. to 9 A.M. while watching the *Today* show (I am aware that I watch too much television). This Bundt could easily have been named The 7 A.M. Cake. And I suppose it is made for morning baking. You can put the cake together in the same amount of time it takes you to brew a cup of coffee—you can actually put it together while you are drinking your morning coffee, and it doesn't require strict attention (or a caffeine buzz). By the time you pop it out of the Bundt pan and drizzle it with icing, it is ready for you to eat and serve (or gift) throughout the day. It's a snack cake in the purest sense. The cake itself is a tight-crumbed vanilla explosion. The key to its robust taste is the amount of vanilla (more than usual) nuanced by the addition of the malted milk powder. The malted milk powder is hard to place in the cake—it's a foreign nuttiness—but the cake would suffer without it. That's often the beauty of malted milk powder: you don't know what you're missing until it's gone.

Yield: One 6-cup Bundt cake

BAKED NOTE: *There is something adorable about this 6-cup Bundt. It seems pleasantly sized for a quaint afternoon with tea and friends. However, if you don't happen to have an embarrassing collection of Bundt pans hanging around the house (like I do), you can absolutely make this cake in the more common 10-cup Bundt pan. It will be shorter, of course—but it will taste exactly the same. You don't necessarily have to adjust the baking time when going from a 6-cup to a 10-cup pan, but check the cake early and often for doneness just to be sure.*

MAKE THE VANILLA BEAN MALT CAKE

Preheat the oven to 325 degrees F. Generously coat the inside of a 6-cup Bundt pan with nonstick cooking spray; alternatively, butter it thoroughly, dust it with flour, and knock out the excess flour.

Place the bourbon in a small bowl. Cut the vanilla bean in half lengthwise and, using the tip of a knife or a small spoon, scrape the seeds into the bourbon. Discard the vanilla bean pod or save it for another use. Stir the mixture to combine. Set aside.

In a medium bowl, whisk together the flour, malted milk powder, baking powder, and salt.

In the bowl of a standing mixer fitted with the paddle attachment, beat the butter and both sugars on medium speed until light and fluffy, about 3 minutes. Add the eggs and egg yolk, one at a time, beating well after each addition. Scrape down the sides and bottom of the bowl and beat again for 15 seconds. Add the bourbon mixture and beat until well blended, about 20 seconds.

Turn the mixer to low, add about half of the flour mixture, then stream in the buttermilk. Add the remaining flour mixture and beat until just combined. Do not overmix.

Pour the batter into the prepared pan, and smooth with an offset spatula. Bake for 35 to 45 minutes, rotating the pan halfway through the baking time, until a small sharp knife inserted into the cake comes out clean.

Transfer the pan to a wire rack to cool for 45 minutes. Gently loosen the sides of the cake from the pan and turn it out onto the rack to cool completely.

MAKE THE VANILLA GLAZE

Whisk all the ingredients together in a medium bowl. The glaze should be loose enough to drizzle. (If it is too thick, add a little more milk; if it is too loose add a little more confectioners' sugar.)

Drizzle the glaze over the cake in a zigzag pattern. Allow the glaze to set for 15 minutes prior to serving.

The cake can be stored at room temperature, covered with a cake dome or in a cake saver, for up to 3 days.

THE AMERICAN CANCER SOCIETY SUGGESTS PUTTING CINNAMON STICKS IN YOUR MOUTH AS ONE WAY TO SUPPRESS THE URGE TO SMOKE

CASSIA IS THE FAKE GUCCI PURSE OF THE CINNAMON WORLD. ALSO KNOWN AS "FAKE CINNAMON," IT IS MORE COMMONLY SOLD IN THE UNITED STATES THAN TRUE CINNAMON, AND IT IS SPICIER AND HOTTER IN FLAVOR.

$38,195,680 WHAT THE UNITED STATES SPENT ON CINNAMON IMPORTS IN 2010

CINNAMON CAN:
- CURE STOMACH AILMENTS
- TREAT NAUSEA & COLDS
- AID DIGESTION
- HELP REDUCE THE RISK OF CARDIOVASCULAR DISEASE

"CINNAMON" RANKED #700   ON THE LIST OF MOST POPULAR BABY NAMES ♪ IN 1969 ♪ the same year that NEIL YOUNG'S "CINNAMON GIRL" WAS RELEASED TO CRITICAL ACCLAIM. THE NAME HAS YET TO REACH THE TOP 1,000 AGAIN.

THE UNITED STATES IMPORTS MOST OF ITS CINNAMON FROM INDONESIA
(but also quite a bit from Sri Lanka, Vietnam, and India)

Cinnamon was once more valuable than gold.

Chapter 7
CINNAMON

Perhaps we apply cinnamon a bit too liberally, like salt. It's a spice with an undeniable punch and warmth, and we might abuse these charms ever so slightly—pushing the boundaries of what is considered an acceptable amount of cinnamon—but we prefer to think we are just pushing the flavor profile to a higher level, a higher appreciation. Renato actually is more of a cinnamaniac. He tries to slip it into various stages of recipe development with a not-so-casual "This could use a little cinnamon." I am glad to oblige (most of the time). Between the two of us we have obscene amounts of cinnamon—it looks like we are preparing for a cinnamon apocalypse—there are jars of ground cinnamon, bags of cinnamon sticks, and various cinnamon things (like tea, soap, candles) scattered throughout our homes. We use cinnamon in a version of almost every baked good, but it's the cookies that send us. Warm cinnamon-scented cookies (snickerdoodles, chocolate chip) equal warm fragrant house. In other words, happy homes are full of cinnamon.

CLASSIC CARROT CAKE

with

CINNAMON CREAM CHEESE FROSTING

For the Classic Carrot Cake

I	cup shredded or flaked sweetened coconut
I	cup walnuts, toasted (page 19), coarsely chopped
2¼	cups all-purpose flour
2	teaspoons baking soda
2	teaspoons baking powder
I	teaspoon salt
2	teaspoons cinnamon
¼	teaspoon freshly grated nutmeg
¼	teaspoon ground ginger
⅛	teaspoon ground cloves
I	cup granulated sugar
I	cup firmly packed dark brown sugar
3	large eggs, plus 2 large egg yolks
I	cup vegetable oil (preferably canola)
4	ounces (I stick) unsalted butter, melted and cooled
2	teaspoons pure vanilla extract
3	cups finely grated peeled carrots (about I pound; see Baked Note)

For the Cinnamon Cream Cheese Frosting

4	ounces (I stick) unsalted butter, softened
8	ounces cream cheese, softened
3	cups confectioners' sugar, sifted
I	tablespoon pure vanilla extract
I½	teaspoons cinnamon
½	teaspoon salt

TO US, CARROT CAKE without cinnamon is like macaroni and cheese without the cheese. And because we are cinnamon enthusiasts (some would say Renato is almost compulsive), we decided to top this cake with a cinnamon cream cheese frosting. But this cake is not just about the cinnamon. This cake is also about the perfectly crafted cake sponge—a nice interplay of moisture and texture provided by the walnuts, coconut, and...well...carrots. It should also be noted that this cake, while perfect for any special occasion (and of course, super easy to transport in its sheet cake form), is eerily well suited for a late-morning breakfast.

/////////////////////////////// *Yield: One 9-inch, single-layer cake* ///////////////////////////////

BAKED NOTE: *How finely should you grate your carrots? Typically, we recommend a really fine shred that is usually achieved by hand by using a Microplane or box-type grater, but ultimately the decision is yours. If you are feeling a hankering to use a machine, you can absolutely chop and grate away in the food processor, though the pieces will be chunkier and so will your cake. But there is nothing wrong with a chunky cake.*

///

MAKE THE CLASSIC CARROT CAKE

Preheat the oven to 325 degrees F. Butter the bottom and sides of a 9-by-13-inch light-colored metal baking pan. Line the pan with parchment paper so that the paper over-hangs the pan on two sides. Butter the parchment. Dust the parchment with flour and knock out the excess flour.

Spread the coconut in an even layer on a rimmed baking sheet and bake until toasted and lightly browned, 5 to 7 minutes (use a spatula to flip the coconut after 3 minutes). Allow the baking sheet to cool for a few minutes, then spread the walnuts over the coconut and toss them together with your hands.

In a large bowl whisk together the flour, baking soda, baking powder, salt, cinnamon, nutmeg, ginger, and cloves. Set aside.

In the bowl of a standing mixer fitted with the paddle attachment, beat both sugars, the eggs, and the egg yolks on medium speed until the mixture comes together and is pale in color. Add the oil and butter and continue beating on medium speed until the mixture emulsifies. Scrape down the sides and bottom of the bowl, add the vanilla, and beat again for 15 seconds.

Using a rubber spatula, gently fold the dry ingredients into the wet ingredients until just incorporated. Scatter the coconut mixture and the carrots over the batter and gently fold them in until they are evenly distributed throughout the batter.

Pour the batter into the prepared pan. Bake for 35 to 40 minutes, rotating the pan halfway through the baking time, until a toothpick inserted in the center of the cake comes out with just a few moist crumbs. Transfer the pan to a wire rack and cool completely.

MAKE THE CINNAMON CREAM CHEESE FROSTING

In the bowl of a standing mixer fitted with the paddle attachment, beat the butter until it is completely smooth. Add the cream cheese and beat until no lumps remain.

Add the confectioners' sugar, vanilla, cinnamon, and salt and beat until smooth (be careful not to overbeat the frosting or it will lose its structure). The frosting can be made a day ahead: after mixing, cover the bowl tightly and refrigerate; let the frosting soften at room temperature before using.

Using an offset spatula, spread the frosting evenly across the top of the cake.

Lift the cake out of the pan using the parchment paper overhang and cut into serving-size pieces.

The cake can be stored in the refrigerator, covered with a cake dome or in a cake saver, for up to 3 days. Bring the cake to almost room temperature before serving.

WHOLE-WHEAT CINNAMON SUGAR PRETZELS

I LIVED A STEREOTYPICAL New York City newbie lifestyle: low bank balance, maxed-out credit card, a small, windowless bedroom in an illegal loft, many (maybe too many) late nights, and buckets of inexpensive Chinese takeout and street vendor soft pretzels. The idea was to save money on food (mere sustenance) to pay for the many late nights. Over time and with much strate-gic initiative, I was able to figure out which street vendors had the best soft pretzels. Of course, all of the pretzels were most likely sourced from the same manufacturer, but some vendors were able to score me "fresh" pretzels (i.e., ones that were warmed recently and only once), while others perfected the heat to smoke to salt ratio. Mostly, though, they were heartbreakingly forgetta-ble—a New York institution best savored in the mind, not the belly. Homemade pretzels are infinitely better. And like most things Baked, these homemade pretzels have a sweet bent. They are still classically puffy with a chewy, dark golden brown exterior, but we slather ours in melted butter—the more butter you can get on your pretzel, the happier you'll be—and sprinkle them with a generous helping of cinnamon sugar. It's the perfect salty sweet treat.

// *Yield: 8 to 10 pretzels* //

BAKED NOTE: We can assure you that your pretzel dough prowess will progress significantly each time you make this recipe. You will start to get a feel for the proper elasticity for rolling, the perfect length for shaping, and the gentle touch required for flipping (in the baking soda bath). Don't worry if you don't master these techniques on the first go-round—pretzel dough is fairly forgiving—just remember to be gentle throughout the process, and know that a misshapen pretzel is just as delicious as a perfectly shaped one.

//

MAKE THE PRETZEL DOUGH

In a large bowl, whisk together the bread flour, whole wheat flour, and salt. Add the butter. Use your fingertips to rub the butter into the flour mixture until the butter is pea size and the mixture resembles coarse sand.

In the bowl of a standing mixer fitted with the dough hook attachment, gently whisk together the yeast, honey, and water. Stop stirring and let stand until the mixture starts to foam, 8 to 10 minutes.

For the Pretzel Dough

- 1½ cups bread flour
- 1½ cups whole wheat flour
- ¼ teaspoon salt
- 1 ounce (¼ stick) unsalted butter, cool but not cold, cut into ½-inch cubes
- 1 packet active dry yeast (2¼ teaspoons)
- 1 tablespoon plus 1 teaspoon honey
- 1 cup warm water (105 to 115 degrees F)
- 2 tablespoons canola oil

For the Baking Soda Bath

- ⅓ cup baking soda

For the Cinnamon Sugar Topping

- ¼ cup sugar
- 3 teaspoons cinnamon
- ¼ teaspoon freshly grated nutmeg
- ⅛ teaspoon salt
- 3 tablespoons unsalted butter, melted

Add the flour mixture to the yeast mixture and mix on low speed until combined. Increase the speed to medium-low and continue mixing until the dough is elastic and pulls away from the sides of the bowl. Remove the dough to a plate. Add the canola oil to the bowl and use your fingers to spread a very thin coating of it onto the bottom and sides of the bowl. Transfer the dough back into the bowl, turn it a few times to coat in the canola oil, and cover the bowl with plastic wrap. Set the bowl in a warm place until the dough doubles in size, about 1 hour.

Grease two half-sheet pans (18 by 13 inches) with a thick coating of nonstick cooking spray. Alternatively, grease the pans with a thin coating of canola oil.

Cut the dough into 8 to 10 equal pieces.

On a flat, slightly oiled surface (or on the prepared pans), roll each dough piece into an 18-inch rope. Then, to make the classic pretzel shape, form each rope into a wide *u* shape, then take each end and drape it across the opposite side, overlapping the bottom half of the *u* shape by an inch or two. Press gently where the dough overlaps so the pieces adhere to each other. Allow the dough to rest at room temperature while you make the baking soda bath.

MAKE THE BAKING SODA BATH

Preheat the oven to 475 degrees F and position the rack in the center.

In a large pot, stir the baking soda into about 7 cups of water. Bring to a rolling boil. In batches of 3, boil the pretzels for about 1 minute on each side (flipping them gently with a heatproof spatula). Use the spatula to remove the pretzels from the water, allowing excess water to drain back into the pot, and place the pretzels on the prepared baking sheets. (If you used the baking sheets to roll out your pretzels, make sure the sheets are still well oiled.)

Once all the pretzels are boiled, bake one sheet at a time for about 15 minutes, or until the pretzels are browned (if you are making smaller, thinner pretzels, check for pretzel doneness around the 10-minute mark). Remove the baking sheet from the oven and let the pretzels cool for a few minutes. Repeat for the second baking sheet.

MAKE THE CINNAMON SUGAR TOPPING

In a shallow bowl, whisk together the sugar, cinnamon, nutmeg, and salt.

Baste the top of each still-warm pretzel with a generous slathering of butter, then sprinkle the sugar mixture over. Serve immediately.

Pretzels taste best if eaten within 12 hours of baking. However, I have been known to munch on leftovers over the course of a few days. Just store them at room temperature, tightly covered, for up to 2 days, and, if you want, pop them in a microwave for 15 seconds to warm them just before eating.

THE PRETZEL AS CANVAS

It's possible to tailor a pretzel—at least our homemade, boiled-and-baked version—to every personality. The pretzel base (pre-cinnamon sugar topping) is versatile enough to stand up to almost any topping or preparation—however ridiculous—so feel free to use a few of our ideas or experiment with your own.

New York City Vendor-Style Pretzel

After the pretzels come out of the baking soda bath, but before they go into the oven, simply brush the pretzel dough with a little bit of egg wash (one egg yolk and a few drops of water, whisked until blended), then sprinkle with chunky salt or fleur de sel. Bake for the same amount of time listed in the recipe. (Omit the cinnamon sugar topping completely.) Serve immediately.

Chocolate-Drizzled Pretzels

This is one of our favorites. Simply bake the pretzels as per the recipe, but omit the cinnamon sugar topping. In a double boiler, melt 2 ounces of good-quality dark chocolate with 2 ounces of good-quality milk chocolate. While the chocolate is still warm, drizzle or spoon the chocolate over the pretzels. Serve warm (yes, this is a bit messy) or allow the chocolate to set briefly before serving.

Cheese Pretzels

In a small bowl, mix about ½ cup each of shredded Parmesan and shredded Asiago. After the pretzels come out of the baking soda bath, but before they go into the oven, simply brush the pretzel dough with a little bit of egg wash (one egg yolk and a few drops of water, whisked until blended), then sprinkle each pretzel with the cheese. Bake for the same amount of time listed in the recipe. (Omit the cinnamon sugar topping completely.)

Garlic-Rosemary Pretzels

After the pretzels come out of the baking soda bath, but before they go into the oven, simply brush the pretzel dough with a little bit of egg wash (one egg yolk and a few drops of water, whisked until blended), then top with freshly minced garlic (3 cloves should be more than enough to cover all the pretzels). Bake for the same amount of time listed in the recipe. After you remove the pretzels from the oven, gently brush each one with a little bit of olive oil and sprinkle with salt and freshly minced rosemary. (Omit the cinnamon sugar topping completely.) Serve immediately.

1¼	cups all-purpose flour
2	tablespoons dark unsweetened cocoa powder (like Valrhona)
1	tablespoon ancho chile powder
2	teaspoons freshly grated cinnamon
1	teaspoon salt
1	tablespoon freshly grated ginger or ½ teaspoon ground ginger
9	ounces good-quality dark chocolate (60 to 72%), coarsely chopped
2	ounces good-quality milk chocolate, coarsely chopped
8	ounces (2 sticks) unsalted butter, cut into 1-inch cubes
1½	cups granulated sugar
½	cup firmly packed light brown sugar
5	large eggs, at room temperature

SPICY BROWNIES

A BAKED BOOK without a brownie recipe is an incomplete book. After all, brownies are the bedrock of our Brooklyn bakery, and they have a supernatural, almost holy sway over our lives. Our original brownie—almost perfectly calibrated to target the exact center of the fudgy/cakey continuum—has won many awards, received an extravagant amount of high praise (duly earned), and generally impresses even non-brownie people (though we feel bad for these non-brownie people—life must be dusty and gray). Our Spicy Brownies are a variation on our basic brownie and are popular with a growing subset of spiced brownie enthusiasts. This recipe has evolved over the years. Originally, the spice was provided by a hard kick of chipotle powder, but it was probably too hard a kick, so we veered toward the smoother, subtler, smokier ancho chile, and we played with the amount of cinnamon until we found the perfect warm spot (anything more felt pushy; anything less felt insignificant). Finally, we added some milk chocolate to the mix. To us, milk chocolate always plays better with spices.

//////////////////////////// **Yield: 12 large or 24 small brownies** ////////////////////////////

BAKED NOTE: *Are you feeling less spicy and more nutty? Our peanut butter brownies at Baked are as popular as our Spicy Brownies and it is very easy to adapt this recipe to make them. Simply omit the chile powder, cinnamon, and ginger and add ⅔ cup slightly warmed smooth peanut butter and 2 teaspoons pure vanilla extract to the brownie batter after adding the eggs.*

///

Preheat the oven to 350 degrees F. Butter the bottom and sides of a 9-by-13-inch glass or light-colored metal baking pan. Line the pan with parchment paper and butter the parchment.

In a medium bowl, whisk together the flour, cocoa powder, chile powder, cinnamon, salt, and ginger and set aside.

Place the chopped chocolates and the butter in the bowl of a double boiler over medium heat and stir occasionally until they are completely melted and combined. Turn off the heat, but keep the bowl over the water of the double boiler. Add both sugars and whisk until completely combined. Remove the bowl from the water and let the mixture come to room temperature.

Add 3 eggs to the chocolate mixture and whisk until just combined. Add the remaining eggs and whisk until just combined. Do not overbeat the batter at this stage or your brownies will be cakey.

Sprinkle the flour mixture over the chocolate. Using a spatula, fold the dry ingredients into the wet ingredients until there is just a trace amount of the flour mixture visible. Pour the batter into the prepared pan and smooth the top with a spatula.

Bake the brownies for 30 minutes, rotating the pan halfway through the baking time, until a toothpick inserted in the center of the pan comes out with a few moist crumbs. Remove the brownies from the oven and transfer to a wire rack to cool completely before cutting and serving.

The brownies can be stored at room temperature, tightly covered, for up to 4 days.

Ingredients

8	ounces (2 sticks) unsalted butter, cut into ½-inch cubes
2¾	cups all-purpose flour
2	teaspoons cream of tartar
I	teaspoon baking soda
I	tablespoon plus 2 teaspoons cinnamon, divided
½	teaspoon salt
2	large eggs
I	tablespoon whole milk
I	cup plus 3 tablespoons granulated sugar, divided
½	cup firmly packed light brown sugar

BROWN BUTTER SNICKERDOODLES

THE SNICKERDOODLE, a very close cousin of the sugar cookie, is a unicorn fairy dream of cinnamon and sweet. It's a feel-good lunchbox nostalgia cookie that tastes like joy and laughter—an all-around, anytime treat—and we hardly feel embarrassed or guilty when devouring more than is appropriate (like 3 or 4 plus) in one sitting. Our version includes a hint of nuttiness via the browned butter to offset the super sweetness, and we have been known to underbake them a tad (usually a no-no in our book) to bring out the chewy texture even more (yes, this is cheating). We encourage you to make these often and year round. The snickerdoodle is the happiest cookie we know.

/////////////////////////////////// *Yield: 24 cookies* ///////////////////////////////////

BAKED NOTE: *Though this recipe calls for straining the brown butter, it is not completely necessary. In fact, some people (myself included), prefer unstrained brown butter. The browned bits add a subtle smoky taste (almost burnt), and I rather appreciate the speckled effect the brown bits impart to the dough.*

In a medium skillet, melt the butter over medium heat swirling the pan occasionally, until the foam subsides and the butter turns nut brown, 8 to 10 minutes. Pour the browned butter through a strainer directly into the bowl of a standing mixer fitted with the paddle attachment. Beat the butter on medium-low speed to release the heat and bring it to room temperature, 5 to 7 minutes.

In a large bowl, whisk together the flour, cream of tartar, baking soda, 1 teaspoon of the cinnamon, and the salt.

In a small bowl, combine the eggs and milk and wisk lightly.

Once the butter is cooled, turn off the mixer, add 1 cup of the granulated sugar and the brown sugar, and beat on medium speed for about 2 minutes. Scrape down the sides and bottom of the bowl and beat again for a few seconds. Turn the mixer to low and stream in the egg mixture. Continue beating on medium speed until thoroughly combined, 30 to 45 seconds.

Add the flour mixture in three parts, beating after each addition for 10 to 15 seconds, or until just barely incorporated. Scrape down the sides of the bowl and gather the

dough into a mound in the middle. Cover the bowl and refrigerate for at least 1 hour or up to 24 hours.

Preheat the oven to 400 degrees F. Line two baking sheets with parchment paper.

In a wide-mouthed bowl, stir together the remaining 3 tablespoons of sugar and 1 tablespoon plus 1 teaspoon of cinnamon until the mixture is uniform in color.

Using a small 2-tablespoon-size ice cream scoop with a release mechanism, scoop the dough into balls and roll the dough balls in the cinnamon sugar mixture. (Alternatively, measure the dough using a tablespoon and use your hands to form it into a ball before rolling in the cinnamon sugar mixture.) Place the cookies about 1½ inches apart on the prepared baking sheets and bake for about 10 minutes, rotating the pans halfway through the baking time, until the cookies are cracked and the fissures are set. (We prefer our snickerdoodles chewy. If you want a slightly crunchier cookie, bake for an additional 1 to 2 minutes, but still take care to not overbake the cookies.)

Set the pans on wire racks to cool for 10 minutes. Use a spatula to transfer the cookies to the racks to cool completely.

The cookies can be stored at room temperature, in an airtight container, for up to 3 days.

CINNAMON CHOCOLATE SOUFFLÉS

THESE SOUFFLÉS—a perfectly matched mix of cinnamon and chocolate wrapped up in the texture of a cloud—taste like the approach of early winter. It is exactly the type of dessert that is created for roaring fireplaces and nightcaps and comfortable sweaters. We have yet to debut this dessert in front of a roaring fireplace (fireplaces being a rare luxury in Brooklyn…or at least affordable Brooklyn), but we can attest to the harmonious pairing of these Cinnamon Chocolate Soufflés with boozy nightcaps and comfy sweaters. This dessert pleases the eye as much as it does the stomach, and contrary to popular opinion, soufflés are fairly hassle free.

//////////////////////////////// *Yield: 4 servings* ////////////////////////////////

BAKED NOTE: *Our soufflés probably don't need a big helping of whipped cream—it's a bit like adding another scoop of ice cream to a fully loaded banana split—but we would be remiss not to recommend our Whiskey Whipped Cream on page 86 should you decide to go that route. If you are going to have an accompaniment, it might as well be full of whiskey.*

1½	teaspoons cinnamon, divided
¼	cup plus 1 tablespoon granulated sugar, divided
5	ounces good-quality dark chocolate (60 to 72%), coarsely chopped
1½	ounces (3 tablespoons) unsalted butter
3	large eggs, separated, plus 1 large egg white
1	teaspoon cream of tartar
⅛	teaspoon salt
1	teaspoon pure vanilla extract
	Confectioners' sugar for dusting
	Whiskey Whipped Cream (optional, page 86)

Preheat the oven to 400 degrees F and position the rack in the center. Lightly butter the bottom and sides of four 6-ounce ramekins. Mix together 1 teaspoon of the cinnamon and 1 tablespoon of the granulated sugar, dust the ramekins with the cinnamon sugar mixture, and knock out the excess cinnamon sugar. Place the ramekins on a baking sheet.

Place the chocolate and butter in the bowl of a double boiler over medium heat and stir occasionally until they are completely melted and combined. Turn off the heat and whisk in the remaining ½ teaspoon cinnamon. Transfer the chocolate mixture to a large bowl and whisk in the egg yolks, one at a time, until blended. Set aside.

In the bowl of a standing mixer fitted with the whisk attachment (or, if you are feeling strong, you can certainly do this without the aid of a machine—you will just need a whisk and bowl and a ready arm), whisk the egg whites on high speed for 1 minute. Sprinkle the cream of tartar and salt over the whites and continue whisking on high speed until the egg whites are foamy. Continue whisking while streaming in the remaining ¼ cup sugar, then the vanilla. Whisk until stiff peaks form.

Gently fold one-quarter of the stiff egg white mixture into the chocolate mixture until almost combined. The chocolate mixture will begin to lighten. Fold another quarter of the egg white mixture into the chocolate mixture until nearly combined. Finally, add the remaining egg white mixture to the chocolate mixture and fold gently until completely combined.

Divide the soufflé mixture equally among the ramekins, then run your thumb around the inside edge of each ramekin to wipe away any stray mixture (this will help provide an even rise). Place the baking sheet in the oven, immediately reduce the oven temperature to 375 degrees F, and bake for 8 minutes. Soufflés are generally finished baking after rising 1½ to 2 inches; the centers should still be jiggly while the perimeter should be almost set. If the soufflés are not done baking after 8 minutes, continue baking, checking them at 2-minute intervals. Remove the baking sheet from the oven, transfer the ramekins to a serving plate, and serve immediately. Garnish the tops with a dusting of confectioners' sugar or dollop of whiskey whipped cream, if desired.

For the Holiday Spice Cake

2¼	cups cake flour
¾	cup all-purpose flour
I	tablespoon baking powder
I	teaspoon baking soda
¾	teaspoon salt
4	ounces (I stick) unsalted butter, softened
½	cup vegetable shortening, softened
2	cups sugar
2½	teaspoons pure vanilla extract
I	large egg, plus 3 large egg whites, at room temperature
1½	cups ice-cold water
I	tablespoon cinnamon
2	teaspoons ground allspice
I	teaspoon freshly grated ginger
3	tablespoons molasses
¼	teaspoon cream of tartar

For the Eggnog Buttercream

1½	cups sugar
⅓	cup all-purpose flour
1½	cups whole milk
⅓	cup heavy cream
12	ounces (3 sticks) unsalted butter, cool but not cold, cut into ½-inch cubes
2	tablespoons good-quality dark rum
I	teaspoon pure vanilla extract
I	tablespoon freshly grated nutmeg
½	teaspoon cinnamon

For the Assembly

Decorations (see Note)

HOLIDAY SPICE CAKE
with
EGGNOG BUTTERCREAM

THIS CAKE IS SPECIAL. More specifically, this is a November/December special-edition cake—a rarity for us. While we usually advocate making any cake you want any time of the year, we specifically created this one to push all the romantic holiday buttons and then disappear from the calendar until the next season arrives. It is a cake that is imbued with a sense of pure snow, sleigh bells, glittering parties, Douglas firs, and hot chocolate—entirely silly, but entirely true. The cake itself is a gentle and light white cake infused with warm spices and molasses, while the frosting and filling is an eggnog riff on our popular buttercream. Together they create an honest holiday cake—a cake that is fantastic and intimate and tasty. It's a snack engineered for quiet times near the Christmas tree or for a festive party drenched in champagne.

////////////////////////// *Yield: One 8-inch, 3-layer cake* //////////////////////////

BAKED NOTE: *Holiday cakes are meant to be decorated, but we'd suggest not overdecorating them (though you don't have to listen to us). We think this cake looks great with a tone-on-tone ensemble. A few carefully placed silver or pearl dragées or an infusion of pearl luster dust in the buttercream really makes this cake stand out in a striking and modern manner.*

MAKE THE HOLIDAY SPICE CAKE

Preheat the oven to 325 degrees F. Butter three 8-inch round cake pans, line the bottoms with parchment paper, and butter the parchment. Dust the parchment with flour and knock out the excess flour.

Sift the flours, baking powder, baking soda, and salt together into a large bowl. Stir to combine.

In the bowl of a standing mixer fitted with the paddle attachment, beat the butter and shortening on medium speed until creamy, 3 to 4 minutes. Add the sugar and vanilla and beat until fluffy, about 3 minutes. Scrape down the sides and bottom of the bowl, add the whole egg, and beat until just combined.

With the mixer on low speed, add the flour mixture in three parts, alternating with the water, beginning and ending with the flour mixture. For each addition, turn the mixer to low to add the ingredients, then to medium speed for a few seconds until incorporated. Scrape down the sides and bottom of the bowl, then mix on low speed for a few more seconds.

In a small bowl, whisk together the cinnamon, allspice, ginger, and molasses until combined. Fold the mixture into the batter.

In a medium bowl, whisk the egg whites and cream of tartar until soft peaks form. (You can do this by hand. Don't be intimidated; it should only take 2 to 3 minutes). Do not overbeat. Gently fold the egg whites into the batter.

Divide the batter among the prepared pans and smooth the tops. Bake for 25 to 28 minutes, rotating the pans halfway through the baking time, until a toothpick inserted in the center of the cakes comes out clean. Transfer the pans to wire racks and let cool for 20 minutes. Turn the cakes out onto the racks and let them cool completely. Remove the parchment.

MAKE THE EGGNOG BUTTERCREAM

In a medium, heavy-bottomed saucepan, whisk together the sugar and flour. Add the milk and cream and cook over medium heat, whisking occasionally, until the mixture comes to a boil and has thickened, 8 to 12 minutes (as the mixture thickens, you may have to stir more often to keep it from sticking to the bottom of the pan).

Transfer the mixture to the bowl of a standing mixer fitted with the paddle attachment. Beat on high speed until cool, at least 7 minutes. (You can speed up the process by pressing bags of frozen berries or frozen corn against the sides and bottom of the mixing bowl.) Reduce the mixer speed to low and add the butter; mix until thoroughly incorporated. Increase the speed to medium-high and beat until the frosting is light and fluffy, 1 to 2 minutes.

Add the rum, vanilla, nutmeg, and cinnamon and continue mixing until combined. If the frosting is too soft, put the bowl in the refrigerator to chill slightly, then beat again until it is the proper consistency. If the frosting is too firm, set the bowl over a pot of simmering water and beat with a wooden spoon until it is the proper consistency.

ASSEMBLE THE CAKE

Place one layer on a serving platter. Trim the top to create a flat surface and, using an offset or flat spatula, evenly spread about 1¼ cups frosting on top. Add the next layer, trim it and frost it, then add the third layer. Spread a very thin layer of frosting over the sides and top of the cake and put it in the refrigerator for about 15 minutes to firm up. (This is known as a crumb coating; it helps keep loose cake crumbs under control when you frost the outside of the cake.) Spread the sides and top of the cake with the remaining frosting. Decorate the cake (see Baked Note) and refrigerate it for 15 minutes to let it firm up before serving.

This cake will keep beautifully at room temperature, covered with a cake dome or in a cake saver, for up to 3 days if the weather is cool and dry. Otherwise, store it in the refrigerator, covered with a cake dome or in a cake saver, for up to 2 days. Let the cake sit at room temperature for at least 2 hours before serving.

For the Cinnamon Spritz Cookies

2	cups all-purpose flour
1	teaspoon cinnamon
¼	teaspoon ground cardamom
¼	teaspoon salt
8	ounces (2 sticks) unsalted butter, at room temperature, cut into ½-inch cubes
¾	cup sugar
1	large egg

For the Soft Meringue Filling

1	large egg white
½	cup sugar
2	teaspoons light corn syrup
½	teaspoon pure vanilla extract

For the Assembly

Confectioners' sugar for dusting

CINNAMON SPRITZ SANDWICH COOKIES

IN COOKIE-SPEAK, we are primarily "scoopers" not "pipers." That is, we prefer scooping dough—the digging, the shaping, the immediate tactile connection—as opposed to piping dough through a cookie press or pastry bag. However, sometimes a strange piping urge strikes. It is lightning quick, usually occurs only during the winter holiday periods (Christmas carolers can ignite the urge almost instantaneously), and it cannot be ignored. We satiate these cravings with our Cinnamon Spritz Cookies. These cookies are adorable—a word we generally avoid at all costs, but in this case there is no other way to describe these mini-sandwich, whoopie pie–like, holiday cookies. By themselves, the Cinnamon Spritz Cookies are a sweet snack—light and holiday spicy. But when two of these cookies sandwich a fluffy meringue filling, both the taste and the textural contrast are magnified: crunchy, gooey, smooth, and sweet.

////////////////////////////// *Yield: 16 sandwich cookies* //////////////////////////////

BAKED NOTE: *Our soft meringue filling is delicious, genuinely easy to make, and quite quick, but we have used "emergency" filling replacements in the past to equal fanfare. Nutella, Speculoos spread, almond butter, and almost any vanilla or chocolate frosting work well with this cookie in a pinch.*

MAKE THE CINNAMON SPRITZ COOKIES

Line two baking sheets with parchment paper.

In a large bowl, whisk together the flour, cinnamon, cardamom, and salt.

In the bowl of a standing mixer fitted with the paddle attachment, beat the butter and sugar on medium-high speed until light and fluffy, about 2 minutes. Scrape down the sides and bottom of the bowl, add the egg, and mix again until combined. Add half of the flour mixture and beat at low speed until just incorporated. Add the remaining flour mixture and beat again at very low speed just until incorporated.

Scrape the dough into a pastry bag fitted with a ½-inch star tip and pipe the dough into 1 ¾-inch rosettes (about 2 inches apart) directly onto the prepared baking sheets. Chill the cookies on the baking sheets in the refrigerator for about 30 minutes. While the cookies are chilling, preheat the oven to 350 degrees F.

Remove the sheets from the refrigerator and bake the cookies for 12 to 14 minutes for cakey cookies or 16 minutes (or until the edges are golden brown) for crispy cookies, rotating the pans halfway through the baking time. Set the baking sheets on a wire rack for 5 minutes to cool. Use a spatula to transfer the cookies to the rack to cool completely.

MAKE THE SOFT MERINGUE FILLING

Place the egg white, sugar, corn syrup, vanilla, and 2 tablespoons of water in the bowl of a standing mixer. Whisk to combine. Set the bowl over a saucepan of simmering water—the bowl should not touch the water. Continue whisking until the sugar is completely dissolved, about 3 minutes. Transfer the bowl to the mixer fitted with the whisk attachment and whisk on medium-high speed until glossy and voluminous, and slightly stiff peaks form, about 5 minutes.

ASSEMBLE THE COOKIES

Immediately scrape the meringue into a piping bag fitted with a ¼-inch star or plain tip. Turn half of the cooled cookies flat side up. Pipe meringue onto the flat side of an upturned cookie, place another cookie flat side down on top of the filling, and press slightly so that the filling spreads to the edges of the cookie. Repeat until all the cookies are used. Dust with confectioners' sugar.

The cookies can be stored at room temperature, tightly covered, for up to 3 days.

AUTHENTIC PARMESAN CHEESE
SOMETIMES CALLED
"THE KING OF CHEESES"
MUST
BE AGED FOR AT LEAST
2 YEARS
AND ALWAYS
HAS ITS OFFICIAL NAME AND
THE YEAR IT WAS MADE
STENCILED ONTO THE RIND

RICOTTA CHEESE IS TECHNICALLY
NOT
A CHEESE, SINCE IT IS MADE OF
WHEY, A CHEESE BY-PRODUCT

CREAM CHEESE
CONSUMPTION

in America

HAS INCREASED 178%
since 1980—
A FACT OFTEN ASSOCIATED WITH
THE RISE OF THE POPULARITY OF
THE BAGEL

ACCORDING TO THE USDA
ALL CREAM CHEESE MUST BE

at least

33% MILK FAT

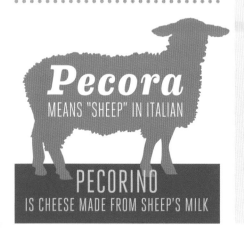

Pecora
MEANS "SHEEP" IN ITALIAN

PECORINO
IS CHEESE MADE FROM SHEEP'S MILK

PECORINO ROMANO
IS MADE USING A SPECIAL
TECHNIQUE CALLED
"RUMMAGING CURD,"
WHICH INVOLVES DRAINING THE
CURD QUICKLY AFTER MOLDING

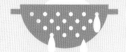

and then
PIERCING THE SURFACES LIGHTLY
BEFORE SALT IS APPLIED.

CREAM CHEESE
CONTAINS ONLY
about
HALF THE FAT
AND CALORIES

of
B U T T E R

Chapter 8

CHEESE

If we weren't in the pastry business, we would most certainly explore employment options in the world of cheese. We would attempt to apprentice with world renowned cheese mongers and study with competent, small-batch cheese makers. Vacations would be planned around important cheese-savvy locales—er, Paris and Rome—and we would consume half our body weight monthly (we actually might be close already) in cheese foodstuffs (research, of course). At the moment, cheese is our hobby. A hobby that invariably creeps into our baking life in the form of a wealth of baked goods made, stuffed, or topped with cheese or multiple cheeses. Baking with cheese is also an easy way to bring a little savory (a needed distraction) into the sweet kitchen, and the riffs are endless. Cakes and brownies (and cookies and pies) are our true loves, and cheese—glorious cheese—is our best friend.

For the Almond Graham Cracker Crust

- ½ cup sliced, blanched almonds, toasted (page 19)
- 3 cups graham cracker crumbs (about 42 whole graham crackers)
- 3 tablespoons firmly packed dark brown sugar
- 6 ounces (1½ sticks) unsalted butter, melted

For the Ricotta Filling

- 2 pounds good-quality ricotta, drained (see "How to Drain Fresh Ricotta" page 152)
- 4 large eggs, separated, plus 1 large egg yolk
- ¾ cup granulated sugar
- 1 tablespoon all-purpose flour
- 2 tablespoons amaretto
- 1 teaspoon pure almond extract
- Zest of 1 orange (about 1 tablespoon)
- ⅛ teaspoon salt

For Serving

- 2 tablespoons confectioners' sugar (optional)
- 2 heaping tablespoons sliced, blanched almonds, toasted (optional, page 19)

ORANGE ALMOND RICOTTA CHEESECAKE

WE BOTH HAVE a preoccupation with cheesecake and, luckily, we both have a preoccupation with ricotta too—fresh ricotta. Unfortunately, the mass-produced, ubiquitous supermarket ricotta does not even closely resemble (in taste or in texture) the real product. Fresh ricotta is creamy, sometimes a little bit sweet, and rich without being heavy. Glum, factory-made ricotta tastes like old plastic. In other words, if you want to be transported—if you want your world to open up and the sun to shine—use fresh ricotta (from sheep, cows, buffalos…) for this cheesecake. Our Orange Almond Ricotta Cheesecake (*torta di ricotta*) is a dessert that you will make multiple times for multiple reasons—it is the type of dessert that prompts guests to request the recipe—and reach for seconds. Ricotta cheesecakes are usually lighter than their cream cheese cousins (equally delicious), and ours is gently flavored with the tang of orange and a bite of almond. Like us, this recipe is a little bit Italian and a little bit American, and we hope you enjoy it as much as we do.

//////////////////////////////// **Yield: One 9-inch cheesecake** ////////////////////////////////

BAKED NOTE: *Invariably, in your quest to find a great ricotta, you will have to decide between cow's milk or sheep's milk. Both (assuming they are good quality) are perfect; however, blind taste tests seem to indicate that sheep's milk (with a slightly more pronounced nuttiness) takes a slight edge. We recommend tasting the cheese before baking. Chances are, if you enjoy it on its own, you will love it in our cheesecake.*

//

MAKE THE ALMOND GRAHAM CRACKER CRUST

Preheat the oven to 325 degrees F. Using nonstick cooking spray, lightly coat both the bottom and sides of a high-sided 9-inch tart pan (2½ to 3 inches tall) with removable bottom. Line the bottom of the pan with parchment and lightly spray the parchment.

In a food processor, pulse the almonds until they are finely chopped (do not worry if you have a few large, coarse pieces). Add the graham cracker crumbs and the brown sugar and pulse until combined. Pour the butter over the crumbs and pulse again to blend the mixture until uniform. Transfer the crumb mixture to the prepared tart pan and press it into the bottom and up the sides. Use the bottom of a large measuring cup or drinking glass to help you create a firm, even crust.

Bake the crust until it is golden brown, 10 to 12 minutes. If it begins to puff while baking, use the back of a spoon to press it gently down. Remove the pan from the oven and transfer to a wire rack to cool completely. Keep the oven on.

MAKE THE RICOTTA FILLING

In a food processor, pulse the ricotta in short bursts until smooth, about 2 minutes. Add the 5 egg yolks, sugar, flour, amaretto, almond extract, and orange zest. Pulse in short bursts until completely smooth and lump free, scraping down the sides and bottom of the food processor bowl once or twice. Turn out the mixture into a large bowl.

In the bowl of a standing mixer fitted with the whisk attachment, beat the egg whites and the salt until stiff peaks form (do not whip past the stiff peak stage or the whites will become dry and unusable).

Fold one-third of the egg white mixture into the ricotta mixture until incorporated. Add half of the remaining egg whites and gently fold until almost incorporated, then fold in the remaining egg whites.

Pour the ricotta mixture into the prepared crust and bake for 55 to 70 minutes. Using an instant read thermometer, take the internal temperature of the center of the cheesecake; when done, it should read 160 degrees F. (If you want to eyeball for doneness—a sometimes difficult task—look for a firm outer ring and a center that is slightly wobbly when shaken.) Do not be alarmed if the cheesecake soufflés up and then falls—this is normal. Remove the cheesecake from the oven and transfer to a wire rack to cool to room temperature. Cover with plastic wrap and refrigerate until thoroughly chilled, 4 to 6 hours.

To serve, gently push up on the tart bottom to release the cheesecake from the pan. Top with a dusting of sifted powdered sugar or sliced almonds—or both.

The cheesecake can be stored in the refrigerator, tightly covered, for up to 3 days.

HOW TO DRAIN FRESH RICOTTA

Line a sieve with a cheesecloth or paper towel and place the sieve over a bowl. Place the ricotta directly on the cloth or towel and let sit overnight in the refrigerator. Drain and discard any liquid (you can gently press the ricotta to release excess liquid, but you do not need to wring it out) and reserve the ricotta in a medium bowl. Use immediately or refrigerate (it will keep for up to 2 days in the refrigerator).

CHEDDAR CORN SOUFFLÉ

YES, THIS INCREDIBLY RICH, creamy, Cheddar Corn Soufflé can be served as a dessert—a studious, old-school, cheese course. It can also be served as an appetizer. Or as a side. Or, less typically, as a main course. We actually encourage you, if you are feeling full of morning pep, to try it out on unsuspecting breakfast or brunch guests. Fact is, we don't really care when you serve this multipurpose concoction, we just encourage you to make it often. Our riff on this venerable dish is punched up with the decidedly unsubtle extra-sharp cheddar (we have classic macaroni and cheese on the brain) and a handful of corn—the two flavors complement each other well, and the corn adds a bright burst of texture. Finally, we think our perfectly golden Cheddar Corn Soufflé is one of those dishes that fancifies the mood with little effort, and everyone knows we could use a bit more fancy in our lives.

////////////////////////// **Yield: 6 main-dish or 10 side-dish servings** //////////////////////////

BAKED NOTE: *If you prefer a more pronounced corn taste, you can increase the corn in the recipe from anywhere up to ¾ cup total without affecting the soufflé.*

//

2	tablespoons finely grated fresh Parmesan cheese
½	teaspoon salt
½	teaspoon freshly grated nutmeg
½	teaspoon freshly ground black pepper
¼	teaspoon ground cayenne
1	cup whole milk
2	ounces (½ stick) unsalted butter
¼	cup all-purpose flour
5	large eggs, separated, plus 1 large egg white, at room temperature
¾	teaspoon cream of tartar
1	cup packed grated extra-sharp cheddar cheese (about 4 ounces)
½	cup fresh corn kernels or frozen corn, thawed

Preheat the oven to 400 degrees F and position the rack in the center. Lightly butter the bottom and sides of a 1½-quart soufflé dish. Dust the soufflé dish with the Parmesan cheese (so that it adheres to the butter) and knock out the excess.

In a small bowl, whisk together the salt, nutmeg, black pepper, and cayenne. Set aside.

In a medium saucepan over medium heat, warm, but do not boil, the milk. Remove from heat once tiny bubbles appear around the pan's perimeter.

In a medium, heavy-bottomed saucepan, melt the butter. Add the flour and whisk until completely combined, 2 to 3 minutes. Remove from the heat, wait 30 seconds, then slowly stream the milk into the butter mixture while whisking constantly. Continue whisking until smooth, and return to the heat. Cook until the mixture bubbles and becomes thick, 8 to 10 minutes. When bubbles appear, remove from the heat and whisk in the spice mixture. Continue stirring vigorously for about 1 minute to release some of the heat. Add the 5 egg yolks, one at a time, whisking after each addition. After all the yolks are completely incorporated, transfer the mixture to a large bowl.

In another large bowl (or in the bowl of a standing mixer fitted with the whisk attachment), whisk the 6 egg whites vigorously for 1 minute. Sprinkle the cream of tartar over the whites and continue beating until the egg whites form stiff peaks.

Fold one-third of the egg white mixture into the soufflé base. Add the cheddar cheese and corn, along with half of the remaining egg whites, and gently fold until almost incorporated. Gently fold in the remaining egg whites until completely but just incorporated.

Transfer the entire mixture to the prepared soufflé dish. Run your thumb around the inside edge of the dish to wipe away any stray mixture (this will provide for an even rise), place the soufflé in the oven, and immediately reduce the oven temperature to 375 degrees F. Bake for 30 to 35 minutes, or until the soufflé is puffy, slightly golden, and the center is just about set.

Transfer the soufflé dish to a serving platter and serve immediately.

POPPY SEED POUND CAKE

with

BROWN BUTTER GLAZE

For the Poppy Seed Filling

- ¼ cup granulated sugar
- ⅓ cup whole milk
- 1 tablespoon unsalted butter, cut into ½-inch cubes
- ½ cup poppy seeds
- ¼ cup graham cracker crumbs (about 4 whole graham crackers)

For the Poppy Seed Pound Cake

- 2½ cups all-purpose flour
- 1½ teaspoons baking powder
- ½ teaspoon salt
- ¼ teaspoon baking soda
- 8 ounces cream cheese, softened
- 8 ounces (2 sticks) unsalted butter, softened
- 1 cup granulated sugar
- ½ cup firmly packed dark brown sugar
- 4 large eggs
- 2 teaspoons pure vanilla extract
- 2 tablespoons freshly grated orange zest (about 2 oranges)

For the Brown Butter Glaze

- 1 tablespoon poppy seeds
- 2 ounces (½ stick) unsalted butter, cut into ½-inch cubes
- 1½ cups confectioners' sugar, sifted
- 1 teaspoon freshly grated orange zest (about ½ orange)
- 2 tablespoons whole milk
- 1 teaspoon orange juice

MY GREAT-GRANDMOTHER TOOK great pains to keep each of her many great-grandchildren well stocked with homemade pound cake. The classic pound cake, wrapped in plastic wrap and aluminum foil and buffered by old newspapers in a postal box, would arrive near holidays, birthdays, and occasionally without reason. Though I loved the handmade loaves, I was physically unable to eat them plain (of course, I never admitted this to my great-grandma—it would have broken her heart). I had to cut the loaves into slices and dip each slice in chocolate, smear them in peanut butter, cover them in ice cream, or toast and butter them. To me, classic pound cake always needed a little help—a little something—to make the pounds worthwhile. I felt the urge to provide a makeover. This recipe is my take on pound cake. The flavor is still subtle (I resisted the urge to add chocolate), yet the poppy seed filling provides a little zing and the glaze is dreamworthy. Great-grandma might not have initially approved—but I am certain that she would have been swayed eventually.

////////////////////// **Yield: One 10- or 12-cup Bundt cake** //////////////////////

BAKED NOTE: *This Bundt, like all great Bundt cakes, tastes delicious without a fancy glaze or frosting—you can simply dust the top with a few tablespoons of confectioners' sugar, cut, and serve. However, sometimes you might be feeling glazy, and if that feeling envelops you while making this cake, we wholeheartedly recommend you serve it with the suggested and delicious glaze.*

MAKE THE POPPY SEED FILLING

In a medium saucepan over low heat, stir together the sugar and the milk. Bring just to a boil and remove from the heat. Whisk in the butter.

In a spice grinder, pulse the poppy seeds until they are almost powdery. Stir the poppy seeds into the milk mixture. Once the milk mixture has cooled to room temperature, stir in the graham cracker crumbs. Let cool completely.

MAKE THE POPPY SEED POUND CAKE

Preheat the oven to 350 degrees F. Generously coat the inside of a 10- or 12-cup Bundt pan with nonstick cooking spray; alternatively, butter it well, dust it with flour, and knock out the excess flour.

In a large bowl, sift together the flour, baking powder, salt, and baking soda. Set aside.

In the bowl of a standing mixer fitted with the paddle attachment, beat the cream cheese, butter, and both sugars on medium speed until light and fluffy, about 3 minutes. Scrape down the sides and bottom of the bowl and add the eggs, one at a time, beating well after each addition. Scrape down the bowl again, add the vanilla and orange zest, and beat until just incorporated.

Add the flour mixture to the cream cheese mixture in two parts, beating after each addition until just combined, about 10 seconds. Scrape down the bowl again and beat for 5 seconds.

Pour half of the cake batter into the Bundt pan. Use an offset spatula or the back of a large spoon to even out the batter. Spoon the poppy seed filling over the cake batter (it does not have to be a perfect, even layer, but you can use the back of the spoon to smooth it out gently), then cover with the remaining cake batter (gently smooth out the batter into an even-ish layer). Bake for about 1 hour, or until a small sharp knife inserted into the center of the cake comes out clean. Transfer the pan to a wire rack to cool completely. Gently loosen the sides of the cake from the pan and turn it out onto the rack.

MAKE THE BROWN BUTTER GLAZE

Place a dry medium skillet over medium heat for 3 minutes. Pour the poppy seeds into the skillet and toast for 1 minute; use a wooden spoon to stir the seeds continuously during toasting. Pour the poppy seeds into a small bowl and set aside.

Return the skillet to the heat and add the butter. Melt the butter, swirling the pan occasionally, until the foam subsides and the butter turns a medium nut brown, about 8 minutes. Pour the browned butter into a large bowl (don't worry if a few of the butter solids—the sediment—end up in the bowl, though you don't want to add all of it).

Add the confectioners' sugar, orange zest, milk, and orange juice to the browned butter. Stir until the glaze comes together and is smooth. Stir in the toasted poppy seeds. Immediately drizzle the glaze along the crown of the Bundt cake, allowing it to drip down the sides. Allow the glaze to set before serving, about 5 minutes.

The cake can be stored at room temperature, tightly covered, for up to 3 days.

LEMON AND BLACK PEPPER QUICHE

THE POPULARITY OF QUICHE surprised us. Actually, the breadth and depth of "quiche people" surprised us. As the evidence gathered at our bakery suggests, quiche eaters vary widely and play against type, at least the type emblazoned on our subconscious by the Bruce Feirstein tome *Real Men Don't Eat Quiche*. Neither of us read the book, but it was such a cultural touchstone that quiche was generally maligned by an entire generation—our generation. But at our bakery, everyone eats quiche. Teachers, truck drivers, dancers, artists, locals, and tourists all partake with equal enthusiasm. It was eye-opening: make a good quiche, and they will come. Our quiche was developed to steer clear of the light, fey, fluffy variety—too quaint for Baked and probably too expected. Instead, all of our quiches are robust, squat, and fully flavored—in other words, our quiche is very "Baked." This quiche, like our Lemon Pecorino Pepper Icebox Cookies (page 162), pays homage to the classic Roman dish *cacio e pepe*, though it is obviously more savory—more of a nod to the original dish. We think it makes for a perfect Sunday brunch, but also qualifies for a suitable late-night snack.

// *Yield: One 9-inch quiche* //

BAKED NOTE: *This recipe is written to accommodate the typical 9-inch tart pan with removable bottom; however, if you can find a high-sided 8-inch tart pan with removable bottom, we suggest you use it. The smaller, taller pan produces a more severe quiche—thicker crust, thicker filling—that feels a tad more substantial.*

//

½	recipe Classic Pie Dough (page 161)
3	tablespoons all-purpose flour
2	large eggs, plus 2 large egg yolks
1	cup half-and-half
1	cup crème fraîche
	Juice of ½ lemon (about 1 tablespoon)
	Zest of 1 lemon (about 1 tablespoon)
1	teaspoon salt
¾	teaspoon ground white pepper
1½	teaspoons freshly ground black pepper, divided
¾	cup loosely packed shredded mozzarella
¾	cup finely grated fresh Parmesan
1	paper-thin slice of lemon for decoration (optional)

Using nonstick cooking spray, coat the bottom and sides of a 9-inch tart pan with a removable bottom. Alternatively, butter the pan well, dust it with flour, and knock out the excess flour.

Dust a work surface with a sprinkling of flour and roll the dough out into an 11-inch round, about ¼ inch thick. Transfer it to the prepared tart pan and carefully work it into the bottom and build up the sides to twice the thickness of the bottom (the dough will shrink once baked). Cover with plastic wrap and place in the freezer for at least 60 minutes. (It will keep this way, tightly wrapped, for up to 3 months.)

Preheat the oven to 375 degrees F. Line a baking sheet with aluminum foil or parchment paper.

Remove the tart pan from the freezer and, using the tines of a fork, prick the bottom of the tart shell. Line the shell with aluminum foil and fill it three-quarters of the way full with pie weights or dried beans. Place the tart shell in the oven and bake for 25 to 30 minutes, or until the edges of the tart just begin to brown. Remove the foil and weights and bake for another 7 to 10 minutes, until the crust is golden brown all over. Transfer the tart pan to a wire rack to cool.

In a large bowl, vigorously whisk together the flour, eggs, and egg yolks until smooth. In another bowl whisk together the half-and-half, crème fraîche, and lemon juice until blended. Add the half-and-half mixture to the flour mixture and whisk gently until combined. Sprinkle the top of the mixture with the lemon zest, salt, white pepper, and ¾ teaspoon of the black pepper and whisk until combined.

Place the cooled tart shell on the prepared baking sheet. Sprinkle the mozzarella over the crust, then sprinkle with Parmesan. Pour the egg mixture over the cheese, filling to the lip of the tart shell (do not let it overflow; you may have some extra filling). Sprinkle the remaining ¾ teaspoon black pepper over the filling and place the lemon slice in the center if you wish.

Bake for 25 to 30 minutes, or until the filling is set and a small paring knife inserted into the center of the quiche comes out clean. Remove the pan from the oven and place on a wire rack to cool for 30 minutes.

To serve, gently push up on the tart bottom to release the quiche from the pan. Cut and serve while still warm.

The completely cooled quiche can be stored in the refrigerator, tightly covered, for up to 3 days. Reheat in the oven at 225 degrees F until warm to the touch before serving.

CLASSIC PIE DOUGH

///////////////////////////// *Two 9-inch, single-crust pies* /////////////////////////////

3	cups all-purpose flour, chilled
1	tablespoon sugar
1	teaspoon fine sea salt
8	ounces (2 sticks) cold unsalted butter, cut into ½-inch cubes

In a medium bowl, whisk the flour, sugar, and salt together. In a measuring cup, stir ¾ cup water with several ice cubes until it is very cold, discarding any remaining ice.

Toss the butter in the flour mixture to coat. Place the mixture in a food processor and pulse in short bursts until the butter pieces are the size of hazelnuts.

Pulsing in 4-second bursts, slowly drizzle the cold water into the food processor through the feed tube. As soon as the dough comes together in a ball, stop adding water.

Remove the dough from the food processor and divide it in half. Flatten each piece into a disk and wrap each disk first in parchment paper and then in plastic wrap. Refrigerate the dough until firm, about 1 hour.

The dough can be stored in the refrigerator for up to 3 days or in the freezer for up to 3 months. If frozen, thaw it in the refrigerator before proceeding with your recipe.

LEMON PECORINO PEPPER ICEBOX COOKIES

8	ounces (2 sticks) unsalted butter, at room temperature, cut into ½-inch cubes
⅔	cup confectioners' sugar, sifted
¼	cup freshly grated Pecorino Romano
I	large egg, plus I large egg yolk
¼	teaspoon salt
I	tablespoon freshly ground black pepper
3	tablespoons lemon zest (about 3 lemons)
I	tablespoon fresh lemon juice
2	cups all-purpose flour
¼	cup sanding sugar or colored sanding sugar (optional)

RIGHTLY OR WRONGLY, I have made whole dinners from a variety of leftover cookies and half-eaten cheeses (and a few glasses or more of lingering red wine). So it only seemed appropriate to somehow combine the two in a more cohesive manner into their own dish, and I took it even further by riffing specifically on *cacio e pepe*—the classic Roman pasta dish of pepper and cheese. The basic, but lovely, icebox cookie (i.e., refrigerated slice-and-bake-dough cookie) seemed like the perfect delivery vehicle for such an experiment. I am rather fond of these icebox cookies—they are simple, light (much lighter than a shortbread), a lot of fun to make, and ideal for afternoon (or late-night) snacking. It's always been my go-to tea cookie. Pecorino Romano, one of my favorite cheeses, provides just enough of a salty kick to enhance the lemon flavor of this icebox without overwhelming it, and the black pepper gives the hint of something spicy without being intense. I promise you, though this is a strange marriage of sweet and savory, it is still very much a delicious cookie—one you will make again and again.

//////////////////////////////////// Yield: 45 to 60 cookies ////////////////////////////////////

BAKED NOTE: *These icebox cookies, like most icebox cookies, are perfectly suited for a "bake on demand" approach. Since the cookies last nearly a month in their frozen, prebaked log form, I suggest cutting and baking only as many you think you will serve and eat in one sitting. Also, feel free to cut the logs into 6 or 8 chunks and roll each smaller log in a different and brightly colored sanding sugar to add a bit of sunshine to your tea cookie table.*

In the bowl of a standing mixer fitted with the paddle attachment, beat the butter until creamy. Add the confectioners' sugar and Pecorino Romano and beat on medium-high speed until smooth and fluffy. Add the egg and egg yolk and beat until just combined. Scrape down the sides and bottom of the bowl and add the salt, pepper, lemon zest, and lemon juice and beat until incorporated.

Add the flour all at once and beat on the lowest speed until just incorporated. Do not overbeat. Gather the dough into a ball, slice it in half, and wrap each piece in plastic wrap. Refrigerate until firm, about 30 minutes.

Turn the first piece of dough out onto a smooth, very lightly floured surface (preferably a cold surface like marble or steel) and use your floured hands to form and roll the dough into a cookie log 1¾ to 2 inches in diameter. Repeat the process with the second piece. Wrap each log in plastic wrap and chill for at least 3 hours. The dough will keep in the refrigerator, tightly wrapped, for 3 to 5 days, or up to 1 month in the freezer.

Preheat the oven to 350 degrees F. Line two baking sheets with parchment paper.

Remove the logs from the refrigerator and roll each one in the sanding sugar to coat the sides. Slice the cookies ⅛ inch thick and place on the prepared baking sheets about ½ inch apart. (Note: You can cut the cookies slightly thicker and bake them slightly longer for a less crunchy cookie, if that is your personal preference.)

Bake for 11 to 13 minutes (no color equals a softer cookie, slightly brown equals a crispier cookie). Remove the baking sheets from the oven and set them on wire racks to cool for 5 minutes. Then use a spatula to transfer the cookies directly to the racks to cool completely.

The cookies can be stored at room temperature, tightly covered, for up to 4 days.

For the Cream Cheese Filling

8	ounces cream cheese, softened
⅓	cup granulated sugar
1	large egg
1	teaspoon pure vanilla extract
¼	teaspoon salt
6	ounces good-quality white chocolate, coarsely chopped

For the Chocolate Cheesecake Muffins

3	cups all-purpose flour
1½	cups granulated sugar
½	cup firmly packed light brown sugar
2	teaspoons baking powder
1	tablespoon espresso powder
2	teaspoons salt
½	cup dark unsweetened cocoa powder (like Valrhona)
8	ounces good-quality dark chocolate (60 to 72%), coarsely chopped, divided
3	ounces (¾ stick) unsalted butter, at room temperature, cut into ½-inch cubes
1	cup hot coffee
¾	cup hot water
¼	cup plus 2 tablespoons canola oil
1	tablespoon white vinegar
3	large eggs
2	tablespoons sanding sugar (optional)

CHOCOLATE CHEESECAKE MUFFINS

THE CHOCOLATE CHEESECAKE muffin was born as a direct, middle-finger-in-the-air response to the viral, kudzu-like growth of the bran muffin. Our muffin, the perfect melding of chocolate and cream cheese, is our volley in the muffin wars. Bran muffins, often the texture of dry hay and aging newspaper, are not really muffins—they are really just ill-advised attempts to make something pseudo-nutritional in muffin form. If you want something entirely wholesome and boringly nutritious for breakfast, eat a bowl of bran. If you want something interesting, tasty, and incredibly fun for breakfast, make and eat these muffins. The ratio of butter to flour to egg to oil in muffins is just shy of the ratio needed for cupcakes (sans frosting), and we celebrate, rather than shun, this connection. This is a perfect breakfast treat—the chocolate portion is dark without being too sweet and is studded with chocolate chunks for texture and flavor, while the cheesecake filling is a welcome tangy surprise. It's our chocolate-for-breakfast philosophy fully realized.

// **Yield: 12 muffins** *//*

BAKED NOTE: *We are slightly hesitant to note that Chocolate Cheesecake Muffins are equally delicious as basic chocolate muffins. In fact, the recipe makes beautiful chocolate muffins—no need to make any serious changes, just leave out the cream cheese filling steps. If you are feeling motivated, the muffins sans filling taste especially interesting sliced, toasted, and lightly buttered—like a toasty cupcake.*

MAKE THE CREAM CHEESE FILLING

In the bowl of a standing mixer fitted with the paddle attachment, beat the cream cheese on medium speed until smooth. Add the sugar and beat until the sugar is incorporated and the mixture is lump free. Scrape down the sides and bottom of the bowl and add the egg, vanilla, and salt, beating until completely incorporated, about 1 minute. Fold in the white chocolate chunks. Refrigerate the filling while you make the muffins. (The cream cheese filling can be stored in the refrigerator, tightly covered, for up to 3 days.)

MAKE THE CHOCOLATE CHEESECAKE MUFFINS

Preheat the oven to 350 degrees F. Lightly spray each cup of a standard 12-cup muffin pan with nonstick cooking spray and use a paper towel to spread the oil evenly along the bottom and up the sides of each cup.

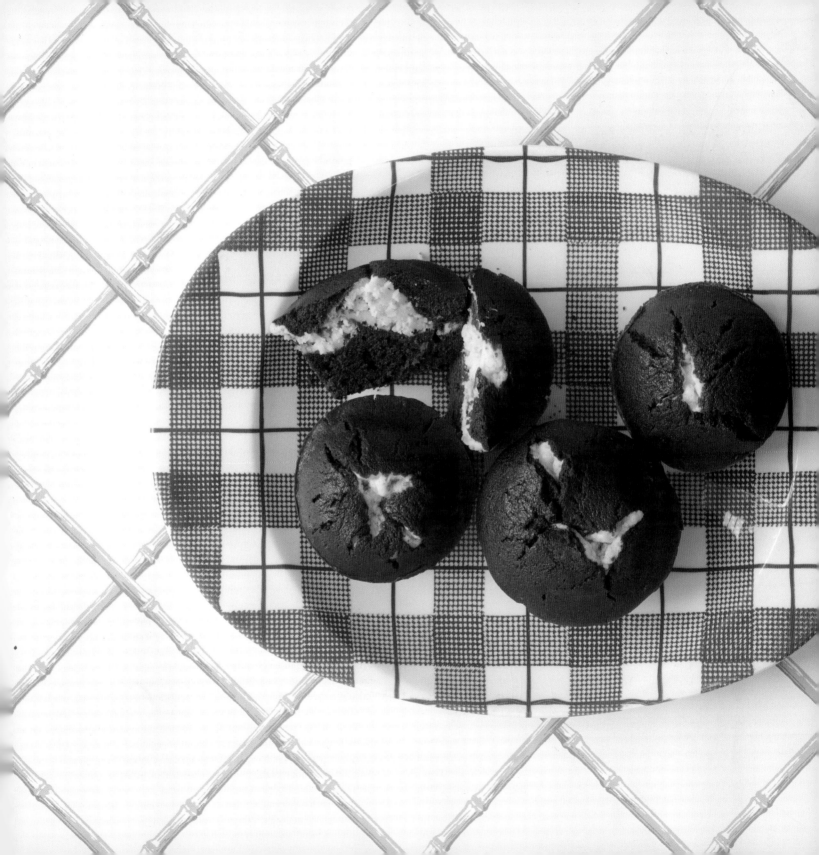

In a large bowl, whisk together the flour, sugars, baking powder, espresso powder, and salt. Set aside.

In another large bowl, place the cocoa powder, 2 ounces of the chocolate, and the butter. Pour the coffee and the hot water over the chocolate and butter and wait 1 minute. Whisk until smooth. Add the oil, vinegar, and eggs and whisk again until the batter is completely smooth.

Make a well in the dry ingredients and pour the wet ingredients into the well. Slowly fold the dry ingredients into the wet until just mixed (be careful not to overmix). Fold in the remaining 6 ounces of the chocolate. Note: If you are using large-ish chocolate chunks you should toss them in flour so that they will not sink to the bottom of the mix.

Spoon about 2 heaping tablespoons of chocolate batter into each prepared muffin cup (about one-quarter full). Tap the bottom of the pan against the counter to level the batter. Add 1 heaping tablespoon of the cream cheese filling to each cup, then cover the cream cheese layer with the remaining chocolate batter. Make sure the batter is just flush with the rim of the pan. If you want, sprinkle the muffin tops with sanding sugar right before baking to create a crunchy muffin top (and who can say no to a crunchy muffin top?).

Bake for 30 to 32 minutes, rotating the pan halfway through the baking time, until a toothpick inserted into the center of a muffin comes out clean.

Move the muffin pan to a wire rack and let cool for 15 minutes. Gently loosen the muffins with an offset spatula or small knife, remove the muffins from the pan, and let them finish cooling on the wire rack.

The muffins can be stored in the refrigerator, in an airtight container, for up to 2 days. Allow them to come to room temperature before serving.

CREAM CHEESE CHOCOLATE SNACKING COOKIES

THESE COOKIES ARE a slight but unique departure from the traditional Baked repertoire. Usually we push flavors and textures to the extreme—cookies on steroids—but we were looking for something a bit less showy this time around: a chocolaty tea cookie that's not part of the shortbread family. We decided to lighten a classic chocolate dough with cream cheese and sprinkle in some chocolate chips (I suppose we are always adding chocolate chips to things). We couldn't be more addicted to this cookie. It is rich yet light, and falls somewhere in between crispy and chewy. Be warned: This is the type of cookie that will sneak up on you, the kind that you will find yourself munching in multiples, the one you can rely on for many occasions—but we like them best for midweek TV nights.

//////////////////////////////////// **Yield: 24 to 36 cookies** ////////////////////////////////////

BAKED NOTE: *Keep this recipe close by for last-minute parties. It is easy to prepare and easy to double (all the ingredients will still fit in one mixing bowl), and the resulting cookie is easy to transport (it's not crumbly at all—perfect for a bumpy ride).*

//

4	ounces cream cheese, at room temperature
8	ounces (2 sticks) unsalted butter, cool but not cold
1	cup granulated sugar
½	cup firmly packed dark brown sugar
2	large eggs
2	tablespoons heavy cream
1	teaspoon pure vanilla extract
2¼	cups all-purpose flour
2	teaspoons baking soda
½	teaspoon salt
¼	cup dark unsweetened cocoa powder (like Valrhona)
3	ounces good-quality dark chocolate (60 to 72%), melted and cooled
8	ounces (about 1⅓ cups) semisweet chocolate chips

In the bowl of a standing mixer fitted with the paddle attachment, beat the cream cheese, butter, and sugars together on medium speed until fluffy, about 3 minutes. Scrape down the bowl and add the eggs, one at a time, beating well after each. Add the cream and vanilla and beat until just incorporated.

In another bowl, whisk together the flour, baking soda, salt, and cocoa powder. Add the dry ingredients to the cream cheese mixture and mix on low speed until just incorporated. Do not overmix. Add the melted chocolate and chocolate chips and stir until just combined. Refrigerate the mixture for about 15 minutes.

Preheat the oven to 350 degrees F. Line two baking sheets with parchment paper.

Using a small ice cream scoop with a release mechanism, drop heaping tablespoons of the dough 1½ inches apart onto the prepared baking sheets. (Alternatively, use a tablespoon to measure then drop the dough.) Bake for 10 to 12 minutes, rotating the baking sheets halfway through the baking time, until cookies are set.

Cool the baking sheets on wire racks for 5 minutes. Transfer the cookies to the racks to cool completely. They can be stored, in an airtight container, for up to 3 days.

For the Focaccia Dough

2½	cups all-purpose flour, plus more as needed
2¼	cups bread flour
2¾	teaspoons instant dry yeast
2¾	teaspoons salt
2	cups lukewarm water (100 to 110 degrees F)
⅓	cup good-quality olive oil, plus more for oiling
	Cornmeal for dusting

For the Topping

¼	cup good-quality olive oil, divided plus more for brushing
1	medium red onion, thinly sliced
3½	cups loosely packed baby spinach
2	tablespoons chopped fresh rosemary
2	tablespoons chopped fresh thyme
	Salt, to taste
	Freshly ground black pepper, to taste
	Dried oregano, to taste
2	cups shredded whole-milk mozzarella or other cheese of your choosing
½	cup freshly grated Pecorino Romano or other hard cheese of your choosing, plus more for sprinkling
	Red pepper flakes, to taste

CHEESY FOCACCIA

with

CARAMELIZED ONIONS AND SAUTÉED SPINACH

FOCACCIA AT BAKED wasn't supposed to be. It just sort of happened in the way that happy fated moments happen: It was random, unexpected, but somehow destined. Baked was founded with a strict mission to push American baking—mainly sweet baking—to the forefront. Savory items were supposed to be afterthoughts, bites and bits to break up a sugary, chocolaty day in the kitchen. Then, one afternoon, a focaccia appeared as if sent by angels—or at least bakers in need of a savory, toothsome bread—and it never left. Our original focaccia was very straightforward: hot and fragrant, herb dusted, olive oiled, and salted. The bread was popular—it was beloved by customers and often sold out while still piping hot—and begat more focaccia, this time with more sophisticated toppings like grated and shredded cheeses, homemade tomato sauce, all manner of veggies, and mounds of leafy greens. Now, our focaccia is a Baked staple and is ever evolving. This recipe adheres closely to the one we use at the bakery. The bread itself is thick and chewy and oozes olive oil (use a good-quality one for this) and the toppings—two cheeses, onions, and spinach—are customer and employee favorites. Join us, and take a walk on the savory side—pizza style. After all, it's probably fated.

//////////////////////// **Yield: One extra-large focaccia (about 12 servings)** *////////////////////////*

BAKED NOTE: *We don't need to tell you that the suggested topping is just that—a suggestion. Feel free to experiment at will (think artichoke hearts, Monterey Jack, sun-dried tomatoes), though, this being part of our cheese chapter, we gently encourage a liberal dose of Pecorino Romano or mozzarella regardless of the other ingredients you choose.*

MAKE THE FOCACCIA DOUGH

Place the flours, yeast, and salt in the bowl of a standing mixer fitted with the paddle attachment and beat on low speed until combined. Add the water and ⅓ cup olive oil and mix on low speed until the dough just begins to come together. Turn off the mixer, switch to the dough hook attachment, and mix on medium speed until the dough is smooth and starts to release from the sides of the bowl (it is okay if the dough still sticks to the bottom of the mixing bowl). If the dough feels too wet and is not releasing, add additional all-purpose flour, 2 tablespoons at a time, until the dough releases.

Dust a work surface with flour and stretch the dough into a rectangle (about 9 by 20 inches). Fold each side onto itself, creating a letterfold. Tuck the dough into a ball and place in a lightly oiled bowl. Cover with plastic wrap and set aside in a warm-ish place (at least 72 degrees F) for 20 to 30 minutes. Repeat this process (stretching the dough into a rectangle, letterfolding, tucking into a ball shape, and placing in covered bowl). Wait another 30 minutes and repeat a third time.

Lightly spray a 13-by-18-inch light-colored metal half-sheet pan or two 9-by-13-inch glass or light-colored metal baking pans with nonstick cooking spray and line with parchment paper. Use your fingers to smear a little olive oil (no more than a table-spoon) evenly across the parchment and sprinkle it with an even dusting of cornmeal. Transfer the dough to the prepared pan(s) and stretch it into a rectangle (don't try to stretch the dough into corners of the pan just yet). Cover with plastic wrap and let the dough rest (still at room temperature) for about 20 minutes. Uncover the dough and stretch it into the corners. (If the dough feels resistant to stretching into the pan cor-ners at this time, cover with plastic wrap and wait 10 more minutes.)

Preheat the oven to 450 degrees F and position the rack in the center. Place a baking pan filled with water on the rack below where you will be baking the focaccia. The steam from the pan will give the crust a nice crunchy exterior while keeping the inte-rior moist and chewy.

MAKE THE TOPPING

In a medium skillet or sauté pan, heat 1 tablespoon of olive oil over medium-low heat. Add the onion and sauté for 20 to 25 minutes, or until it is soft and translucent. Set the onion aside. Add the spinach to the skillet, cover, and cook until the spinach is cooked through, about 5 minutes. Turn off the heat and set aside until cool. Squeeze the spin-ach dry and set it aside.

Poke the dough in the pan. If your finger leaves a dent, it is ready; if not, wait 5 min-utes and test again. Toss the rosemary with the remaining 3 tablespoons of oil. Brush the oil onto the top of the dough. Sprinkle with thyme, salt, pepper, and oregano.

Place the focaccia in the oven, one rack above the pan filled with (now boiling) water, and bake for 10 minutes, rotating the pan halfway through the baking time, until the dough starts to brown on top. Then remove the pan from the oven and, leaving a small border of crust, top the dough with the onion, spinach, cheeses, and red pepper flakes. Continue baking the focaccia until the cheese is bubbly and browned.

Remove from the oven, sprinkle with more Pecorino Romano and salt to taste, and brush the edges with a little bit more olive oil. Serve immediately.

Focaccia tastes best directly from the oven, though leftover focaccia can be stored in the refrigerator, tightly covered, for up to 2 days. Reheat at 275 degrees F for about 10 minutes or until warm to the touch before serving.

GUILT FREE

COCOA POWDER IS MADE BY REMOVING THE FAT, OR COCOA BUTTER, FROM COCOA BEANS

95 TO 200

HERSHEY'S KISSES

=

CAFFEINE FOUND IN ONE CUP OF COFFEE

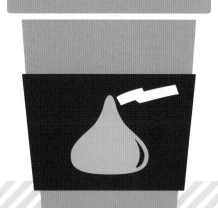

XOCOATL

THE ORIGIN OF THE WORD "CHOCOLATE" IS THOUGHT TO COME FROM THIS AZTEC WORD USED TO DESCRIBE A DRINK MADE FROM CACAO BEANS

CHOCOLATE KISSES

STUDIES HAVE SHOWN THAT CHOCOLATE MELTING ON YOUR TONGUE CREATES A MORE

INTENSE !

& pleasing ●

EFFECT THAN A PASSIONATE KISS, DUE TO THE PRESENCE OF

PHENYLETHYLAMINE

which increases THE PRODUCTION OF

ENDORPHINS

CELEBRATE *with* CHOCOLATE

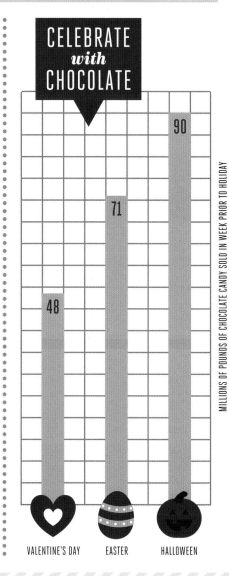

48 — VALENTINE'S DAY
71 — EASTER
90 — HALLOWEEN

MILLIONS OF POUNDS OF CHOCOLATE CANDY SOLD IN WEEK PRIOR TO HOLIDAY

Chapter 9
CHOCOLATE

We are not unique in our slavish devotion to chocolate (and cocoa powder) as an ingredient. It is the most celebrated legal substance on this planet, and it's the rare item that is as popular in Pittsburgh as it is in Paris and beyond. Chocolate is a natural part of our lives, as important to us as oxygen and sleep. We usually incorporate it into our breakfasts and lunches, and always after dinner. Neither of us can recall the last day we went without. In fact, if we had to play favorites—if we had to choose one ingredient in a book full of favorite ingredients—it would be chocolate. It's not the most interesting or unique choice, but it is the honest choice. Load us up with bags of Callebaut and slabs of Valrhona and send us on our way to the imaginary but oft-referenced desert island (with a working oven and small hot plate, of course).

CHOCOLATE MAYONNAISE CUPCAKES

AT FIRST THOUGHT, using mayonnaise in this recipe might seem like a quick and easy parlor trick—a "you'll never guess the secret ingredient"–type game. But once you make these chocolate cupcakes, you will be hard-pressed not to reverse engineer (or at least consider reverse engineering) several of your other dessert recipes to add a mayonnaise component. Mayo is much more than a nimble replacement for the traditional oil and/or butter in this batter. It actually serves a higher purpose, creating a transcendental effect: moist, chocolaty perfection with a light crumb and a smooth, rich flavor. It's easy. It's quick. And it's fast becoming our go-to chocolate birthday cake recipe.

//////////////////////////////////// *Yield: 24 cupcakes* ////////////////////////////////////

> **BAKED NOTE:** *You will be doing no one any favors by using reduced-fat or fat-free mayonnaise in this recipe. This cake, like all great chocolate cakes, is meant to be enjoyed in all its caloric glory.*

//

MAKE THE CHOCOLATE MAYONNAISE CUPCAKES

Preheat the oven to 325 degrees F. Line two 12-cup cupcake pans with paper liners.

In a medium heatproof bowl, stir together the chocolate and cocoa powder. Add the water and whisk until smooth.

In another medium bowl, sift together the flour, baking soda, and baking powder.

In the bowl of a standing mixer fitted with the paddle attachment, beat both sugars and the mayo together until well blended, 2 to 3 minutes. Add the eggs, one at a time, beating well after each addition, then beat the mixture until it is completely combined and uniform in color. Add the vanilla and beat again.

Scrape down the sides and the bottom of the bowl. Add the flour mixture in three parts, alternating with the chocolate mixture, beginning and ending with the flour mixture. Beat just until incorporated.

Fill the cupcake liners about three-quarters full. Bake the cupcakes for 17 to 20 minutes, rotating the pans halfway through the baking time, until a toothpick inserted in the center of a cupcake comes out clean.

For the Chocolate Mayonnaise Cupcakes

2	ounces good-quality dark chocolate (60 to 72%), coarsely chopped
⅔	cup dark unsweetened cocoa powder (like Valrhona)
1¾	cups boiling water
2¾	cups all-purpose flour
1¼	teaspoons baking soda
¼	teaspoon baking powder
1	cup granulated sugar
1	cup firmly packed dark brown sugar
1⅓	cups mayonnaise
2	large eggs
1	teaspoon pure vanilla extract

For the Chocolate Frosting

12	ounces (3 sticks), unsalted butter, softened
3	cups confectioners' sugar, sifted
1½	tablespoons pure vanilla extract
10	ounces good-quality dark chocolate (60 to 72%), melted and cooled

Allow the cupcakes to cool for 15 minutes in the pan, then turn them out onto wire racks to cool completely.

MAKE THE CHOCOLATE FROSTING

In the bowl of a standing mixer fitted with the paddle attachment, beat the butter on high speed until creamy, about 2 minutes. Add the confectioners' sugar all at once and beat until completely blended, about 2 minutes. Add the vanilla extract and beat for 15 seconds. Scrape down the sides and bottom of the bowl and add the chocolate. Beat until smooth, continuing to scrape down the sides as needed until the frosting is uniform in color.

ASSEMBLE THE CUPCAKES

There are many ways to frost a cupcake. If you have a pastry bag, simply fit it with the largest tip, fill the bag with frosting, and pipe enough to cover the cupcake in a big mound. If you do not have a pastry bag, use an ice cream scoop with a release mechanism to scoop the frosting and dispense it onto the top of the cupcake. You can also use an offset spatula to frost the cupcakes.

MILE-HIGH CHOCOLATE CAKE

with

VANILLA BUTTERCREAM

MILE-HIGH DESSERTS—pies piled with mountains of meringue and cakes stacked, undulating, and reaching for the stars—are undeniably sexy. They are fun and centerpieceworthy, and when executed appropriately, they have a smile-inducing appeal: sly, cartoony, and Dr. Seuss-ish. The trick with a mile-high dessert is to keep the taste buds as engaged as the eyes. Common missteps include meringue overload (too much meringue, not enough pie or cake) and taste imbalance (too much of a filling or too many flavors). In other words, keep it beautiful by keeping it simple.

Our Mile-High Chocolate Cake is both visually appealing and incredibly tasty. The bones of the cake are created using six layers of our moist and flavorful classic chocolate cake, and then filled with a simple vanilla buttercream (not too rich, not too sweet). We left the sides exposed to eliminate the problem of having too much frosting, further enhancing its architectural charm. Finally, the top layer is drenched in a velvety chocolate ganache that just barely drips down the exposed sides. Make this cake when you want to make a statement.

/////////////////////////// *Yield: One 8-inch, 6-layer cake* ///////////////////////////

BAKED NOTE: *Even if you have no previous cake stacking experience, we promise you will be able to stack this one. Just go slowly and feel free to refrigerate the cake for 5 minutes in between frosting each layer, which should improve stability. Also, if you are traveling with the cake, we suggest adding the glaze once you have reached your final destination.*

//

MAKE THE CLASSIC CHOCOLATE CAKE

Preheat the oven to 325 degrees F. Butter three 8-by-2-inch round cake pans, line the bottoms with parchment paper, and butter the parchment. Dust the parchment with flour and knock out the excess flour.

Place the cocoa powder in a medium heatproof bowl. Pour the hot water directly over the cocoa and whisk until combined. Add the sour cream and whisk again until smooth. Set aside to cool.

For the Classic Chocolate Cake

¾	cup dark unsweetened cocoa powder (like Valrhona)
1¼	cups hot water
⅔	cup sour cream
2⅔	cups all-purpose flour
2	teaspoons baking powder
1	teaspoon baking soda
½	teaspoon salt
6	ounces (1½ sticks) unsalted butter, softened
½	cup vegetable shortening, at room temperature
1½	cups granulated sugar
1	cup firmly packed dark brown sugar
3	large eggs
1	tablespoon pure vanilla extract

For the Vanilla Buttercream

1⅔	cups granulated sugar, divided
5	large egg whites
1	pound (4 sticks) unsalted butter, at room temperature, cut into tablespoons
2	teaspoons vanilla bean paste

For the Milk Chocolate Glaze

5	ounces good-quality milk chocolate, coarsely chopped
5	ounces good-quality dark chocolate (60 to 72%), coarsely chopped
1¼	cups heavy cream
2	tablespoons light corn syrup
1	ounce (¼ stick) unsalted butter, at room temperature, cut into ½-inch cubes

In another bowl, sift the flour, baking powder, baking soda, and salt and set aside.

In the bowl of a standing mixer fitted with the paddle attachment, beat the butter and shortening on medium speed about 5 minutes, until the mixture appears to ribbon throughout the bowl. Add the sugars and beat until light and fluffy, about 5 minutes more. Add the eggs, one at a time, beating well after each addition, then add the vanilla and beat until incorporated. Scrape down the sides and bottom of the bowl and beat again for 30 seconds.

Add the flour mixture in three parts, alternating with the cocoa mixture, beginning and ending with the flour mixture. Beat just until incorporated.

Divide the batter among the prepared pans (about 2¾ cup batter for each) and smooth the tops with an offset spatula. Bake the cakes for 35 to 40 minutes, rotating the pans halfway through the baking time, until a toothpick inserted in the center of the cakes comes out clean. Transfer the pans to wire racks and let cool for 20 minutes. Turn the cakes out onto the racks and let them cool completely. Remove the parchment.

Wrap each cake layer in plastic and place in the freezer while you make the buttercream (this makes them easier to slice in half horizontally later).

MAKE THE VANILLA BUTTERCREAM

In a medium, heavy-bottomed saucepan, combine 1⅛ cups sugar with ⅓ cup water (be careful not to splash the sides of the pan). Stir gently and cook over medium heat until the sugar is dissolved. Clip a candy thermometer to the side of the pan, making sure the bulb of the thermometer is immersed in the syrup. Stop stirring and increase the heat. Boil the mixture until it reaches the soft ball stage (238 to 240 degrees F), about 5 minutes.

Meanwhile, place the egg whites and the remaining ⅓ cup sugar in the bowl of a standing mixer fitted with the whisk attachment. Beat on medium speed until very soft peaks form (the mixture will be slightly opaque).

Decrease the mixer speed to low and slowly pour the hot syrup down the side of the bowl into the egg white mixture in a slow steady stream, then increase the mixer speed to high and beat until stiff peaks form. Let the meringue cool in the bowl until the mixture is lukewarm (about 100 degrees F), 10 to 25 minutes.

Turn the mixer speed to medium and gradually add the butter, 2 to 3 tablespoons at a time, beating each addition until it is entirely incorporated before adding more. Continue beating until the buttercream is smooth, light, and fluffy. Add the vanilla bean paste and beat again for 15 seconds to incorporate. (If the buttercream looks broken or curdled, place the mixer bowl over a pot of simmering water on medium heat and whisk with a large whisk for 5 to 10 seconds to warm the mixture slightly. Then remove from the heat and whisk vigorously or attach the bowl to the standing mixer and beat again on medium speed. Repeat the process of warming and beating the buttercream as many times as needed until it is smooth and no longer curdled.)

ASSEMBLE THE CAKE

Remove the layers from the freezer and, if necessary, trim any domed tops to form even layers, and using a serrated knife, cut each cake in half horizontally, forming six layers in total. Place one cake layer on a platter. Drop tablespoonfuls of buttercream (about ¾ cup in total) over the top of the cake layer and spread evenly to the edges with an offset spatula. Top with a second cake layer and then another ¾ cup buttercream. Repeat until the sixth layer is stacked—do NOT spread buttercream on the top cake layer. Chill the cake in the refrigerator for at least 1 hour.

MAKE THE MILK CHOCOLATE GLAZE

Place the chopped chocolates in a large heatproof bowl and set aside.

In a small saucepan over medium heat, combine the heavy cream and corn syrup and bring just to a boil. Remove from the heat and pour over the chocolate. Let sit for 2 minutes, then slowly wisk the chocolate and cream together until the chocolate is completely melted and the mixture is smooth. Whisk for another 2 to 3 minutes to release excess heat from the mixture. Add the butter and whisk again until it is completely melted and incorporated. Chill the glaze for 30 to 45 minutes, until slightly thickened (it should drip thickly when poured slowly from the spoon).

Spoon teaspoonfuls of glaze up to 2 inches apart around the top edge of the cake, allowing glaze to drip down the sides. Spoon the remaining glaze over the top center of the cake and smooth with an offset spatula, covering the top completely. Chill the cake until the glaze sets, at least 1 hour.

This cake tastes best when eaten within 24 hours. Refrigerate any leftover cake, tented in foil, for up to 3 days. Let the cake come to room temperature before serving.

CANDY BAR COOKIES

THERE IS SOMETHING almost maniacal about stuffing a candy bar inside a cookie and dipping the whole thing in chocolate. It suggests a more-is-more attitude, a winner-take-all approach to crafting dessert that so often leads one down the depraved path. Thankfully, this cookie perseveres—it is not morally corrupt. It is, in fact, just about as sweet as a baby kitten. Renato first crossed paths with the Candy Bar Cookie in Germany (there, they are called *riegel*) by way of a Christmas cookie platter. He was instantly smitten—and surprised—by the chewy candy bar center lurking inside the simple butter cookie exterior. Though the original German cookie is sans chocolate shell, Renato decided to update this recipe. He dips each cookie in whatever chocolate is on hand (double dipping encouraged), adds a dash of color via decorations, and presents them as large, jewel-like truffles. The cookies are beautiful and delicious, and tailor-made for special occasions.

/////////////////////////////////// **Yield: 40 cookies** ///////////////////////////////////

> **BAKED NOTE**: *This recipe was tested using a variety of candy bars; however, we think it works best with halved, fun-size Bounty (probably hard to find in some areas), Mounds, and 3 Musketeers bars. Whole Rolo caramels and Reese's Mini Peanut Butter Cups are also great choices.*

//

MAKE THE CANDY BAR COOKIES

In a medium bowl, whisk together the flour, sugar, cocoa powder, and salt.

In the bowl of a standing mixer fitted with the paddle attachment, beat the butter on medium speed until creamy. Add the egg yolk and beat until combined. Add the flour mixture and mix on low speed until just incorporated. The dough will look sandy.

Shape the dough into a disk, wrap the disk in plastic wrap, and refrigerate until chilled, about 1 hour.

Preheat the oven to 350 degrees F. Line two large baking sheets with parchment paper.

Dust a work surface with a sprinkling of flour. Unwrap the chilled dough and place it directly on the work surface. Roll the dough into a ¼-inch-thick round. Using a 2¼-inch (or thereabouts) round cookie cutter, cut the dough into circles and transfer them to the prepared baking sheets. Reroll the dough scraps and cut out more circles.

Use your hands to roll the candy pieces into the shape of a ball (or vaguely in the shape of a ball). Place each candy ball on a circle of dough and wrap the dough around the

For the Candy Bar Cookies

2	cups all-purpose flour
½	cup sugar
1	tablespoon dark unsweetened cocoa powder (like Valrhona)
⅛	teaspoon salt
7	ounces (1¾ sticks) unsalted butter, at room temperature
1	large egg yolk
20	fun-size Mounds, cut in half, or 40 Reese's Mini Peanut Butter Cups

For the Assembly

4	ounces good-quality dark chocolate (60 to 72%), coarsely chopped
4	ounces good-quality white chocolate, coarsely chopped
3	tablespoons sprinkles (optional)
3	tablespoons nonpareils (optional)
3	tablespoons pistachios, coarsely chopped (optional)

candy, covering it completely. Use your fingers to pinch together and smooth over any tears in the dough. Place the dough balls, about 1 inch apart, on the prepared baking sheets.

Bake for 12 to 15 minutes, rotating the sheets halfway through the baking time, until the cookies are firm and just slightly brown. Remove the baking sheets from the oven and place on wire racks to cool for 5 minutes, then transfer the cookies directly to the wire racks to cool completely.

ASSEMBLE THE CANDY BAR COOKIES

Using a double boiler or microwave, melt the dark chocolate in one bowl and the white chocolate in another bowl. If you are using sprinkles or nonpareils, place them in small ramekins. Line two baking sheets with parchment paper.

Dip or cover a cookie in the dark or white, allowing the excess chocolate to drip back into the bowl. Dip the top of the cookie in sprinkles, nonpareils, or pistachios. Place the cookie on the prepared baking sheet. Repeat with the remaining cookies and allow the chocolate coating to firm up before serving.

Alternatively, to create a multilayered look, dip each cookie completely in white chocolate. Let the chocolate set (you can even put the baking sheet in the refrigerator for a few minutes). Then re-dip the cookies in dark chocolate, decorate as desired, and allow the chocolate coating to set completely.

CHOCOLATE-CHIP ORANGE PANETTONE

I DO NOT UNDERSTAND Renato's panettone fascination. I appreciate it and respect it, but I do not understand it—in the same way I appreciate and respect but ultimately don't understand opera and camping. Renato's romance with panettone began when he was a teenager during a New Year's Eve celebration. The bread was accompanied by champagne and good cheer, and suddenly he saw panettone as much more than a strange, candied bread; it was a formidable dessert. He began to search for it outside the constraints of the holidays, navigating supermarket aisles, damp with anticipation, in a post–New Year's Day haze. Eventually he decided to make his own. This recipe is Renato's riff on the panettone that enveloped him that New Year's Eve. He swapped out the omnipresent raisins for chocolate chips and added a little bit of cocoa powder, because everything tastes better with a little bit of cocoa. And he kept the candied orange studded throughout—a classic ingredient absolutely worth keeping. Though I am not a panettone person, I am definitely a Chocolate-Chip Orange Panettone person, and I am slowly starting to see the light.

/////////////////////////// *Yield: One 6-inch panettone, 4 inches tall* ///////////////////////////

BAKED NOTE: *Panettone leftovers are the best kind of leftovers. They make a fantastic bread pudding and a faultless French toast. This recipe also happens to meld well with Nutella (or any chocolate spread) and almond butter—just slice, toast, and slather.*

I	panettone paper mold (see "Breaking the Mold," page 183)
3	cups bread flour, divided
I	packet active dry yeast (2¼ teaspoons)
½	cup lukewarm whole milk (100 to 110 degrees F)
¼	cup dark unsweetened cocoa powder (like Valrhona)
½	teaspoon salt
½	cup sugar
3	large eggs, plus 2 large egg yolks
	Zest of 2 oranges (about 2 tablespoons)
I	teaspoon vanilla bean paste or pure vanilla extract
5	ounces (1¼ sticks) unsalted butter, softened, cut into ½-inch cubes
6	ounces (about I cup) semisweet chocolate chips
½	cup Homemade Candied Orange Peel, diced (page 182)

Lightly spray a 6-inch-round-by-4-inch-tall panettone paper mold with vegetable oil (preferably canola) and place on a baking sheet.

In a small bowl, stir together 1 cup of flour and the yeast. Add the milk and stir to combine. Turn the mixture out into a clean, lightly greased bowl, cover with plastic wrap, and set aside until the dough doubles in bulk, about 1 hour.

Sift the remaining flour, the cocoa powder, and the salt into the bowl of a standing mixer fitted with the paddle attachment. Stir in the sugar. Add the dough and mix on low speed until the mixture is shaggy.

Add the eggs, egg yolks, zest, and vanilla bean paste and mix again until the dough comes together and has a distinct shiny appearance, 4 to 5 minutes (the amount of time needed can change depending on humidity and temperature).

HOMEMADE CANDIED ORANGE PEEL

IT'S SUPER SIMPLE to make your own candied orange peel for the Chocolate Chip Orange Panettone. Since this recipe yields slightly more than 1 cup, feel free to use the leftover peel for simple snacks (just roll in sugar or dry and dip in chocolate) or to add to loaf cakes and cookie batters at will (cake batters are usually too light to keep the peel in suspension—it might sink to the bottom of the pan).

////////////////////////////////////// *Yield: 1 cup* //////////////////////////////////////

4	medium oranges
2	cups sugar
¾	cup light corn syrup

Wash the oranges thoroughly. With a knife or a sharp peeler, peel each orange in large strips, leaving the white pith behind; remove any remaining white pith from the peels with a paring knife.

Place the peel in a large, heavy-bottomed saucepan and cover with 1 cup cold water. Bring to a boil and strain. Cover with water, bring to a boil, and strain three more times.

Place the peels, 4 cups water, and the sugar and corn syrup in a medium saucepan and bring to a simmer over medium heat. Reduce the heat to low and simmer for 15 to 20 minutes, until the mixture forms a thick syrup and the peel becomes translucent. Set aside to cool.

When the syrup has cooled, remove the peel and cut it into strips. Return the strips to the syrup. When using in a panettone, loaf cake, or cookie batter, remove the peels from the syrup and dice. If you want to eat them as a snack, remove them from the syrup and roll them in granulated sugar.

The peel can be stored in the syrup in an airtight container in the refrigerator for up to 3 days, or dry the peels on a rack overnight and store in an airtight container at room temperature for up to 3 days.

Switch from the paddle attachment to the dough hook attachment. Turn the mixer to low and gradually add the butter in three additions, mixing until each addition is thoroughly incorporated. Continue mixing the dough until it is elastic and smooth, 10 to 15 minutes.

Add the chocolate chips and orange peel and mix for a few more seconds. Turn the dough out onto a lightly floured surface and knead it by hand until the chocolate chips and orange peel are evenly incorporated. Pat the dough into a small (5-by-5-inch), thick square and tuck all four corners underneath to form a tight dome shape. Place the dough, dome side up, into the prepared mold, cover with a damp tea towel, and allow to rise in a dry place at room temperature for at least 2 hours, or until it has doubled in bulk. (It should not rise beyond the top of the panettone mold at this point; at most it should reach right up to the lip.)

Preheat the oven to 350 degrees F and position the rack in the center.

Bake the panettone for 50 to 70 minutes until the inside center temperature of the bread registers 175 to 180 degrees F on an instant read thermometer. If the top of the bread darkens before it is cooked all the way through, tent it with aluminum foil until it is finished baking.

Place the panettone on a wire rack to cool completely before slicing. It can be stored at room temperature, tightly covered, for up to 5 days.

BREAKING THE MOLD: ALTERNATIVES TO PANETTONE PAPER MOLDS

We realize that the occasional (er, once-a-year) panettone baker probably has very few reasons to keep official panettone paper molds on hand. We also realize that panettone paper molds are not readily available to the vast majority of bakers. Yes, you can source them on the Internet, but it requires some serious forward thinking, perhaps killing the spontaneous joy that so often accompanies baking. So here are a few alternative options to actual panettone paper.

Coffee Can

The most common panettone paper mold substitute is the ordinary coffee can, one that is as close in size and shape to the requested mold as possible, though it does not need to be exact. Wash and dry the can thoroughly. Then cut out a round of parchment paper to cover the inside bottom of the can and grease the round with butter. Next, cut out a rectangle of parchment to line the inside of the coffee can: it should cover the entire inside surface and extend an inch or two above the height of the can. Before inserting the parchment into the can, butter one side of the rectangle and make sure the buttered side is facing into the center of the can. You might have to adjust your bake time based on the size of the coffee can. Generally speaking, if the can is smaller than the suggested panettone mold, it will require less baking time. If it is larger, it will require more.

Soup Cans

If you have unlined (i.e., full tin) regular soup cans, you can make about three mini panettones from one recipe. Follow the directions as for the coffee can method above (greased parchment circle on the bottom, greased parchment lining on the sides) and bake for less time than the current recipe states (start checking for doneness after 35 minutes).

Ephemera

We have seen people bake panettones in a variety of creative vessels such as paper bags and flowerpots. Though we haven't been able to test the latest and greatest in substitutions, we are fairly certain you will achieve panettone happiness as long as you use a heatproof vessel that approximates the size and shape of a mold. Just be sure to line it and grease it properly.

1½	cups plus 2 tablespoons all-purpose flour
¾	cup dark unsweetened cocoa powder (like Valrhona)
1½	teaspoons baking soda
½	teaspoon salt
8	ounces (about 1½ cups) chocolate chunks
1	large egg white
½	cup light corn syrup
1½	tablespoons pure peppermint extract
1	teaspoon pure vanilla extract
6	ounces (1½ sticks) unsalted butter, cool but not cold, cut into ½-inch cubes
⅔	cup firmly packed dark brown sugar
¼	cup granulated sugar

CHEWY CHOCOLATE MINT COOKIES

with

CHOCOLATE CHUNKS

SOME (WELL, MOST) cookies are designed for snacking. They can be nibbled on throughout the day to provide a quick sugar rush (see Cream Cheese Chocolate Snacking Cookies on page 167 or Lemon Pecorino Pepper Icebox Cookies on page 162) or tossed back with a glass of milk before bedtime. Then there is a subset of cookies—a very small subset at that—primarily designed as a dessert experience. Our Chewy Chocolate Mint Cookies with Chocolate Chunks fall into the latter category. They are extremely chocolaty, yet elegant—rich without being ridiculous—and one or two seem to satisfy the sweet craving perfectly. We find these cookies are suitable for well-mannered (or, I suppose, even ill-mannered) dinner parties, fancier affairs, and high-end holiday cookie assortments. Truthfully, they are inordinately suited to accompany a good glass (or two) of red wine.

/////////////////////////////////////// *Yield: About 24 cookies* ///////////////////////////////////////

BAKED NOTE: *This cookie really does benefit from the peppermint extract—it adds a clean edge to the chocolate overload. However, if you are baking for the mint averse, leave out the peppermint extract and add a few chopped, toasted nuts for balance.*

In a large bowl, whisk together the flour, cocoa powder, baking soda, and salt. Stir in the chocolate chunks and set aside.

In a medium bowl, whisk together the egg white, corn syrup, peppermint extract, and vanilla. Set aside.

In the bowl of a standing mixer fitted with the paddle attachment, beat the butter and brown sugar on medium speed until light and fluffy, about 3 minutes. Scrape down the sides and bottom of the bowl, add the egg white mixture, and beat until incorporated, about 1 more minute.

Add the flour mixture all at once to the wet mixture and beat until just incorporated. Scrape down the bowl again and mix for a few more seconds. Cover the dough in plastic wrap and refrigerate for at least 24 hours.

Preheat the oven to 350 degrees F. Line two baking sheets with parchment paper. Place the granulated sugar in a shallow bowl.

Using a small ice cream scoop with a release mechanism, scoop the dough into 2 tablespoon–size balls and roll the dough balls in the granulated sugar. (Alternatively, measure the dough using a tablespoon and use your hands to form it into a ball before rolling in the sugar.) Place the cookies about 1 inch apart on the prepared baking sheets and bake for about 10 minutes, rotating the pans halfway through the baking time, until the cookies have wet fissures and cracks on top.

Set the pan on a wire rack for 10 minutes to cool. Then, using a spatula, transfer the cookies to the rack to cool completely. The cookies taste best if eaten within 24 hours; however, they also freeze extremely well (and taste great straight from the freezer). Freeze any leftovers, tightly wrapped, for up to 3 weeks.

2 cups hazelnuts, toasted (page 19) and skinned

2 cups all-purpose flour

1 teaspoon salt

2 cups confectioners' sugar, plus more for dusting

¾ cup dark unsweetened cocoa powder (like Valrhona)

10 ounces (2½ sticks) unsalted butter, at room temperature, cut into ½-inch cubes

1 cup granulated sugar

¾ cup firmly packed dark brown sugar

3 large eggs, plus 3 large egg yolks

¼ cup vegetable oil

1 tablespoon pure vanilla extract

TUNNEL OF HAZELNUT FUDGE CAKE

UNLIKE SOME OTHER classic American desserts, the Tunnel of Hazelnut Fudge Cake has a well-documented history. In short, Ella Helfrich created a Bundt cake with a gooey ribbon of fudge running through the center by using a now-discontinued Pillsbury Two Layer Size Double Dutch Fudge Buttercream Frosting Mix. Ella and her cake won second prize at the Pillsbury Bake-Off in 1966, and the cake (and to some degree, Ella) went on to achieve a certain kind of fame. Over the years, the cake has been redeveloped by several people in several iterations to re-create the recipe without the former secret ingredient. We decided to give it yet another attempt by substituting hazelnuts for the original walnuts and skipping the glaze entirely—the glaze is not needed, and it actually distracts from the fudgy center. Though this cake is rightfully known for its ribbon of fudge—a somewhat gimmicky device—the cake is rich and dark and toasty all on its own. In fact, if you freeze the leftover Bundt and bring it back to almost room temperature (so it is cold but not rock solid), the cake tastes like a homemade scoop of Nutella.

/////////////////////////////// *Yield: One 10-cup Bundt cake* ///////////////////////////////

BAKED NOTE: *The only difficulty with this cake is properly checking for doneness. It's not impossible, but it does require slightly more attention than the average cake. In addition to the tips offered in the recipe directions, we would also like to offer the following advice: (a) do not open the oven door every 30 seconds to check for doneness—maybe every 2 minutes, (b) the cake will be delicious even if it is 2 minutes over- or underdone, and (c) make this cake—you won't be disappointed.*

///

Preheat the oven to 350 degrees F. Generously spray the inside of a 10-cup Bundt pan with nonstick cooking spray; alternatively, butter it thoroughly, dust it with cocoa powder, and knock out the excess cocoa.

In a food processor, pulse the nuts until they are somewhere between coarsely chopped and almost powdery (you do not want to pulse until they become nut butter). Pour the chopped nuts into a medium bowl, add the flour and salt, and whisk until combined.

Sift together the confectioners' sugar and cocoa powder into a small bowl.

In the bowl of a standing mixer fitted with the paddle attachment, beat the butter and both sugars until pale and fluffy. Scrape down the sides and bottom of the bowl, turn the mixer to low, and add the eggs and egg yolks, one at time, beating until just incorporated. Add the oil and vanilla and beat until the batter is uniform. Add the confectioners' sugar mixture and beat on low speed until just combined. Remove the bowl from the mixer and gently fold in the nut mixture.

Spoon the batter into the prepared pan, smooth the top, and bake for 38 to 45 minutes, rotating the pan halfway through the baking time. Very important note: due to the presence of the fudgy cake center you will not be able to test the cake for doneness using the traditional "toothpick test." Instead, make sure your oven temperature is accurate and watch the time carefully. The cake is technically done when it just begins to pull away from the sides of the pan or when it springs back when gently pressed—though this is not a fail-safe test. My best advice is to keep an eye on this cake after the 35-minute mark and pull it out the moment you think it's done.

Transfer the Bundt to a wire rack to cool for 2 hours in the pan. A great tip we picked up from a Shirley O. Corriher recipe: To prevent the cake from cracking and sinking (if you care about these things—it is the bottom of the cake after all), simply use your fingers to gently press the surface of the cake where it touches the inner and outer edges of the Bundt pan.

Gently loosen the sides of the cake from the pan and turn it out onto a serving platter. Sprinkle with a little sifted confectioners' sugar, if you like, and serve immediately.

Freeze any leftover cake, tightly covered, for up to 7 days. Before serving, let the cake come to almost room temperature (we think the leftovers taste better cold than at room temperature).

BROOKSTERS

THE TALE OF THE BROOKSTER naming is long, noirish, and slightly ridiculous. Suffice it to say, we thought the name Brookie (brownie + cookie + Brooklyn-based baking business = Brookie) was incredibly creative and perhaps original. It wasn't. We were just naive. The Brookie name, though incredibly apt, was weighed down by legal wrangling and trademarks, emotional baggage, and tales of woe. So we decided to remove ourselves from the legal shenanigans and rechristen them "Brooksters."

The Brookster is beautiful in its simplicity—a chocolate chip cookie baked inside a brownie shell—though it is actually deceiving. It is more than the sum of its parts. The cookie portion, the rich brown sugar chocolate chip filling, melds to the dark chocolate brownie bottom in a way that creates a symbiosis of dessert euphoria, an Americana textural explosion. It is familiar, yet altogether new and exciting. The Brookster is one of those high-low treats—it is perfect as an afternoon snack (see muffin tin preparation) and equally at home masquerading as a fancy after-dinner tart (preferably warmed and served with ice cream).

// **Yield: 6 Brooksters** //

> **BAKED NOTE**: *This recipe is fairly straightforward and easy; however, it does require some plan-ahead time. Make sure to read through the whole recipe first, as there are many steps (simple ones, but quite a few). Don't be tempted to rush the specified refrigeration time—it's important for the dough and batter to cool and thicken slightly for a perfect bake. You can do all the prep work ahead of time, then bake at your leisure.*

///

MAKE THE CHOCOLATE CHIP COOKIE FILLING

In a large mixing bowl, whisk together the flour, salt, and baking soda. Set aside.

In the bowl of a standing mixer fitted with the paddle attachment, beat the butter and sugars on medium speed until smooth and creamy. Scrape down the sides and bottom of the bowl and add the eggs, one at a time, beating well after each addition. The mixture will look light and fluffy. Add the vanilla and beat for 5 seconds.

Add half of the flour mixture and beat for 15 seconds. Add the remaining flour mixture and beat until just incorporated.

Remove the bowl from the mixer and fold in the chocolate chips until evenly combined. Cover the bowl tightly and chill in the refrigerator for 3 hours.

For the Chocolate Chip Cookie Filling

2¼	cups all-purpose flour
1	teaspoon salt
1	teaspoon baking soda
8	ounces (2 sticks) unsalted butter, softened
1	cup firmly packed dark brown sugar
½	cup granulated sugar
2	large eggs
2	teaspoons pure vanilla extract
12	ounces (about 2 cups) good-quality semisweet chocolate chips

For the Brownie Shells

¾	cup all-purpose flour
1	tablespoon dark unsweetened cocoa powder (like Valrhona)
½	teaspoon salt
5	ounces good-quality dark chocolate (60 to 72%), coarsely chopped
4	ounces (1 stick) unsalted butter, cut into 1-inch cubes
¾	cup granulated sugar
¼	cup firmly packed light brown sugar
3	large eggs, at room temperature
1	teaspoon pure vanilla extract

MAKE THE BROWNIE SHELLS

Butter the bottoms and sides of 6 individual (4-inch) pie plates, or lightly spray with nonstick cooking spray, and place the pie plates on a baking sheet. (See "How to Make Brooksters in Muffin or Cupcake Pans" for alternative baking instructions.)

In a medium bowl, whisk together the flour, cocoa powder, and salt.

Place the chocolate and the butter in the bowl of a double boiler over medium heat and stir occasionally until they are completely melted and combined. Turn off the heat, but keep the bowl over the water of the double boiler and add both sugars, whisking until completely combined. Remove the bowl from the water and let the mixture cool to room temperature.

Add one egg at a time to the chocolate mixture, whisking after each addition until just combined. Add the vanilla and stir until combined. Do not overbeat the batter at this stage or your brownies will be cakey.

Sprinkle the flour mixture over the chocolate mixture. Using a spatula (do not use a whisk) fold the dry ingredients into the wet ingredients until there is just a trace amount of the flour mixture visible.

Fill each pie plate with brownie batter until it is just under halfway full. Place the baking sheet in the refrigerator and chill for 3 hours.

ASSEMBLE THE BROOKSTERS

After the cookie dough and brownie batter have chilled for 3 hours, preheat the oven to 375 degrees F.

Using an ice cream scoop with a release mechanism, scoop the dough into ¼ cup–size balls and use your hands to shape the dough into perfect spheres. Gently flatten each ball into a disk. The disks should be slightly smaller than the tops of the pie plates.

Remove the baking sheet containing the brownie batter from the refrigerator and gently press a cookie dough disk into the batter in each pie plate. (You may have some leftover chocolate chip cookie batter. If so, feel free to scoop it into 2 tablespoon–size balls and bake on a separate cookie sheet for 12 to 14 minutes.)

Bake for 20 to 25 minutes, rotating the sheet halfway through the baking time. The Brooksters are done when the cookie part is golden brown.

Cool to room temperature or serve warm with ice cream.

¼	cup dark unsweetened cocoa powder (like Valrhona)
1	cup sugar
¼	teaspoon salt

SIMPLE CHOCOLATE SYRUP

THIS SYRUP IS truly a syrup and not a sauce. There is a time and place for rich chocolate sauce (usually made with chunks of chocolate and heavy cream or milk), but there are equally as many recipes (like the Semifreddi on page 124 or the Bourbon, Vanilla, and Chocolate Milkshakes on page 78) that are more suited toward a thinner, straightforward syrup. This syrup packs a cocoa wallop—an intense chocolatey surge—that is not obscured or muted by the presence of dairy. It is less heavy (and perhaps contains a few less calories) than most sauces and we really do use (or abuse) it for just about everything. We are certain that, if left unchecked, we would drizzle it over plates of pasta.

// **Yield: 1 cup** //

> **BAKED NOTE**: *When we say to use a large saucepan in this recipe, we mean it: use a large saucepan. This mixture will bubble up considerably while cooking and you might have to reduce the heat for a minute or two during the process.*

In a large saucepan over medium heat, whisk together the cocoa powder and ½ cup of water until dissolved. Whisk in the sugar and increase the heat to medium-high. Boil the mixture for about 3 minutes, then reduce the heat to low and simmer for another 1 to 2 minutes. Remove from the heat and stir in the salt. Let cool to room temperature. The sauce can be stored in the refrigerator, tightly covered, for up to 3 weeks. Warm it gently to use it as a topping or use it directly from the refrigerator as a milk shake mix-in.

USES FOR LEFTOVER CHOCOLATE SYRUP

Our chocolate syrup yields approximately 1 cup—enough for a lot of Milk Chocolate Malt Semifreddo (page 124) and Bourbon, Vanilla, and Chocolate Milk Shakes (page 78). Thankfully, the syrup is über versatile, and you can use the leftovers any way you like (and since the syrup is dairy free, it keeps really well in the fridge).

- Stir a few tablespoons into milk to make your own chocolate milk.

- Gently warm it and pour it over ice cream.

- Use it as the perfect base for a homemade mocha.

- Poke holes in your chocolate cake sponge (before icing) and brush with ¼ cup syrup to add moisture and chocolate flavor.

- Drizzle it over frozen bananas for the heck of it—we've been known to do it.

CHOCOLATE VELVET WALNUT FUDGE

with

OLIVE OIL AND FLEUR DE SEL

⅔	cup evaporated milk
2¼	cups Homemade Marshmallow Cream (page 195)
2	ounces (½ stick) unsalted butter, cut into ½-inch cubes
1	cup granulated sugar
1	cup firmly packed dark brown sugar
½	teaspoon salt
6	ounces good-quality dark chocolate (60 to 72%), coarsely chopped
6	ounces good-quality milk chocolate, coarsely chopped
2	cups walnuts, toasted extra dark (page 19), coarsely chopped
1½	teaspoons pure vanilla extract
2	tablespoons good-quality extra-virgin olive oil
1	tablespoon fleur de sel

FUDGE NEEDS A REBOOT. It has become stilted and weary, and is in dire need of some love and affection. Lately, fudge as we know it is barely surviving, located almost exclusively in pained-looking shops in kitschy and touristy American towns—usually abutting tacky T-shirt and memento shops. Honestly, fudge has never been our mania, but we knew that there was a greater and more interesting version possible than what was currently available. We wanted to create a version that was smooth in both texture and flavor—we aimed for the chocolate to radiate and the bite to be toothsome (no fake-tasting oils, no awkward sugar crystals)—and we wanted balance. Most fudge is very sweet (even Grandma's delicious fudge is super sweet—good, but *sweet*), so we tried to balance the sugar with a little drizzle of olive oil, a sprinkling of fleur de sel, and a whole bunch of toasty, almost savory walnuts, and it worked beautifully. Our chocolate velvet fudge is a proper fudge. A fudge you can be proud of. A fudge you will want to make, send, and receive. If you have given up on fudge, we hope you will try ours and give it another whirl.

/// *Yield: 24 pieces* ///

BAKED NOTE: *If you are looking to make a gift of this fudge (as many grandmothers across America used to do), may we suggest including a mini bottle of olive oil and a small box of fleur de sel as part of the package along with serving (drizzling and sprinkling) suggestions. It's not necessary of course—the recipient can always add his or her own prior to serving—but it certainly makes the package a little more gifty (and cute).*

///

Lightly spray an 8-inch square baking pan with nonstick cooking spray, line it with aluminum foil, and lightly spray the foil.

In a medium saucepan, stir together the evaporated milk, marshmallow cream, butter, both sugars, and salt. Set the saucepan over low heat and continue to stir gently until the sugars dissolve. Turn the heat up to medium-low and, stirring continuously, bring the mixture to a boil. Clip a candy thermometer to the side of the pan, making sure the bulb of the thermometer is immersed in the syrup. Continue to stir gently and wait for the mixture to reach about 230 degrees F, 6 to 10 minutes (depending on outside temperature and humidity).

Remove from the heat. Carefully add the chopped chocolates and stir until completely melted. Stir in the nuts and vanilla. Keep stirring the fudge until the mixture turns from glossy to matte (it might look a tiny bit oily when spreading it into the pan, but it will change appearance as it cools). Spread the fudge into the prepared pan and let it cool to room temperature. Before the fudge sets completely (wait about 10 minutes after spreading into the pan), use the tip of a small spoon to score 16 equal X patterns on the fudge. The impression should only be about ½ inch deep. Divide the fudge into 16 equal bars.

The fudge can be stored at room temperature, tightly covered, for up to 1 week.

Before serving, drizzle some olive oil into the X impression and sprinkle with fleur de sel.

HOMEMADE MARSHMALLOW CREAM

THIS RICH AND DREAMY recipe makes enough marshmallow cream for two batches of fudge. We have been known to use leftover marshmallow cream for almost anything—ice cream topping, peanut butter and marshmallow sandwiches (a favorite), or even, on occasion, as a quick and dirty cupcake frosting.

/////////////////////////////////// **Yield: 4 cups** ///////////////////////////////////

4	large egg whites
1	teaspoon cream of tartar
⅛	teaspoon salt
⅔	cup plus 3 tablespoons sugar, divided
¾	cup light corn syrup
1	teaspoon pure vanilla extract

In the bowl of a standing mixer fitted with the whisk attachment, whisk the egg whites vigorously for 1 minute. Sprinkle the cream of tartar and salt over the whites and continue beating until the egg whites are foamy. Continue beating while sprinkling in 3 tablespoons of the sugar. Beat until soft peaks form.

In a medium saucepan, gently stir together the remaining ⅔ cup sugar, ¼ cup of water, and the corn syrup. Set the saucepan over low heat and continue to stir gently until the sugar and syrup dissolve. Turn the heat up to medium and bring the mixture to a boil. Clip a candy thermometer to the side of the pan, making sure the bulb of the thermometer is immersed in the syrup. Turn the heat up to medium-high and wait for the mixture to reach firm ball stage, 246 to 248 degrees F, about 10 minutes.

Turn the mixer to low speed. Slowly stream the hot sugar mixture into the egg whites. Once all of the sugar mixture has been added, increase the mixer speed to high and beat until the marshmallow cream is near room temperature and fluffy. Add the vanilla and beat again for 5 more seconds or until incorporated. You can check the temperature of the mixture by touching the bottom of the mixing bowl.

Use immediately or refrigerate, tightly covered, for up to 3 days.

THE BANANA CONTAINS
3 TYPES
OF SUGARS:
FRUCTOSE, SUCROSE
and
GLUCOSE
(along with fiber)

THIS HELPS BANANAS GIVE AN IMMEDIATE ENERGY BOOST.

800+
VIDEOS ON YOUTUBE
DEVOTED TO PEOPLE SLIPPING
ON BANANA PEELS

BANANA PEELS
CONTAIN
A HALLUCINOGENIC
CALLED BUFOTENINE, ALSO FOUND IN THE SKIN OF TOADS

THE LONGEST BANANA SPLIT

made in

PENNSYLVANIA IN 1988
WAS REPORTEDLY 4.55 MILES LONG

— IT WOULD TAKE ABOUT 67 OF THEM TO SPAN THE STATE —

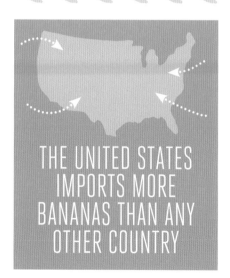

THE UNITED STATES IMPORTS MORE BANANAS THAN ANY OTHER COUNTRY

EATING BANANAS

- can help cure a hangover, as they replenish one's depleted potassium

- are useful in helping alleviate depression because they contain tryptophan, which manufactures serotonin, a naturally occurring relaxant

THERE ARE OVER
500
DIFFERENT TYPES OF BANANAS

Chapter 10
BANANA

The banana—the simple, inexpensive banana—is as much a part of our kitchen as flour, butter, and eggs. We have banana puree in the refrigerator, peeled bananas in the freezer (smoothie fest), and bunches of bananas in various stages of ripeness scattered throughout our respective apartments. We are, ridiculously, bananas about bananas. Our banana euphoria is probably best encapsulated by banana bread—the bread of a thousand sense memories, potlucks, and church cookbooks. It is a showcase for the banana and its uniquely transformative effect on baked goods—the automatic moisture, the round flavor, the effortless sweetness, the unexpected texture, and the homey speckled appearance. In other words, a banana is much more than a banana. It is a secret baking weapon, disguised in a peel, just waiting to be deployed.

For the Bananas Cake

3	cups cake flour
1¼	teaspoons baking powder
1	teaspoon baking soda
½	teaspoon salt
4	ounces (1 stick) unsalted butter, at room temperature, cut into ½-inch cubes
⅓	cup vegetable shortening
1¾	cups plus 1 tablespoon sugar
2	large eggs
2	teaspoons pure vanilla extract
3	large very ripe bananas, mashed (about 1 cup)
½	cup plus 1 tablespoon well-shaken buttermilk

For the Milk Chocolate Ganache Frosting

8	ounces good-quality bittersweet chocolate (60 to 72%), finely chopped
8	ounces good-quality milk chocolate, finely chopped
1½	cups heavy cream
2	tablespoons light corn syrup
12	ounces (3 sticks) unsalted butter, cool but not cold, cut into ½-inch cubes

For the Assembly

	Peanut Butter Filling (page 28)
8	ounces good-quality dark chocolate (60 to 72%), coarsely chopped
6	ounces (1½ sticks) unsalted butter, softened, cut into ½-inch cubes
1	tablespoon light corn syrup

For the Garnish

¼	cup coarsely chopped salted peanuts

BANANAS CAKE

IT WOULD BE almost silly to mention that this cake, when assembled and presented, is more (much more) than the sum of its parts. We say *silly* only because the banana cake sponge alone is quite impressive (moist and banana-y) and delicious even without a drop of frosting or filling—just dust it with confectioners' sugar and serve it with tea. However, this cake is a wunderkind—even a conversation piece—when assembled and presented at celebrations. And then there is the taste. It is no surprise that the layering of fluffy banana cake, sweet peanut butter filling, milk chocolate ganache frosting, and dark chocolate glaze is a perfect ten (or eleven) every single time. We are also certain that a full slice of this cake is an adequate—and extremely enjoyable—dinner replacement. We encourage you to "go big" when slicing.

/// *Yield: One 8-inch, 3-layer cake* ///

BAKED NOTE: *Though this recipe has many steps, all the steps are fairly easy. That said, if you want to break up this recipe, we suggest you make and freeze (wrapped in a double layer of plastic wrap) the cake layers the night before finishing the cake, and measure out (or mise en place) all of your filling ingredients while your cakes are baking. The following day—the day you plan on serving the cake—putting it all together will be effortless (or at least easier).*

///

MAKE THE BANANAS CAKE

Preheat the oven to 325 degrees F. Butter three 8-inch round cake pans, line the bottoms with parchment paper, and butter the parchment. Dust the parchment with flour and knock out the excess flour.

In a medium bowl, whisk together the cake flour, baking powder, baking soda, and salt and set aside.

In the bowl of a standing mixer fitted with the paddle attachment, beat the butter and shortening on medium speed until light and fluffy, about 5 minutes (the mixture will appear to string or ribbon throughout the bowl). Add the sugar and beat on medium speed until light and fluffy, about 5 more minutes. Add the eggs, one at a time, mixing for 10 to 15 seconds after each addition, until the egg is incorporated into the mixture. Then turn the mixer to low, add the vanilla and bananas, and beat until incorporated. (If the mixture appears curdled, keep beating slowly until the mixture looks like it is coming back together.) Scrape down the sides and bottom of the bowl and mix again for 30 seconds. Add the flour mixture in three parts, alternating with the buttermilk, beginning and ending with the flour mixture. Beat for 10 to 15 seconds, or until incorporated, after each addition.

Divide the batter among the prepared pans and use an offset spatula to smooth the tops. Bake for 35 to 40 minutes, rotating the pans halfway through the baking time, until a toothpick inserted in the center of the cake comes out clean. Transfer the pans to a wire rack and cool for 30 to 45 minutes. Turn the cakes out onto the rack and let them cool completely. Remove the parchment.

MAKE THE MILK CHOCOLATE GANACHE FROSTING

Place both chocolates in the bowl of a standing mixer. In a small saucepan, bring the cream and corn syrup to a boil, then remove from the heat and immediately pour the mixture over the chocolate. Let stand for 2 to 3 minutes. Starting in the center of the bowl and working your way out to the edges, whisk the chocolate mixture by hand until it is completely smooth. Set aside to cool to room temperature.

Returning the bowl to the standing mixer fitted with the paddle attachment, on medium speed, gradually add the butter to the chocolate mixture and mix until thoroughly incorporated. The frosting should be completely smooth and have a silky look.

ASSEMBLE THE CAKE

Place one cake layer on a serving platter. Trim the top to create a flat surface and evenly spread half of the peanut butter filling on top. Top with about 1¼ cups of the frosting and gently smooth it out. Add the next cake layer, trim it, spread with the remaining peanut butter filling and top with another 1¼ cups of the frosting. Add the third layer. Spread a very thin layer of frosting over the sides and top of the cake and put it in the refrigerator for about 15 minutes to firm up. (This is known as crumb coating and will help to keep loose cake crumbs under control when you frost the outside of the cake.) Frost the sides and top of the cake with the remaining frosting and refrigerate for 15 minutes to firm it up.

Meanwhile, place the chocolate, butter, and corn syrup in the bowl of a double boiler over medium heat. Using a rubber spatula, stir the mixture until the chocolate and butter are completely melted and smooth. Remove the bowl from the water and stir the glaze to release excess heat.

Line a rimmed baking sheet with parchment paper. Place the cake on a wire rack on the baking sheet. Slowly pour about ¾ cup of the warm glaze over the cake. Use a small offset spatula to smooth it out to the edges. Place the cake in the refrigerator for 5 minutes to set the glaze. Remove from the refrigerator and slowly pour the rest of the glaze over the cake. It should run down the edges in a thick stream. You should be able to control the size and length of the streams by how quickly you pour. Feel free to experiment and have no fear in playing around; this is the fun part and there is no right or wrong way. Garnish around the edge of the cake with the peanuts. Chill the entire cake for about 20 minutes, or until the glaze is set, then transfer to a cake plate. Serve at room temperature.

The cake can be stored at room temperature, covered with a cake dome or in a cake saver, for up to 3 days.

BANANA MOUSSE PARFAITS

BANANA MOUSSE WAS originally conceived as the alternative choice—the "just in case" dessert. We made it just in case a party guest (or guests) might be allergic to nuts or gluten, or just in case someone might have an aversion to chocolate (chocolate factors heavily into most of our social gatherings). Then a funny thing happened. We slowly, and ever so unexpectedly, fell in love with this simple Banana Mousse recipe, and we started to make it often—regardless of the allergies and preferences of our guests. The recipe itself is by far the quickest one in our repertoire—it can be put together in about 5 minutes—but the taste is deceptively complex in a good way. And true to the "just in case" dessert it is—just in case you want something a bit more complicated—the flavor and texture works well with a wide variety of sweets. Thus we are presenting you with a parfait recipe. Of course, if you just want to eat the mousse as is, don't feel obligated to parfait.

////////////////////////////////////// *Yield: 4 servings* //////////////////////////////////////

BAKED NOTE: *To freeze or not to freeze? Whenever we make mousse in large batches. we refrigerate half and freeze the rest. Both versions are heavenly. The chilled banana mousse is silky, lighter than pudding. and just a tiny bit firm. Frozen mousse closely resembles ice cream in both texture and flavor and is delightful in sundaes and parfaits.*

MAKE THE BANANA MOUSSE

In the chilled bowl of a standing mixer fitted with the whisk attachment, whip the heavy cream until soft peaks form. (Alternatively, you can hand whisk in a chilled bowl.) Set aside.

Place the milk, bananas, sugar, and vanilla bean paste in a blender and blend until smooth. Pour the mixture into a large bowl. Fold half of the whipped cream into the banana mixture, then gently fold in the remaining whipped cream. Wrap the entire bowl tightly in plastic wrap and chill for 2 hours.

MAKE THE PARFAITS

Chill four large parfait cups at least 30 minutes before assembling.

Remove the chilled mousse and stir gently with a wooden spoon to loosen mixture. Sprinkle enough brownies (you might want to press them into place gently) to evenly cover the bottom of each parfait cup. Add a layer of mousse, then add a layer of banana slices to cover the mousse, then cover with a layer of granola. End with another layer of mousse and some more brownies. Cover each cup with plastic wrap and chill for 2 more hours. To serve, drizzle each parfait with chocolate syrup and whipped cream.

For the Banana Mousse

- 1 cup cold heavy cream
- ¼ cup cold whole or 2% milk
- 2 large, ripe bananas, cut into large chunks
- ¼ cup sugar
- 2 teaspoons vanilla bean paste

For the Assembly

- 2 large fudgy brownies, chopped coarsely
- 2 medium bananas, sliced
- ½ cup granola
- ¼ cup Simple Chocolate Syrup (page 192)
- ½ cup Whiskey Whipped Cream (page 86)

For the Banana Whoopies

3 ¾	cups all-purpose flour
1 ¼	teaspoon baking powder
1 ¼	teaspoon baking soda
1	teaspoon salt
1	teaspoon cinnamon
2	cups firmly packed light brown sugar
¾	cup canola oil
1	cup sour cream
1½	bananas, mashed (about ½ cup)
2	large eggs

For the Milk Chocolate Swiss Meringue

5	large egg whites
1½	cups granulated sugar
1	pound (4 sticks) unsalted butter, cool but not cold, cut into ½-inch cubes
¼	teaspoon salt
½	teaspoon pure vanilla extract
6	ounces good-quality milk chocolate, melted and cooled

For the Assembly

	Dried banana chips (optional)
	Sliced fresh bananas (optional)

BANANA WHOOPIE PIES

WHOOPIE PIES CONTINUE their forward march across the American dessert-scape with a ferocity only outpaced by the ubiquitous cupcake. There are justifiable reasons for their popularity. Like cupcakes, whoopies can be conceived in just about every imaginable flavor with every kind of frosting, and both share a cuteness factor that has inevitably helped their rapid expansion. And, when executed correctly, whoopies satiate that hard to describe "cake plus cookie plus frosting" craving. They scratch an invisible, hardly recognizable itch. We are whoopie fans, but our friend and pastry chef, Eric Wolitzky, is near fanatical. He creates new versions with focused speed and dedication, but his Banana Whoopie Pie is an all-around favorite. The cookie base is akin to a perfect homespun banana bread, and the filling is light milk chocolate goodness; when combined, the treat is the essence of a flawless day, if we don't say so ourselves. We normally enjoy these at room temperature, however, we think it's also fun and worthwhile to sample this whoopie when it has been slightly chilled (the frosting really firms up).

////////////////////////////////////// *Yield: 15 to 20 whoopie pies* //////////////////////////////////////

BAKED NOTE: Our Banana Whoopie Pies make stunning minis—a fun, eye-catching hors d'oeuvre for the dessert set. Use our recipe as is, but make the whoopies using a smaller ice cream scoop and reduce the bake time by half (smaller whoopie equals shorter bake time).

MAKE THE BANANA WHOOPIES

Preheat the oven to 350 degrees F. Line two baking sheets with parchment paper.

In a large bowl, whisk together the flour, baking powder, baking soda, salt, and cinnamon and set aside.

In a medium bowl, stir the brown sugar and oil together (you might have to use your hands to break up the larger chunks of brown sugar). Add the sour cream and bananas and whisk until combined. Add the eggs and whisk until smooth.

Use a rubber spatula to gently fold the dry ingredients into the wet ingredients. Make sure to scrape down the sides and bottom of the bowl as you fold.

Using a small ice cream scoop with a release mechanism, drop heaping tablespoons of the dough about 1 inch apart onto the prepared baking sheets. Bake for 10 to 12 minutes, until the cookies are just starting to brown on top and a toothpick inserted into the center of a cookie comes out clean. Transfer the pans to wire racks. Let the cookies cool completely on the pans.

MAKE THE MILK CHOCOLATE SWISS MERINGUE

In a medium bowl, whisk the egg whites and sugar together. Set the bowl over a pan of simmering water (do not let the water touch the bottom of the bowl). Heat the mixture until the sugar is completely dissolved and the color is milk white, 2 to 3 minutes.

Transfer the mixture to the bowl of a standing mixer fitted with the whisk attachment and, starting slowly, increase the speed to medium-high; beat until smooth and fluffy, about 5 minutes. Remove the whisk attachment and replace with the paddle attachment. Add the butter and beat on medium-high speed (again starting slowly at first) until smooth and fluffy, about 5 minutes. If the buttercream looks like it is separating, don't worry; it will eventually come together. Add the salt and vanilla and beat for 5 seconds to combine. Gently fold in the chocolate until the mixture is even in color.

ASSEMBLE THE BANANA WHOOPIE PIES

Turn half of the cooled cookies flat side up. Using a small ice cream scoop with a release mechanism, or a tablespoon, drop a large dollop of filling onto the flat side of a cookie. Place another cookie, flat side down, on top of the filling. Press slightly so that the filling spreads to the edges of the cookie. Repeat until all the cookies are used.

Place a banana chip or a slice of fresh banana directly on top and in the center of each cookie if you like. Skewer the chip or banana slice and most of the cookie with a toothpick, hors d'oeuvre style. Put the whoopie pies in the refrigerator for about 30 minutes to firm up before serving.

The whoopie pies will keep in the refrigerator on a parchment-lined baking sheet, tightly covered, for up to 3 days (though they taste best if eaten within 2 days). Bring the whoopie pies to room temperature before serving.

CHOCOLATE BANANA TART

For the Classic Sweet Tart Crust

- 4 ounces (1 stick) cold unsalted butter, cut into ½-inch cubes
- ¼ cup granulated sugar
- ¼ teaspoon salt
- 1 large egg
- 1½ cups all-purpose flour

For the Chocolate Ganache Filling

- 6 ounces good-quality dark chocolate (60 to 72%), chopped coarsely
- 6 ounces good-quality milk chocolate, chopped coarsely
- ⅔ cup plus 1 tablespoon heavy cream
- 1 tablespoon unsalted butter, at room temperature

For the Bananas and Caramel

- 2 ripe bananas
- 2½ ounces (5 tablespoons) unsalted butter, at room temperature, cut into ½-inch cubes
- ½ cup firmly packed light brown sugar
- 2 tablespoons heavy cream

For the Assembly

- 1½ ripe bananas
- 1 tablespoon orange juice

WE ARE BANANAS about bananas, but we are borderline mad for its caramelized self—a perfect blend of crunchy, smoky, sticky, and sweet. Regular bananas may be dependable, but caramelized bananas have all the fun. They are bananas with sass. In fact, we basically created this tart, our Chocolate Banana Tart, as a vehicle for the sassy banana—and it has evolved into a must-make dessert. It is a simple concoction of four essential and bold food groups: chocolate ganache, caramel, sweet crust, and (of course) banana, cobbled together into the guise of a dainty and delicate tart.

////////////////////////////////////// *Yield: One 9-inch tart* //////////////////////////////////////

BAKED NOTE: *You do not need to make this tart as an excuse to make caramelized bananas. We make them frequently and for many uses including: pancake and oatmeal toppings, Greek yogurt stir-ins, cake decor, and peanut butter sandwich add-ins.*

MAKE THE CLASSIC SWEET TART CRUST

In the bowl of a standing mixer fitted with the paddle attachment, beat the butter, sugar, and salt until light and fluffy. Add the egg, and beat just until incorporated. Scrape down the sides and bottom of the bowl, add the flour all at once, and beat just until the dough comes together in a ball. Do not overbeat or your crust will be tough.

Remove the dough from the bowl, shape it into a disk with your hands, wrap it tightly in plastic wrap, and refrigerate for at least 30 minutes.

Dust a work surface with a sprinkling of flour. Use a rolling pin to roll the dough into a 10-inch circle about ¼ inch thick. (Note: The dough will be sticky. Make sure to turn it over with a bench knife or offset spatula as needed and keep the work surface floured.)

Ever so gently guide the dough, without pulling it, into a 9-inch tart pan with removable bottom and lightly press it into place. Roll the rolling pin over the pan to trim off the excess. Place the pan in the freezer for 30 minutes.

Preheat the oven to 375 degrees F.

Line the tart shell with aluminum foil and fill it three-quarters full with pie weights or dried beans. Bake for 15 minutes, then remove the foil and weights and bake for another 10 minutes, or until lightly browned. Transfer the tart pan to a wire rack to cool.

MAKE THE CHOCOLATE GANACHE FILLING

Place the chopped chocolates in a small heatproof bowl (or a large pourable glass measuring cup).

In a small saucepan, gently heat the cream just to boiling. Pour the hot cream over the chocolate and wait 30 seconds, then whisk until smooth. Add the butter and stir until it is completely melted and incorporated. Set aside to cool.

MAKE THE BANANAS AND CARAMEL

Slice the bananas on the diagonal into just-under-1-inch slices.

In a medium, heavy-bottomed skillet, melt the butter over medium heat. Add the brown sugar and stir (with a rubber spatula) until dissolved. Once the mixture starts to bubble, add the bananas, flat sides down, and cook for about 45 seconds or until browned on the bottom. Then carefully flip the bananas (you might want to use tongs to flip each banana slice individually) and cook on the other side until browned, about 45 seconds. Remove the caramelized banana slices to a plate. Dab the slices with a paper towel to remove excess moisture.

Add the cream to the pan and stir to combine. Cook on medium heat until the mixture forms a thick caramel sauce, about 2 minutes, then immediately remove from heat and pour into a small bowl or ramekin to cool. (The caramel will overcook or blacken if you leave it in the skillet, even with the heat turned off.)

ASSEMBLE THE TART

Pour half of the cooled ganache into the tart shell. Place in the refrigerator for 5 minutes to set.

Thinly slice the raw bananas on a diagonal. In a medium bowl, toss the slices in the orange juice, then transfer them to a paper towel and pat dry. Arrange them in a single layer over the chilled ganache to cover the bottom of the tart completely. Top with the remaining ganache. (If the ganache has already started to set, warm it in short bursts in the microwave.) Return the tart to the refrigerator for 5 more minutes.

Decorate the top of the tart with the caramelized bananas and reserved caramel. Serve immediately.

The tart can be stored in the refrigerator, tightly covered, for up to 24 hours, but it tastes best within a few hours of assembling. That said, a few taste testers have claimed that they like the consistency of the tart once it has been refrigerated overnight. To each his own!

BANANA CARAMEL PUDDING

with

MERINGUE TOPPING

For the Caramel Base

1½	cups sugar
1	cup heavy cream

For the Banana Pudding

2	large eggs, plus 2 large egg yolks
4	cups half-and-half, divided
⅓	cup cornstarch
¼	teaspoon salt
2	ounces (½ stick) unsalted butter, cut into ½-inch cubes
1	teaspoon vanilla bean paste or pure vanilla extract
5 or 6	bananas, not quite ripe, yet not green
30	vanilla wafer cookies (about 6 ounces), cut or crushed into large chunks

For the Meringue Topping

4	large egg whites
¼	teaspoon cream of tartar
½	cup sugar

THE CRAVING (to put it mildly) started innocently. It started with just one order of banana pudding, split between the two of us, while we were making a swing through the southern half of the United States. Neither of us was expecting to be transported, and neither of us was expecting this dessert to preoccupy our future thoughts. But it did. I believe that prior to that day, our banana pudding experience had been marred by versions of slimy bananas engulfed in boxed pudding mix. We did not know the joys of a true homemade Southern banana pudding (this is not something our grandmothers made): sweet vanilla custard, chewy vanilla wafers (the cookies get moist and chewy over time in the custard), and a crunchy meringue top. It's at once a simple and joyous dessert. Our recipe is a slight variation on the pudding we discovered that fateful day. We decided to flavor our custard with a little bit of caramel, and we pulled back a tiny bit on the overall sugar for a decidedly less sweet version.

Yield: 8 servings

BAKED NOTE: *Ninety-nine percent of the banana puddings we encountered (yes, there was research involved) are made with vanilla wafer cookies (whether the famous Nabisco brand or a homemade version). Obviously they work wonderfully in this dessert. However, don't be afraid to experiment with other types of cookies. Shortbread will work perfectly, as well as some types of biscotti and even, strangely, crispy chocolate chip cookies.*

MAKE THE CARAMEL BASE

In a large saucepan with high sides, combine the sugar and ⅓ cup of water. Stir the mixture gently so you don't splash any of it up on the sides of the pan. Turn the heat to medium-high and continue stirring until the sugar dissolves. Increase the heat to high, stop stirring, and allow the mixture to boil. Once it begins to turn a rich caramel color, remove it from the heat and gently stream in the cream (it will bubble up, so add the cream slowly at first). Stir until combined. Set aside.

MAKE THE BANANA PUDDING

In a medium bowl, whisk the eggs and egg yolks until pale and blended.

In another medium bowl, whisk together 1 cup of the half-and-half, the cornstarch, and the salt until the mixture is uniform and the cornstarch has dissolved. Whisk this mixture into the caramel base. Place the caramel mixture over medium-high heat and whisk in the remaining 3 cups of half-and-half. While whisking constantly but

gently, bring the mixture to a boil, reduce the heat to medium, and boil (still whisking) for about 15 seconds. The mixture will thicken. Remove from the heat and continue whisking vigorously for about 15 seconds to release excess heat.

Pour one-third of the caramel mixture into the egg mixture, whisking the egg mixture constantly. Transfer the egg mixture into the saucepan with the caramel mixture and, whisking constantly, bring back to a boil. Cook for 1 to 2 minutes, until the custard is very thick. Remove from the heat and whisk in the butter, then the vanilla bean paste. Push the custard through a fine-mesh sieve into a separate bowl and allow the custard to come to room temperature, about 1 hour. Stir the custard, cover the bowl, and place in the refrigerator for about 1 hour to chill. (The custard can be made up to 24 hours ahead of time and should be stored in the refrigerator, tightly covered.)

ASSEMBLE THE PUDDING

Thirty minutes before the custard is entirely chilled, place eight 6-ounce ramekins or a large 1½-quart soufflé or baking dish on a baking sheet and use one of the following methods for assembling the final dish, then return the pudding, uncovered, to the refrigerator to chill while you make the Meringue Topping.

Layer method: Spread a small amount of pudding on the bottom of each ramekin or of the large dish. Thinly slice the bananas and arrange in a single layer on top. Sprinkle one-third of the cookies on top of the bananas, then cover with one-third of the remaining pudding. Repeat twice more (bananas, cookies, pudding) so that your top layer is pudding.

No-layer method (a.k.a. lazy method): Thinly slice the bananas and sprinkle them over the chilled pudding. Sprinkle the cookies over the bananas. Using a wooden spoon, fold the bananas and cookies into the pudding until completely combined. Divide the mixture equally among the ramekins or pour into the large dish.

MAKE THE MERINGUE TOPPING

Preheat the oven to 350 degrees F.

Place the egg whites in the bowl of a standing mixer fitted with the whisk attachment, and sprinkle them with the cream of tartar. Beat on medium-high speed until soft peaks just begin to form, 4 to 5 minutes. Reduce the speed to medium, slowly stream in the sugar, and continue beating until the whites are glossy and stiff but not dry.

Pile the meringue high and with a little artistic flair directly onto the pudding. Be sure to spread it all the way to the edges.

Bake for 12 to 15 minutes or until the meringue turns golden brown. Place the sheet pan with the pudding on a wire rack to cool for 30 to 40 minutes.

Banana pudding tastes great slightly warm (though it will be very runny) and even better thoroughly chilled. It can be stored in the refrigerator, tightly covered, for up to 3 days; note that the cookies will continue to soften as time goes on.

BANANA IN A BLANKET

WE ARE NOT known for fanciful or whimsical cakes. Our cakes are usually straightforward, with a heavy emphasis on clean lines and superior tastes. It's always been flavor over form (we just don't understand the shaped-cake craze). However, sometimes a dessert idea will spring forth that is slightly amusing—either by name or presentation or both—and delicious, and when that happens we feel absurdly lucky and sometimes just absurd. Our Banana in a Blanket is a fun dessert to make and serve. It is ever so slightly tongue-in-cheek and extremely tasty and simple. First, we slather my grandmother's über-classic chocolate cake roll recipe with a generous amount of banana chocolate whipped cream and walnuts, then we gently wrap the whole thing up around a semifrozen banana. We are always freezing bananas for future breads and cakes and smoothies, and this seemed like the perfect dessert to utilize a beautifully chilled banana—a good-humored addition to a perfectly delicious cake.

///////////////////////////////// *Yield: Makes 10 servings* /////////////////////////////////

BAKED NOTE: *Do not fear the roll cake. As long as the cake is rolled while warm, you should manage to have very few, if any, breaking problems. However, if it does tear or break, you can always piece it back together using the filling as a sort of glue, and no one will know the difference.*

//

MAKE THE CHOCOLATE ROLL CAKE

Preheat the oven to 325 degrees F. Lightly coat a jelly-roll pan (10 by 15 inches) with nonstick cooking spray and line it with parchment paper, allowing the parchment to overhang slightly on two sides.

Place the flour, cocoa powder, and salt on the center of a sheet of parchment paper. Sift the ingredients into a small bowl. Turn the sifted ingredients back onto the parchment paper and sift together two more times. Set aside.

In a medium bowl, whisk the egg yolks and vanilla vigorously until thick and pale yellow (almost lemony) in color, 1 to 2 minutes.

Place the egg whites in the bowl of a standing mixer fitted with the whisk attachment, and sprinkle the cream of tartar over the egg whites. Beat on medium-high speed until soft peaks just begin to form, 4 to 5 minutes. Reduce the speed to medium, slowly stream in the granulated sugar, and continue beating until the whites are glossy and stiff but not dry.

Gradually fold one-third of the beaten egg whites into the yolk mixture. Fold half of the

For the Chocolate Roll Cake

- ¼ cup all-purpose flour
- 3 tablespoons dark unsweetened cocoa powder (like Valrhona)
- ¼ teaspoon salt
- 5 large eggs, at room temperature, separated
- 1 teaspoon pure vanilla extract
- ½ teaspoon cream of tartar
- ½ cup granulated sugar
- 2 tablespoons confectioners' sugar, divided

For the Filling and Assembly

- 4½ ounces good-quality dark chocolate (60 to 72%), coarsely chopped
- 4 medium-size ripe bananas, peeled, divided
- 1 cup heavy cream
- 2 tablespoons granulated sugar
- ½ cup walnuts, toasted (page 19), coarsely chopped, plus additional for garnish (optional)
- Confectioners' sugar for sprinkling

sifted flour mixture into the egg mixture and then gently fold in half of the remaining egg whites. Fold in the remaining flour mixture followed by the remaining egg whites. Pour the batter into the prepared pan and smooth the top. Bake for 20 to 25 minutes, rotating the pan halfway through the baking time, or until a toothpick inserted in the center comes out clean (the cake may still appear wobbly, but it should be dry).

Transfer the pan to a cooling rack, cover the cake with a few damp (but not wet) paper towels, and cool for 10 minutes. Run a hot knife around the edges of the cake, remove the towels, and sift 1 tablespoon of the confectioners' sugar over the cake. Place a very thin tea towel over the cake, then place a half-sheet pan right side up on top of the tea towel. With a quick motion, invert the cake onto the back of the pan and gently remove the parchment paper. Sift the remaining tablespoon of confectioners' sugar over the cake. Starting with one of the short ends of the cake, roll the cake up ever so gently, using the towel to support the cake as you go (it's almost like a lift and turn motion). Let the cake cool all rolled up in the towel.

MAKE THE FILLING AND ASSEMBLE THE CAKE

Place the chocolate in the bowl of a double boiler over medium heat and stir occasionally until the chocolate is 90 percent melted. Remove the bowl from the water and continue stirring until it is completely melted and smooth. (Alternatively, in a microwave-safe bowl, cook the chocolate at 50% power (medium) for 15-second bursts, stirring between each blast, until melted and smooth.) Set aside to cool completely.

Wrap 2 bananas in aluminum foil and place in the freezer while you prepare the whipped cream. (Note: If you want to use frozen bananas that are already in your freezer, be sure to let them thaw to a semifrozen state before using—you want them firm, but you do not want them to be completely frozen.) Slice the remaining bananas into a microwave-safe bowl. Microwave the bananas on high for 30 seconds, remove from the microwave, and mash them completely. Set aside to cool.

In a large chilled metal bowl (or in the bowl of a standing mixer fitted with the whisk attachment), whisk the cream vigorously for about 1 minute. Stop and sprinkle the sugar over the cream, then continue to beat until soft peaks form. Fold half of the whipped cream into the chocolate until almost combined, then add the remaining whipped cream and fold in until uniform in color. Stir in the mashed banana.

Gently remove the cake from the towel, unroll it, and place it on the parchment. Place a sheet of parchment on a flat surface. Spread the filling in an even layer over the cake. Sprinkle the walnuts over the filling. Remove the bananas from the freezer and place them end to end at one short end of the cake, cutting to fit if they are too long. Starting at the banana end, gently roll up the cake. Cover it tightly in plastic wrap, and refrigerate for 1 hour.

To serve, place the cake seam side down on a serving plate, garnish with the extra walnuts, if desired, and sprinkle with confectioners' sugar; slice and serve it immediately. The cake can be stored, tightly covered, in the refrigerator for 2 days. Bring to room temperature before serving.

1½	cups all-purpose flour
1	cup sugar
1	teaspoon baking soda
½	teaspoon salt
3	large very ripe bananas, mashed (about 1 cup)
⅓	cup vegetable oil
¼	cup whole milk
¼	cup honey
2	large eggs
2	tablespoons poppy seeds

HONEY BANANA POPPY SEED BREAD

WE HAVE A banana bread problem in the same way that a shoe hoarder has a shoe problem. The problem comes down to one of editing. Shoe collectors want shoes in every shape in every color for every occasion and every outfit, and we want banana bread recipes in every shape and every variation for every occasion and every month of the year. Shoe people fill closets and garages, and we fill recipe books and hard drives (and, oddly enough, shoe boxes). We think each banana bread recipe is a different and enthralling narrative with an ever-changing cast of characters like nuts, chocolate chunks, seeds, zests, sour cream, yogurt, milk, and honey. We don't feel comfortable selecting one recipe as our favorite—and there are actually two banana bread recipes in this book (see also Crunchy Peanut Butter Banana Bread, page 25)—but our Honey Banana Poppy Seed Bread ranks highly in our hearts. This bread is basic and hearty. The honey flavor is noticeable but not overbearing, and the poppy seeds add a pleasant bite, a counterbalance to the sweet bananas, and a slight nutty taste. This recipe is a dear friend worth visiting often.

Yield: One 9-by-5-inch loaf

BAKED NOTE: *The poppy seeds aren't essential to this recipe, but we think they provide a pleasant textural contrast. The bread base itself is completely malleable. so feel free to swap out the poppies with either ½ cup toasted chopped nuts (for a more traditional loaf) or ½ cup chocolate chips (a Baked favorite).*

Preheat the oven to 350 degrees F and position the rack in the center. Butter a 9-by-5-inch loaf pan, dust it with flour, and knock out the excess flour.

In a large bowl, whisk together the flour, sugar, baking soda, and salt.

In another large bowl, whisk together the bananas, vegetable oil, milk, honey, and eggs.

Make a well in the center of the dry ingredients and pour the wet ingredients into it. Fold the dry ingredients into the wet ever so gently until just combined. Stir in the poppy seeds.

Pour the batter into the prepared pan and bake for 1 hour to 1 hour and 10 minutes, or until a toothpick inserted into the center of the loaf comes out with a few moist crumbs.

Let the loaf cool in the pan for 15 minutes, then turn it out onto a wire rack to cool completely. The loaf will keep at room temperature, tightly covered, for up to 3 days.

Acknowledgments

As with our previous books, we are grateful to a large swath of people for keeping us sane in the midst of a flurry of tear-stained pages and chocolate-smudged keyboards. We could not have produced this volume without the following decent folks:

A big shout out to Jessie Sheehan—interpreter of our sweet dreams (and recipes) and cookie-of-the-month advocate. Her Good Morning Sunshine Bars are worthy of a book-length thesis themselves.

Thank you to Alison Fargis—super special agent and friend—for the figurative and literal protective hugs.

Kind words all around for the patience and guidance of our editors: Elinor Hutton wins a special place in our hearts for providing lots of hand-holding through crippling bouts of our New York Neurosis—and she can attack a manuscript with stealth ninjalike skills; Natalie Kaire, for keeping us on the straight and narrow though we are neither straight nor narrow; and all of our other friends at STC.

Extra special love to all of our recipe testers and their crafty ways: Nathan Noland, Sheri Codiana, Heidi Gastler, Liz Moore, Diana Vassar, David Mahon, Joann Tamburro, Julie Halpin, Caitlin Kenney, and Rachel Boller (aka Cake Lady).

Nancy Mongiovi, Stephanie Felton, Francesco, Stephen and the boys (including Michelle), and our respective families for following us down the rabbit hole of bananas and chocolate and booze.

Hugs to Bret Hansen, Sven Weidmann, and Tina, just because.

A joyous round of applause to Tina Rupp for another batch of beautiful, good-enough-to-eat photos, Leslie Siegel for propping the hell out of our treats, Liza Jernow for styling them and Alissa Faden for tying all the bits and pieces together.

Special thanks to Amy Geduldig and the New York Public Library for making us appear bookish and intelligent, and to Brian Kennedy for the snazzy author shot.

We wouldn't have a single book without a bakery and we wouldn't have a functioning bakery without such an amazing, dedicated staff. Special callouts to Molly, Veronika, Amy, Melissa, Kathleen, Jordan, Alexandra, Pascual, Misael, Emma, and all of our baristas, who always pour coffee and slice cake with a smile.

A special shout-out to our entire team at Williams-Sonoma; we appreciate it very much.

Finally, we always like to thank the people who helped push Baked up a very steep hill: Martha Stewart, Lesli Heffler Flick, Kristine Moberg, Eric Wolitzky, and, as always, Rafi Avarmovitz.

As always, if we forgot anyone, we apologize in advance and we know we owe you a boatload of brownies.

MATT + RENATO

Sources

CANDY, CHOCOLATE, AND OTHER SPECIALTY INGREDIENTS

Bob's Red Mill
800-349-2173
www.bobsredmill.com
Grits and specialty flours

Callebaut Chocolate
312-496-7300
www.worldwidechocolate.com

Economy Candy
212-254-1531
www.economycandy.com
Maltesers, milk chocolate–covered peanuts, and a multitude of other candies and chocolates

India Tree
800-369-4848
www.indiatree.com
Great resource for specialty sugars

Jacques Torres
212-414-2462
www.mrchocolate.com

Koppers Chocolate
800-325-0026
www.kopperschocolate.com
Malted milk balls (Whoppers), chocolate-covered peanuts available in bulk quantities

Neilsen Massey
800-525-7873
www.nielsenmassey.com
Great source for vanilla bean paste and coffee extract (and, of course, pure vanilla extract)

Saltworks
800-353-7258
www.saltworks.us
Wide variety of salts sold in bulk portions

Scharffen Berger
866-608-6944
www.scharffenberger.com
Available in most grocery/specialty stores

TCHO Chocolate
415-981-0189
www.tcho.com
Addictive milk chocolate

Valrhona Chocolate
888-682-5746
www.valrhona-chocolate.com
Also available in many specialty stores

Whole Foods
512-477-4455
www.wholefoodsmarket.com
Organic foods as well as a great variety of high-grade chocolates and cheeses (often locally sourced)

KITCHEN & BAKING EQUIPMENT

Crate & Barrel
800-967-6696
www.crateandbarrel.com

JB Prince
800-473-0577
www.jbprince.com

King Arthur Flour
800-827-6836
www.kingarthurflour.com

KitchenAid Appliances
800-334-6889
www.kitchenaid.com

New York Cake & Bake
800-942-2539
www.nycake.com
A fantastic resource for the New York–based baker: pans, tools, and decorating equipment

Nordic Ware
877-466-7342
www.nordicware.com
Feed your Bundt pan obsession with the original heavy-duty creator. Nordic Ware products are also featured at Williams-Sonoma stores.

Pfeil & Holing
800-247-7955
www.cakedeco.com
Decorating supplies sold in bulk

Williams-Sonoma
800-541-1262
www.williams-sonoma.com
Best resource for all of your baking and kitchen needs—including some signature Baked items

CERAMICS

Elephant Ceramics
www.elephantceramics.com
Hand-crafted, lovingly made ceramics, which are featured throughout this book

Conversion Charts

WEIGHT EQUIVALENTS: *The metric weights given in this chart are not exact equivalents, but have been rounded up or down slightly to make measuring easier.*

AVOIRDUPOIS	METRIC
¼ oz	7 g
½ oz	15 g
1 oz	30 g
2 oz	60 g
3 oz	90 g
4 oz	115 g
5 oz	150 g
6 oz	175 g
7 oz	200 g
8 oz (½ lb)	225 g
9 oz	250 g
10 oz	300 g
11 oz	325 g
12 oz	350 g
13 oz	375 g
14 oz	400 g
15 oz	425 g
16 oz (1 lb)	450 g
1½ lb	750 g
2 lb	900 g
2¼ lb	1 kg
3 lb	1.4 kg
4 lb	1.8 kg

VOLUME EQUIVALENTS: *These are not exact equivalents for American cups and spoons, but have been rounded up or down slightly to make measuring easier.*

AMERICAN	METRIC	IMPERIAL
¼ tsp	1.2 ml	
½ tsp	2.5 ml	
1 tsp	5.0 ml	
½ Tbsp (1.5 tsp)	7.5 ml	
1 Tbsp (3 tsp)	15 ml	
¼ cup (4 Tbsp)	60 ml	2 fl oz
⅓ cup (5 Tbsp)	75 ml	2.5 fl oz
½ cup (8 Tbsp)	125 ml	4 fl oz
⅔ cup (10 Tbsp)	150 ml	5 fl oz
¾ cup (12 Tbsp)	175 ml	6 fl oz
1 cup (16 Tbsp)	250 ml	8 fl oz
1¼ cups	300 ml	10 fl oz (½ pint)
1½ cups	350 ml	12 fl oz
2 cups (1 pint)	500 ml	16 fl oz
2½ cups	625 ml	20 fl oz (1 pint)
1 quart	1 liter	32 fl oz

OVEN MARK	F	C	GAS
Very cool	250–275	130–140	½–1
Cool	300	150	2
Warm	325	170	3
Moderate	350	180	4
Moderately hot	375	190	5
	400	200	6
Hot	425	220	7
	450	230	8
Very hot	475	250	9

Infographic Source Notes

PEANUT BUTTER

www.newyorker.com/online/blogs/
cartoonlounge/2009/01/fear-itself.html

www.guardian.co.uk/film/2011/oct/05/mister-
ed-hollywood-remake

www.bloomberg.com/news/2011-12-06/christmas-
tree-spending-rises-to-highest-since-before-
recession.html

oklahoma4h.okstate.edu/aitc/lessons/extras/
recipes/peanuts.pdf

www.gapeanuts.com/aboutgpc.asp

www.nationalpeanutboard.org/classroom-funfacts.php

www.peanutsusa.org.uk/Europe

LEMON AND LIME

headrush.discovery.com/science-experiments/
fruit-battery-experiment-02.html

www.britannica.com/EBchecked/topic/305150/
John-Pennekamp-Coral-Reef-
State-Park

www.npr.org/2011/02/03/133432767/food-fight-
maine-legislature-takes-on-whoopie-pies

www.sunkist.com/products/lemons.aspx

thewondrous.com/50-extreme-guinness-world-
records/

cookinglight.com/cooking-101/essential-ingredients/
lemons-benefits-facts-00400000065198

CARAMEL

blogs.smithsonianmag.com/food/2011/01/a-search-
for-the-origins-of-grandmothers-caramels/

www.nytimes.com/2008/12/31/dining/31cara
.html?pagewanted=all

www.kraftrecipes.com/recipes/caramel-dipped-
apples-55497.aspx

sptimes.com/News/102401/Taste/dish.shtml

www.britannica.com/EBchecked/topic/86729/
butterscotch?anchor=ref4151

www.britannica.com/EBchecked/
topic/92513/candy/50509/Caramels-and-
toffee?anchor=ref502152

www.huffingtonpost.com/2011/06/28/peanuts-
cracker-jacks-dont_n_886151.html

cooking.stackexchange.com/questions/3158/
what-is-the-difference-between-butterscotch-
caramel-and-toffee

BOOZE

www.bbc.co.uk/food/whisky

www.history.com/videos/life-aboard-a-pirate-
ship#life-aboard-a-pirate-ship

corporate.discovery.com/blog/tag/how-
whiskey-made-america/

www.history.com/videos/from-whiskey-
to-bourbon#from-whiskey-to-bourbon

www1.american.edu/ted/kentuckybourbon.htm

www.merriam-webster.com/dictionary/rum-running

www.merriam-webster.com/dictionary/bootlegger

PUMPKIN

www.agday.org/education/fun_facts.php

www.allaboutpumpkins.com/qanda.html

www.punkinchunkin.com/history

www.sunset.com/garden/fruits-veggies/
unusual-pumpkins-00418000069308/

www.harrisseeds.com/

www.huffingtonpost.com/2011/10/21/worlds-
largest-pumpkin-on_n_1024291.html

bangordailynews.com/2011/10/28/living/
7-things-you-don%E2%80%99t-know-about-
the-great-pumpkin/

MALTED MILK POWDER

www.ovaltine.co.uk/en/article.asp?chco_id=23

blogs.kcrw.com/goodfood/2011/10/using-malt-
powder-in-pizza-dough/

www.thehersheycompany.com/brands/whoppers/
milk-chocolate-malted-milk-balls.aspx

racine.wi.net/c2f5.html

www.theworldsstrongestman.com/hall-of-fame/
mariusz-pudzianowski/

CINNAMON

www.britannica.com/EBchecked/topic/118117/cinnamon

https://usatradeonline.gov/

www.ssa.gov/cgi-bin/popularnames.cgi

www.amazon.com/Greatest-Hits-Neil-Young=
dPB00063EMJ6

www.cancer.org/Healthy/StayAwayfromTobacco/

www.naturalhomeandgarden.com/natural-health/
natural-medicine-cabinet-cinnamon-for-diabetes-
infections-and-stomach-problems.aspx

www.womenshealthmag.com/nutrition/
cinnamon-benefits-explained

www.britannica.com/EBchecked/topic/118117/cinnamon

CHEESE

www.britannica.com/EBchecked/topic/444397/
Parmesan

www.wipo.int/wipo_magazine/en/2011/01/
article_0005.html

translate.google.com

www.census.gov/compendia/statab/cats/health_
nutrition.html and www.slate.com/articles/life/
food/2008/11/a_short_history_of_the_bagel.html

blogs.riverfronttimes.com/gutcheck/2009/
02/fun_facts_ricotta_cheese_steven_jenkins_
st_louis_food_blog_021209.php

www.ams.usda.gov

recipes.howstuffworks.com/food-facts/cream-
cheese-questions.htm

CHOCOLATE

www.marketingcharts.com/topics/behavioral-
marketing/easter-beats-valentine%E2%80%99s-
day-for-chocolate-candy-lovers-8596/

www.mayoclinic.com/health/caffeine/AN01211

www.britannica.com/EBchecked/topic/
113885/chocolate

www.smithsonianmag.com/arts-culture/brief-
history-of-chocolate.html

news.bbc.co.uk/2/hi/health/6558775.stm

BANANAS

www.agday.org/education/fun_facts.php

www.census.gov/compendia/statab/cats/health_
nutrition.html

www.britannica.com/EBchecked/topic/51297/banana

www.youtube.com/results?search_query=
slip+on+banana+peel

www.britannica.com/EBchecked/topic/252931/
hallucinogen

library.thinkquest.org/11960/fun/records.htm

www.naturalremediesforbetterhealth.com/banana.html

video.planetgreen.discovery.com/go-green/new-
years/new-years-party.html

planetgreen.discovery.com/food-health/bananas-
fight-blues.html

Index

Note: Page numbers in *italics* indicate photographs

Published in 2012 by Stewart, Tabori & Chang
An imprint of ABRAMS

Library of Congress Cataloging-in-Publication Data

Lewis, Matt.
Baked elements : our 10 favorite ingredients
Matt Lewis and Renato Poliafito ; photographs by Tina Rupp.
p. cm.
Includes bibliographical references and index.
ISBN 978-1-58479-985-6 (alk. paper)
1. Desserts. 2. Baking. 3. Baked (Bakery) I. Poliafito, Renato. II.
Title.
TX773.L469 2012
641.86—dc23
2012004079

Editor: Elinor Hutton
Designer: Alissa Faden
Production Manager: Kathleen Gaffney
Prop Styling: Leslie Siegel
Food Styling: Liza Jernow

The text of this book was composed in Eames Century Modern, Heroic Condensed, and Knockout.

Printed and bound in the United States

10 9 8 7 6 5 4 3 2 1

Stewart, Tabori & Chang books are available at special discounts when purchased in quantity for
premiums and promotions as well as fundraising or educational use. Special editions can also be
created to specification. For details, contact specialsales@abramsbooks.com or the address below.

115 West 18th Street
New York, NY 10011
www.abramsbooks.com

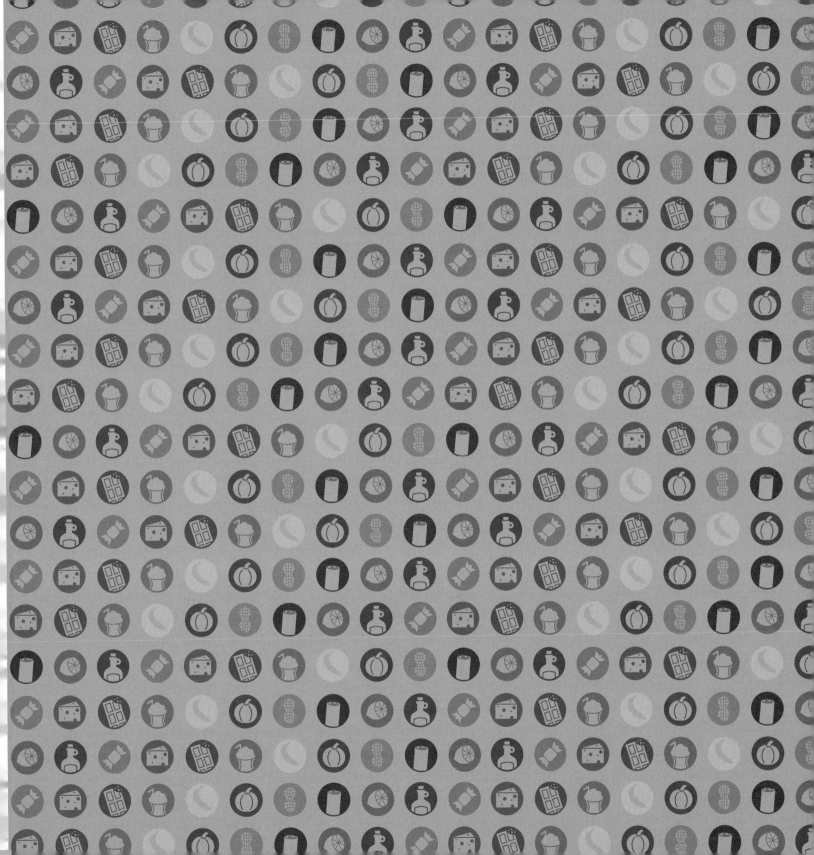

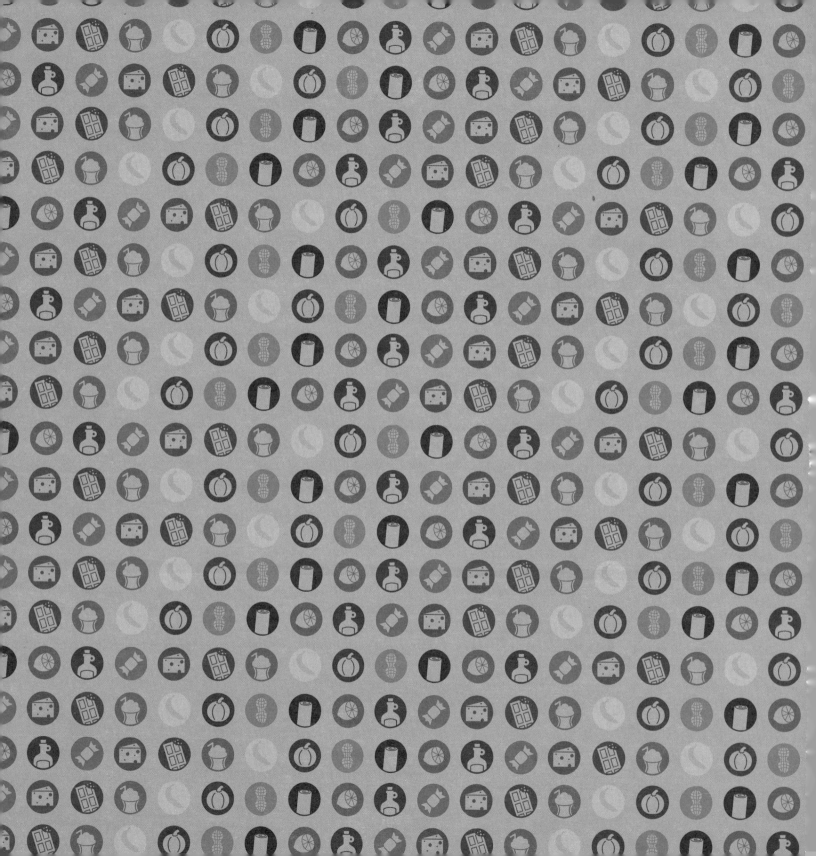